MAY THE ROAD RISE TO MEET YOU

Daily Thoughts On Life And Faith

To HALEY!
May you and
yours always
have all the
love you need!

ALSO BY RONNIE McBRAYER

But God Meant It for Good

Keeping the Faith: Passages, Proverbs, and Parables

Leaving Religion, Following Jesus

Keeping the Faith, Volume 2

The Jesus Tribe

Esther

How Far Is Heaven?

The Gospel According to Waffle House

Fruits of the Cotton Patch

Wild Wild Walton

MAY THE ROAD RISE TO MEET YOU

Daily Thoughts On Life And Faith

Ronnie McBrayer

May the road rise to meet you.
May the wind always be at your back.
May the sun shine warm upon your face.
May the rains fall soft upon your fields.
And until we meet again,
May God hold you in the palm of His hand.

- An Irish Blessing

In Memory of Chris Hale
1949 - 2014

Published by Bird on a Wire Media.

Cover design, book layout, and formatting for publishing completed by Tim Ryals.

Cover Art by Vincent Van Gogh, *Country Road*, Pencil Drawing, 1882.

Interior Art by Vincent Van Gogh, *A Pair of Shoes*, Oil on Canvas, 1885.

ISBN-13: 978-1522792345
ISBN-10: 1522792341

TABLE OF CONTENTS

PREFACE

Bertrand Russell, the famous British atheist, would not become a Christian because religion - all religion he said - is based on fear; and fear could only lead to savagery. "It is no wonder that cruelty and religion have gone hand in hand," he said, "because fear is at the basis of both things."

Soren Kierkegaard, who was a committed Christian, said something similar: "Fearful religion is sinful religion," he wrote. Both men were correct. Any approach to faith that is based on fear is a faith that has not matured and can hardly lead to life.

The crux to most everything I say and write pushes back against this very subject: Too much of Christianity is based on anxiety and fear. Thus, it can become an exercise in shaming people, a cruelty, rather than liberating and showing people the infinite love God has for them.

As simply as I can say it, I believe that genuine faith leads to love, not fear; to ultimate freedom, not spiritual enslavement. That is the spirit in which I offer these "daily thoughts on life and faith."

A few more observations are in order as you begin: First, you will find no footnotes or references in the text. This is not for the purpose of infringing upon the work of others, as customarily I eagerly site my sources. This is to keep the content as focused as possible.

Second, each daily "devotional" is intentionally simple. While topics are varied, ranging far and wide, each reading can be completed in only a few short minutes.

Finally, I write, not to impose my thoughts on you, but to awaken something already burning within your heart, a spark you know to be true: "Where God's love is, there is no fear, because God's perfect love drives it away."

Ronnie McBrayer
Freeport, Florida
Advent 2015

JANUARY

January 1: Still Called Today

Imagine that tomorrow morning I deposit into your personal bank account $86,400. Not only am I going to deposit this amount into your account tomorrow, I'm going to do the same thing every day next week. That is a combined $604,800 that will be waiting for you. But I'm just getting started. I'm going to do this every day for the next year. At the conclusion of twelve months you will have received more than $31.5 million.

Now, what if I told you that you have in your possession, today, something even more valuable than $31 million? Would you believe me? You do, because every day that you wake, you receive that daily deposit, not measured in dollars, but in seconds. Every day contains 86,400 seconds; every week more than 600,000; and every year more than 31 million. They are yours to spend as you please. The only catch is, when each day is over, your "funds" expire. They have to be spent with urgency, for tomorrow your account will reset. And because it will reset, what we do with those seconds matters a great deal.

The temptation, Frederick Buechner said, "Is to believe that we have all the time in the world, whereas the truth of it is we do not...For each of us there comes a point of no return, a point from which we no longer have life enough left to go back and start over."

There is an unmerciful ruthlessness to time that demands we spend what we have - all we have - while today is still called today. Today we still have opportunity. Today we still have time. We cannot, then, put off until tomorrow, next week, or next year what must and can only be done while there are seconds left in our banks.

January 2: Lighten Your Load

In Paulo Coelho's brilliant book, *The Alchemist,* a boy is sent to a wise man to discover the secret of happiness. Upon his arrival, the sage hands him a teaspoon containing two tiny drops of oil, with the instructions to wander the castle for two hours without spilling the oil.

The lad did as instructed, carefully climbing the stairwells and creeping down the hallways of the palace, his eyes always fixed on the teaspoon. When he returned to the wise man he was asked, "Did you see my Persian tapestries, my gardens, my parchments in the library?" Embarrassed, the boy replied that he had not. He had been focused solely on the oil in the spoon.

Thus, the boy was sent back to tour the castle, and this time he focused all his attention on the beauty that surrounded him. He returned to the wise man with excitement, thrilled at all he had seen. The wise man then asked, "And where are the two drops of oil I gave you?" The boy realized that he had spilt them along the way.

The wise man then revealed his "secret" to happiness: "Happiness lies in looking at all the wonders of the world and never forgetting the two drops of oil in the spoon."

This parabolic story calls for a much needed balance in our lives. We must be in tune with the world around us, while also caring for the few precious things we have been given to carry on our journey.

Thankfully, what we carry - what is most important to us - can be reduced to a few drops, as there is so little that is absolutely essential in life. So if life seems burdensome, and you can't see the wonder around you, it might be time to lighten your load.

January 3: Older And Wiser

Dilip Jeste and Thomas Meeks study human wisdom. Among their findings are two obvious, enlightening discoveries. First, true wisdom - the ability to skillfully apply knowledge and understanding to one's life - is extremely rare. There just aren't many sages or gurus among us. And second, those who are genuinely wise have the benefit of age and experience on their side - and more often than not, bad experiences.

You have to live a while, get kicked in the head a few times, fall on your face more than once, get caught in a self-manufactured disaster or two, and then wisdom - mercifully - begins to take root. Thus, the older you are, by this logic, the smarter you should be. And by the way, it was Jack Weinberg in the 1960s who said, "Don't trust anyone over 30" - a marvelous anti-establishment statement I love. But I bet he would no longer stand by that statement.

Youth may give us much of what we need: Audacity, vision, zeal, and a healthy dose of revolutionary chaos. But like a fine wine, only time gives us wisdom. Therefore, it should be no surprise that our world is in its current condition. It is a world that values youth, childish rhetoric, toned bodies, and this month's fresh face from L.A. or Nashville more than it values reason, understanding, and the invaluable wisdom that comes from age.

It is a culture that sacrifices on the altar of youthful stupidity the wizened experience of its elders; and it does so at its own tragic expense. For a society that will not listen to its grandparents or the voice of history, is a society that is doomed. So don't be too upset about getting a year older. It will make you wiser, and the world needs your wisdom.

January 4: Spirituality 101

If you have ever struggled with addiction, you know this to be true: Addiction devours. It consumes a person's physical, spiritual, and emotional well-being, using up her or her identity.

Of course, addiction is not limited to alcohol or cocaine. Sex, food, video games, smoking, religion, gambling, shopping, the internet, relationships, or work: The list is exhaustive. Anything that initially empowers us can enslave us.

When such enslavement begins to gobble up our lives, it is easy to decide that we want something better. We want transformation; we want change. But our attempts to revolutionize our lives almost always fail. This is because the recognition that life must change is not enough. Transformation is not accomplished by giving up what is bad for you. The bad has to be replaced with what is healthy.

I think this is what Blaise Pascal meant when he said, "There is a God-shaped vacuum in the heart of every man and woman which cannot be filled by any created thing, but only by God." I think this is the express intent of Paul when he wrote, "I have been crucified with Christ and I no longer live, but it is Christ who now lives in me."

And I think that this is exactly what Bill Wilson, co-founder of Alcoholics Anonymous, was talking about when he articulated those necessary steps toward sobriety, where one must acknowledge his or her powerlessness and turn life over to a Higher Power who is the only source of health and sanity.

This isn't mere self-help. This is Spirituality 101. This is the essence of the Christian life: Our desires, impulses, and very lives have to be crucified, and replaced, so that the life God has for us can be born and lived in its stead.

January 5: Submission

My son's motto is: "Never submit." He practices this maxim rigorously, and it serves him well in some situations, but when he cannot impose his demands upon people or circumstances, then "Never Submit" leads to terrible frustration.

Nevertheless, he is at least speaking the truth, as only youngsters can. This is precisely how many of us live. We refuse to submit - not even to a way of life that would be better for us – and not even to God. This shows up even when we pray.

Prayer can be very self-centered, scripturally-laced ransom letters, demanding that the Almighty do things our way and comply with our plans. We cling to our personal agendas, and conveying these to God, require him to make us as comfortable as possible.

Such an attitude is not unlike checking into a luxurious penthouse. We want something to eat, so room service is called and the kitchen goes into full operational mode to bring us whatever we want when we want it. Our favorite shirt is dirty. No problem, send for the maid. She will quickly take it to the laundry and return it before dinner.

Do you need a cab? Ring the bell; the concierge lives to serve you. Not enough clean towels? Want your bed made twice a day? Need an extra chocolate on your pillow at bedtime? It's easy-peasy: Pick up the phone and the management will be happy to attend to your every whim and impulse.

Does prayer really work this way? I don't think so. Prayer is not a method for getting everything we want. Rather, it is the means by which we surrender to what God wants. It is an act of submission; the letting go of our will, to be shaped by the will of God.

January 6: The Life You Have

An American investor took a vacation on the Pacific coast of Mexico. One morning he met a local fisherman carrying a string of the most beautiful fish the American had ever seen. While talking to the angler, the investor discovered that the man had a simple daily routine.

He got up early to fish, returned to shore to sell his catch at the market, went home to play with his children, took a siesta with his wife, and then strolled into the village each evening where he drank cerveza and played guitar with his friends. The American scoffed.

"Listen," he said, "I am an Ivy League MBA, and I can help you. If you spent more time fishing, with the proceeds you could then buy a bigger boat. With the success of the bigger boat you could then buy several boats, until eventually you would have a whole fleet of fishing vessels.

"Instead of selling your small catch to the market, you could sell directly to the processor, eventually opening your own cannery. You could control the product, processing, and distribution. You could move to the city, and leave this beachside dock all together."

The Mexican fisherman, bewildered, asked, "But señor, what then?" The American laughed and said, "Easy! You sell it all and become very rich. Then you retire, move to the coast, fish early in the morning, play with your children, take a siesta with your wife, and stroll to the village each evening where you can drink cerveza and play guitar with your friends."

The lesson is obvious, though not an easy one to learn: You may already be living the life you are looking for. Rapaciously grasping for "more" may not be worth giving up the peaceful, gratifying, fulfilling life; the life that is already yours.

January 7: My Life To Live Over

"You can't unfry an egg, but there is no law against thinking about it. So if I had my life to live over, I would try to make more mistakes. I would relax. I would be sillier. I know of very few things that I would take seriously...

"I would pay less attention to people who teach tension, who cry at us to be serious... I would seek out more teachers who inspire relaxation and fun. I had a few of them, fortunately, and I figure it was they who kept me from going entirely to the dogs. From them I learned how to gather what few scraggly daisies I have gathered along life's cindery pathway.

"I would start barefooted a little earlier in the spring and stay that way a little later in the fall. I would play hooky more. I would shoot more paper wads. I would have more dogs. I would keep later hours. I'd have more sweethearts. I would fish more. I would go to more circuses. I would go to more dances. I would ride on more merry-go-rounds. I would be carefree as long as I could, or at least until I got some care - instead of having my cares in advance.

"G.K. Chesterton once said, 'A characteristic of the great saints is their power of levity. Angels can fly because they can take themselves lightly.' In a world in which practically everybody else seems to be consecrated to the gravity of the situation, I would rise to glorify the levity of the situation...

"I doubt that I'll do much damage with my creed. The opposition is too strong. There are too many serious people trying to get everybody else to be too darned serious." - by Don Herold, Reader's Digest, October 1953

January 8: Birthing Babies

After years as a pastor and chaplain (not to mention, being a father), I have been present at many births. Births after their mothers labored for hours; births alarmingly sudden; births only by means of surgical intervention; births in maternity wards, ERs, in homes, and once in the floorboard of a Buick.

As varied as childbirth is, every newborn needs the same thing: All the help he or she can get, to ensure good health. Likewise, this is the calling of the church and individual Christians.

Christians should provide safe, welcoming environments for faith to be born within people. Churches should strive to be delivery rooms where the new in faith can grow, be nurtured, and become the people God wants them to be.

There are many helpful images that define the church's mission. It is a hospital providing healing to the sick and injured. It is a fuel station for those who are exhausted. It is a banquet hall of grace open to all who will feast at God's table. But let us not forget our role as incubators of developing faith, skilled midwives assisting with spiritual birth.

And as it is with physical birth, spiritual birth is not an invariable experience. Some come to faith easily, like they can't wait to get here, and all you have to do is catch them. Others get wedged in the birth canal with philosophical, spiritual, and emotional sticking points. Some arrive in grand fashion, genuinely born again, but quickly lose their way.

There are the doubters, the skeptics, the seekers, the confused, the angry, the stuck, the ready, the breeched, the premature, and those needing intensive care. All are precious people on the road to some kind of spiritual birth. Our role is to simply help their personal, unique faith emerge.

January 9: The Joy Of Now

There is an ancient Zen parable about a man who surprised a sleeping tiger while walking through the jungle. The ferocious animal pursued the man, causing him to throw down his bag and walking stick, as he ran for his life.

With the tiger tightly on his heels, the man came to a steep cliff. He saw a vine dangling over the edge, quickly grabbed it, and began shimmying down the vine just narrowly escaping the teeth of the tiger who now leered hungrily at him from the rim above.

This put the traveler in a real predicament. He was high in the air with no place to go. The vicious tiger was overhead; jagged rocks were below; and he was clinging to a vine that was not nearly long enough to lower him to the ground. Then, as if things could not be direr, a mouse emerged from its den and began to nibble at the vine.

At this precise moment the traveler saw a perfect, plump strawberry right there within arm's reach, growing out of the face of the cliff. He picked it, ate it, and exclaimed, "Wow!!! That is the best strawberry I've ever tasted in my entire life!"

The story ends there (leaving the man hanging in a lurch), but the lesson keeps going: If the man had been preoccupied with the rocks below (his possible future), or the tiger above (his past troubles), or the mouse chewing away at the vine (his vanishing present), he would have missed the strawberry within the present moment. He would have missed the joy of now.

Right now, that is today, might not be your greatest moment, but now is all you have. Give now all you have, and you might be surprised at the joy you will discover.

January 10: On The Same Team

Is there anything that can bring healing to our divisive society, ripped apart by so many bitter rivalries? As a Christian, maybe I should answer that question by returning to the mantra: "Jesus is the Answer." And I don't mean that in a trite sort of way that only leads to more division. I mean it in the cosmic, sweeping, unifying sense.

The Apostle Paul made clear that Jesus came not to create a new religion (again, another tool of division), but to create a new humanity. He came to obliterate rivalry and competition, and to erase the lines that divide us. As Paul said, "We are all one in Jesus Christ."

Consider this practical example: Fans at a football game. Have you ever noticed how diverse said crowd is? There are rednecks and rappers. Hillbillies and hipsters. College alumni and dropouts. Rightists and leftists. Men and women. Blacks and whites. Legals and illegals. They are all sitting, cheering, laughing, eating, and drinking together. This type of unity would be impossible without there being something transcendent to put them on the same team (In this case, a mere sporting event).

By saying, "Jesus is the Answer," I am talking about this kind of solidarity. While we are often divided by so many little tribal allegiances, in Christ we can find that something transcendent that can unite us. When Jesus becomes more important to we who are people of faith, than all the other lesser things, then we can experience unity.

What wonderful things could truly take place if those who call themselves Christians could unite in Christ, rather than wrongly use Christ to strengthen the divisions already so deeply entrenched in the world! I'd like to think that we just might have a new opportunity to learn to live together.

January 11: The Salesman

Rabbi Albert Lewis often told a story he called, "The Salesman," It goes: "A salesman knocks on a door. The man who answers says, 'I don't need anything.' The next day, the salesman returns. 'Stay away,' he is told, and the man gets very angry.

"On the third day the salesman returns once again. 'You again!' the man screams. 'I warned you!' He gets so angry, he spits in the salesman's face. The salesman wipes the spit off with a handkerchief, then looks to the sky and says, 'It must be raining.'"

Rabbi Lewis explains that love is just like that. Love keeps knocking, and goes back tomorrow. Love stays at it. Lewis would agree, I think, that such love mimics the relentless love of God. He stays at it.

This isn't warm and fuzzy talk. This is the real love and grace of God poured out on us without condition and without end. God's love for us does not depend upon who we are, the good or bad we have done, or the mistakes we have made. God's love depends upon his own nature and goodness. Even when we spit in his face, he keeps coming back.

That is why the worst of your personal failures, the worst crimes you have committed, your divorce, your drug abuse, your emotional baggage and weakness, your arrest record, your selfishness, your adultery, your addiction, your dishonesty, stupidity, and your bone-headed decisions - fill in the blank - can never separate you from God's love. Never.

So even if we shake our fist at him in rage, spit in his face, and do everything we think possible to spurn his love, God will be back; standing on the porch in the rain of our refusal, eager and ready to love us through our rejection.

January 12: Getting Through

"If there was one last crust of bread in this town, it would be mine." That's a quote from a rather pretentious member of the clergy, stating how God would take care of him should the world come unhinged tomorrow.

"I have never seen the godly abandoned or their children out begging for bread," he quoted. This man considered himself godly, thus, no deprivation would ever befall him, as bread from heaven would always fall into his lap. For him, the corollary was also true: "If you are ungodly, then you will not always have what you need."

To hear advocates of this position explain, those who please God always land on top of the heap. Their cupboards are always full, their gas tanks never empty, their tables are always running over, and their checks never bounce.

But what about the suffering and needy? Is there something wrong with the faith of these poor people? Does suffering only come upon those who are unrighteous? No, this position will not hold up for long; this idea that righteous living always leads to the good life.

Countless numbers of godly people have suffered, have gone without, have been tortured, have been chained in prison, and have died by stoning, firing squad, holocaust, and worse. They suffered, not because they possessed an inferior faith, a faith not strong enough to get them out of trouble, but because of their unwavering belief.

The writer of the book of Hebrews concludes that those who suffer this way are "too good for this world and earn a good reputation because of faith." Just because we don't have as much as others, an empty cupboard, or sometimes suffer, doesn't mean our faith is defective. Faith isn't for getting us what we want, but for getting us through.

January 13: Wade In The Water

January 13, 1982, was a cold, snowy day in Washington D.C., with a massive blizzard threatening the city. At the height of the storm, Air Florida Flight 90, just seconds in the air with its wings heavy with snow and ice, struck the 14th Street Bridge and plunged into the icy waters of the Potomac River.

Hundreds of onlookers gathered on the damaged bridge and the snow covered banks of the river to watch the scene. One man was twenty-eight-year-old Lenny Skutnik, a congressional staffer. When he saw a woman, Priscilla Tirado, blinded by shock and jet fuel, too weak to grasp the rings being lowered to her by the rescuers, Lenny quickly went from being an observer to a participant. He jumped into the freezing water, pulling her to shore and to safety.

Later that month President Ronald Reagan seated Lenny Skutnik next to the First Lady as his special guest for the State of the Union Address. Lenny was the first ever "ordinary" American to receive such an honor. Skutnik resisted all efforts to make his risky act into something extraordinary, however, and said, "Nobody else was doing anything. I just did it."

Heroes, spiritual or otherwise, are not those who have special powers, bulging muscles, and colorful costumes. Nothing could be further from the truth. Heroes are simply those who, even in throat-strangling fear, say their prayers and jump into the water.

It's true that you can't solve every knotty problem or rescue every person in need, but you can do what you can do. You can respond in faith, knowing that the water might be cold, the dangers many, and the risks great. But you need not be afraid. Wade on in, and don't let fear keep you on the sidelines.

January 14: Unforced Rhythms Of Grace

Two monks were walking along when they come to a shallow, muddy river. A beautiful woman in a long white dress was standing there. She couldn't figure out how to continue her journey without ruining her outfit. So one of the monks picked her up in his arms - something he was forbidden to do, for touching a woman was against his vows - and carried her across to the other side.

After a few hours, the second monk was unable to remain silent about this breach of conduct. He blurted out, "How could you pick up that woman when you knew it was against the rules?" The first monk replied, "Are you still carrying her around? I put her down hours ago."

This is an instructive tale about two different approaches to spirituality. One can view faith as a tightly controlled, carefully managed list of "dos and don'ts," or one can move with the spirit. One can carry around faith as a heavy burden, or "put it down," to live lighter and happier.

This point is eloquently driven home by Eugene Peterson's artistic rendering of Matthew 11: "Are you tired? Worn out? Burned out on religion? Come to me. You'll recover your life. Learn the unforced rhythms of grace."

The "unforced rhythms of grace." There is no more incomparable phrase, and nothing any higher to which anyone could aspire: To express the life of faith with freedom, harmony, and buoyancy.

Do you want to live the free and gracious life? Then partner with Jesus. When the music of mercy plays, follow his lead, and you'll find yourself enjoying faith - actually living it - rather than enduring it. Following Jesus leads, invariably, to recovery, not religion; to empowerment, not exhaustion; it leads to the laying down of our burdens. It leads to grace.

January 15: The Red Hills Of Georgia

We are many years removed from the work of Dr. Martin Luther King, Jr. whose birthday is today. Yet, racism continues, and more horrifying, racism endures within the church, a people who profess allegiance to One who welcomed all people regardless of their nationality, skin color, or any of the other factors that divide people.

For we who are Christians, love for our neighbor must be our calling card. Grace must be the currency which we exchange, and when people who allege faith in Christ refuse those he readily accepts, we must declare the truth that racism and bigotry are unequivocally and explicitly wrong.

For me, this has become more than theory. It is personal. I have a multi-racial son, a beautiful young man with eyes as dark as night and skin that is rich, mocha-brown. Though I am his adoptive father, we are more accurately, to quote King, "the sons of former slaves and the sons of former slave owners from the red hills of Georgia."

I want my son to grow up in a culture without the prejudice that has plagued these hundreds of years. I want him to be a part of a nation where "he will not be judged by the color of his skin, but by the content of his character." But even if such achievements are not brought to bear in the greater society in his lifetime, I want him to know that within the community of Christ.

Society may be slow in changing its attitudes. Governments may delay the changing of policies. Individuals may go to their graves clinging to hate and hard-heartedness. But in the church that carries the name of Jesus, we cannot simultaneously express our love for God and refute the love that Christ has for all.

January 16: Steep Grade Ahead

The steepest railroad track in the United States is the Saluda Grade in the mountains of North Carolina. It is a boiler-busting, brake-burning section of track that Norfolk Southern finally closed because it took too much time to cross over.

The train would chug up the mountain, huffing and puffing, wheezing and groaning. Finally at the top, the engine would begin the descent down the other side. But the engine descended more slowly than during the ascent, because the majority of the train - hundreds of feet and thousands of pounds - was pulling against the engine.

The railroad learned, after a number of chaotic mishaps, to employ "helper engines" at Saluda. These were big engines that waited at the bottom of the mountain. When a train went by, a helper engine - or sometimes two or three if the load was really heavy - would fall in behind to push slow and steady to the top. Then the helper engines would then ride their brakes down the other side to keep the train steady and safely on the tracks.

For the ten decades that passenger trains crossed over Saluda Grade, not a single train passenger was ever injured or killed on the journey. That incredible safety record was the result of taking the necessary time and care to move people patiently along on their journey.

We all travel with precious, precious cargo - and that's more than a sticker on a soccer mom's SUV - that's the truth. So why get in such a hurry? Slow down.

Some people are traveling dangerous roads. Take some time to help them get over the steepest grades. It will involve huffing, puffing, pulling, pushing, and the pressures from all sides will be crushing. But life is at stake, and living is more important than our schedules.

January 17: Fight Like A Butterfly

Muhammad Ali, on the eve of a championship fight, said he would, "Float like a butterfly and sting like a bee." I'd like to slightly amend his famous phrase.

A boy came upon a cocoon in the forest. He took it home and waited for the butterfly to emerge. One day a small tear in the pouch finally appeared, and the butterfly began to emerge. But it was such a desperate struggle for the poor thing to get out! So, the boy took scissors and carefully cut the cocoon open to rescue the beautiful butterfly.

But it wasn't beautiful; it was fat and swollen. Its wings were wilted, and over time it never learned to fly. It could only crawl around in a shoebox. When the boy told his science teacher this tale, he learned that the butterfly's laborious effort to emerge from its shell was nature's way of circulating dormant blood and strengthening its new wings. The fight was preparation for transformation, and the boy's "help" had actually hurt the butterfly.

What is true in nature is also true of human nature: Some suffering is necessary. We have to struggle. We must face resistance – we must – if we will ever gain the strength we need to fly. This reveals the supreme spiritual principle: There is no resurrection without a cross, no greatness without grief, and no strength apart from suffering. The struggle is vitally necessary to the maturation process.

When we avoid suffering at all costs, we fail to see that such behavior will cost us everything, for if we cannot tolerate anything that hurts or discomforts us now, we will never become people of faith, character, or maturity later. With apologies to Ali, we will never "float like a butterfly" until we have learned to fight like one.

January 18: Finishing

There is a vast difference, a world of difference, between saying "I quit" and saying "I'm finished."

Case in point: At the 1968 Olympic Games in Mexico City, Mexico, the last marathon runner entered Olympic Stadium more than an hour behind the winner and other competitors. Most of the spectators had gone home, the sun had already set, and there was no way he could win. But still, John Stephen Akhwari of Tanzania ran.

Akhwari was in terrible condition. He needed stitches, was bandaged and bleeding, and was limping along with a dislocated knee cap. He had suffered a fall earlier in the day, and his ragged appearance proved as much.

As he entered the stadium's tunnel, car headlights lighting his path, those few left in the stands began to cheer wildly. Akhwari hobbled onto the track and triumphantly across the finish line. It was one of those great, courageous, enduring Olympic moments. Why did Akhwari stay in the race? He told reporters, "My country did not send me 5,000 miles to start a race. They sent me 5,000 miles to finish."

Akhwari finished 57th of the 74 competitors who started the race: Dead last. But he finished, unlike 17 other runners with "DNF" marked beside their name: Did Not Finish.

The encouragement from Scripture is almost universal: "Fight the good fight... Finish the course... Keep the faith... Forgetting what is behind, press on... Finish the race and complete the task the Lord Jesus has given you... Let us run with endurance... Run to win... We will harvest a good crop if we don't give up, or quit... Remain faithful and you will receive the crown of life."

It matters not if you finish first or last. Simply, finish your race. The end of it all will be worth it.

January 19: A Harborous Disposition

Robert Putnam wrote a book some years ago entitled, *Bowling Alone*. Bowling, unbelievably, is the most participated in sport in America. Annually, more people bowl than any other single sport. But, fewer people are bowling in leagues. Thus, they are "bowling alone," not in community or connection with others.

Putnam uses this as a metaphor for our society. We are disconnected from our neighbors (in spite of all our technology), resulting in less social cohesiveness, fragmentation into special interest groups, and less cooperation and trust toward those outside our immediate circle.

People of faith, ironically enough, have a solution for this problem. It is hospitality. Hospitality is not the act of being nice, though a little kindness would go a long way in this world. Rather, hospitality is openness to the stranger. Hospitality is the intentional act of removing the barriers that stand in the way of community, and the opening of arms and hearts to those in need.

William Tyndale, an early translator of the Bible into English, translated hospitality as, "a harborous disposition." To create safe harbors, safe places for others to come in from the storm and find safety, wholeness, and welcome; this is hospitality.

A cursory look at the word "hospitality" shows "hospital" is the root of the word, and a hospital, originally, wasn't a high-tech medical facility. It was a guest house for pilgrims that took in travelers. It provided them with food, care, and gave them a safe place to rest.

Hospitality, practiced properly, is to do no less than fulfill the words of Jesus: "As you do for the least of these, you do for me. For I was hungry, and you fed me. I was thirsty, and you gave me a drink. I was a stranger, and you invited me in."

January 20: Anxious For Approval

Acceptance is a good thing. It is validating to be welcomed by others or to gain the respect and admiration of your peers. But it doesn't take long for the valid need for acceptance to slide into some very dark territory.

We go from enjoying the approval of others to needing it. We grow desperately addicted to the fawning endorsements of others and will do anything to get these. That's what makes forty-year-olds behave as adolescents. You can have a house in the burbs, a nearly four-figure car payment, three kids in soccer and still act like a 7th grader trying to make it with the "in" crowd.

Splintered, needy, clingy, and anxious, we spend the lion's share of our energy and years chasing after the validation of others, a validation that we think will make us whole. We become slaves to the expectations of others while simultaneously manipulating those expectations to get what we feel we need.

And for what? A few emotional strokes, the fleeting approval of someone who is as fractured as we are, approval that lasts for about five minutes, and then the grueling exercise must begin all over again?

Here's some good news: When you are deeply, madly, unconditionally, and fiercely loved - as God loves us - you can let the foolish exercise of chasing the approval of others go. If we could get this down into the basement of our hearts, then we might enjoy a degree of confidence and freedom that we never thought possible.

We can reach the point in life where we no longer need the love and validation of people, because we have come to know and experience the unconditional love of God. Then we can be free from the ruthless, unmerciful demands of uncertain and provisional affections.

January 21: Lasting Kindness

When I was a child my family lived hand to mouth. We were loved and cared for, but the cupboards were often more bare than full. I often say that we ate a lot of "Hamburger Helper" in those days, but with only the "Helper."

My dad's job was at a textile mill, a job he maintains to this day (though he should retire). At the mill, a couple of my father's co-workers would help us, as such salt-of-the-earth people do. One of them was an old Baptist preacher named Gene Clark. Gene worked the mill during the week and preached on the weekend to a congregation of less than a hundred people out in the sticks.

During the hardest years Gene would slip my dad a wad of cash on Friday afternoons and say, "The church has plenty of money. You need this more than they do." And, honestly, we did. Another man was Bobby Gentry. One Saturday morning Bobby pulled up in the driveway of our home and got out of the car dressed in a way I had never seen him before. Rather than donning his usual coveralls, he was wearing a suit.

Three other men from his church dressed in suits got out of the car with him. Then another car with four more men pulled up. These eight men began heaving brown paper sacks of groceries through our front door for what seemed like an hour. It wasn't Christmas. It wasn't Thanksgiving. It was just on time.

Those groceries were gone in a matter of weeks, consumed by little hungry mouths, but the memory of those men's kindness will last my entire life. So today, be kind to those you meet. Your generosity will last longer than any gift you give.

January 22: Kingdom Curriculum

The animals decided they must do something to help humanity face the challenges of the world, so they organized a school. They adopted a systematic curriculum consisting of running, climbing, swimming, and flying.

The duck was excellent in swimming and flying, but was extremely poor at running. He had to drop swimming and stay after school for additional track practice. This gave the duck's poor webbed feet callouses, so much so, that he became only average at swimming.

Meanwhile, the rabbit was one of the best at running, but had a mental breakdown because of his swimming class. The squirrel was excellent in climbing, but when her flying teacher made her start from the ground rather than from the treetops, all her grades plummeted.

The maverick in the school was the eagle. He was hardly a team player, and gloated in climbing class that he could beat everyone else to the top of the tree, but he always used his own way to get there.

The prairie dogs stayed out of the school altogether because digging was not added to the curriculum. They later joined with the badger and gophers to start a successful charter school.

At the end of the year, none of the animals did very well. An eel that was an exceedingly good swimmer, but that could also run, climb and fly a little, had the highest cumulative score and was selected as the valedictorian.

Not everyone will fit into the church's well-ordered, highly structured, cookie-cutter curriculum. As we are all gifted differently, people must be given space and place to "do their part," whatever part that is, but not try to be something they are not. It's a principle that works, not only in the animal kingdom, but also in the kingdom of God.

January 23: Take A Load Off

Accumulate. It's a dangerous little word that describes gently falling snow; the harmless growth of lint on the top bookshelf; or the inevitable gathering of ragged boxes, rusty tools, kits and caboodles found inside our garages.

But those things that slowly accumulate can become merciless blizzards, a horde of cascading dust bunnies, and a backlog of space-stealing, flea market junk. Indeed, accumulate is a dangerous word.

What the Bible calls "trials and tribulations" accumulate too. Gradually, imperceptibly at first, the flakes fall silently down. A setback here. A disappointment there. A protracted illness. A wayward child. Deep, wordless pain. Anxiety about tomorrow. Without a sound, the weariness of life gathers until one day a look out the window reveals drifts the size of sand dunes crushing against the soul.

And sometimes it's not the accumulation of various difficulties that grows so heavy; it's the accumulation of time. A single burden, a load that was once manageable, becomes impossible to bear if it is carried too long.

For example, take into your hand a single bottle of water. It weighs about a pound. Hold it in your outstretched arm. How long can you maintain such a position? A few minutes and you won't be aware of the weight. Hold it for an hour and you will develop pain, tremors, and weakness. Hold it for hours on end and you will end up in need of a chiropractor, surgeon, or orthopedist.

All of us carry burdens. All of us suffer from accumulation: The accumulation of multiple hardships or the accumulation of time – what we used to bear with ease, is now too much. So be careful taking on too many "small" burdens. They tend to become crushing millstones, and no one is strong enough to carry even the lightest load forever.

January 24: No More Enemies

When Spanish dictator Francisco Franco was on his deathbed, a priest was called. The priest asked Franco, "My son, have you forgiven all of your enemies?" The dictator replied, "Father, I have no enemies." The priest asked, "Then you have made peace with them?" Franco reportedly answered, "No. I killed them all."

That deathbed conversation defined the two ways – the only two ways – that we can be rid of our enemies. We can destroy them, the way of the world; or we can forgive them, the way of Christ. We have a great deal of experience with the former, but can we learn to practice the art of forgiveness?

Forgiveness is not clean. It is a tangled, bloody mess. It is a storm of emotion and confusion; a process of starting, stopping, circling, advancing, backtracking, building, collapsing, doing better, doing worse, wallowing, and recovering. Yet, it is the Christ-prescribed path for healing. Healing, yes, but forgiveness is not a magic wand that puts everything marvelously back into place. Forgiveness doesn't save every marriage. It doesn't restore every family. It doesn't repair every broken relationship.

It won't necessarily make you feel good about your son-in-law, your ex-wife, or your step-son. And it is a guarantee that when you try to forgive or reconcile with some people, it will bounce off of them like a rock skipping across flat water.

Our example is Christ: Many will never acknowledge his love for them. They will never embrace it or be changed by it. He loves them still, and his scars prove as much. For his scars are unending symbols, not of the damage that humans inflict on one another, but hopeful signs that love will one day end all animosities, not by means of revenge, but with forgiveness.

January 25: Giving Up On The Past

Dr. Fred Luskin said, "To forgive is to give up all hope for a better past." According to Luskin, what keeps people frozen solid with the regrets and shame of yesteryear is the lingering optimism that they might go back and change it.

Forget that, Dr. Luskin says – not the past – but the prospects of adjusting anything that is now in the rearview mirror. The Apostle Paul said something similar in the New Testament. He made peace with his past and his past self (the self is the hardest person in the world with whom to make peace) with this formula: "Forgetting the past and I press on toward what is ahead."

Can we really forget the past? No. Painful memories, bad choices we have made, ways we have been harmed or harmed others, the heartbreaking losses of offense and betrayal – none of these can be changed. There is no supernatural whitewash for our memory banks or a little recessed button in the back of our skulls that will reboot our brains.

Yet, we can forget the past if forgetting is as Luskin defines it; learning to live so that the past no longer controls us. Forgetting is not an act of ignoring our past experiences. It is integrating those experiences with the present. Forgetting the past is not an act of erasing memories. It is an act of hopeful defiance, whereby we keep living, keep moving, and keep keeping on.

Will we have to let go of some painful memories time and again? Count on it. Will some things from the past haunt us longer than others? Absolutely. Will we have to recycle some heartaches a few times? It is likely. But the challenge will always be the same: To put the past where it belongs - in the past.

January 26: Holy Agitation

An ancient story, often retold but never without relevance, has one of the Egyptian Pharaohs making a strange request of his priests. As the sacrificial ox was being slain at the altar, the Pharaoh demands that the holy men bring to him the holiest portion of the animal, and that part of the animal most evil. In the end, the priests brought Pharaoh only the tongue.

This reflects the parallel wisdom of an equally olden Jewish proverb: "Death and life are in the power of one's words; they hold both poison and fruit." The ancients knew this – the power of words – but we seem to have forgotten it. For all the trouble afflicting this world today, one of the more insidious but overlooked concerns is the failure of basic civility.

Caustic cable news sound bites, scathing social media comments, political mudslinging, rants and tirades against enemies and neighbors: There is a devilish eagerness to rip others apart with our dehumanizing, violent words. This loss of healthy, respectful communication is as big a factor in the loss of a society's soul as institutional and economic collapse.

What can we do about it? Not much if we continue the cycle of spewing poison and death from our mouths. Yet, venomous words are not the only option. Our words also hold the power of life and healing. What if we put the same energy, enthusiasm, and creativity into plotting others' betterment as we did their demise?

"Think of ways to motivate one another to acts of love and good works," the Bible says. "Motivate" means "to incite," to "enflame." The Bible gives us license to be agitators – not to cause trouble – but to be instigators of love and excellence in others, and there's no better way to do that than with good words.

January 27: Take It With You

My friend, Father Thad, once led a parish that desperately needed to expand its ministry. But one man in the congregation absolutely resisted, always squelching prospective change by saying something like, "My grandfather gave the land for this church; my daddy cleared the trees for the building; and we're not going to change a thing (Catholics don't have a monopoly on this sentiment)."

Thad finally had enough. He secured a diocese blessing and obtained a piece of land on the other side of town. He called the local house builders, and had the church relocated! I have this charming picture in my mind of the church, steeple atop, rolling down the road on stilts led by a vestment-clad Father Thad, reading the gospel and splashing holy water along the way.

Truth told, that is pretty good ecclesiology, a word seminarians use to answer the question: "What is the nature of the church?" After several hundred years of religious institutionalism, more and more people are recognizing that the church is not a building. Sure, we say, "I go to church at such-and-such place," but the real church is a people, not a place.

When the last homilies, sermons, songs, testimonies, and prayers are offered at your congregation or parish on Sunday morning, you don't leave the church. You will leave a specific gathering of the church, certainly, but you take the church with you – because the church is you.

And whether we are Catholic, Baptist, Pentecostal, sprinkled, dipped, dunked, or barely damp, we will not be defined so much by "where we go to church," but by whether or not we will be the church once we leave the building. As Father Thad put it so accurately: "Why start another church, when you can take it with you?"

January 28: Settle Down

"Maybe it's time to settle down." Those were my words to a friend who was seeking a bit of help with his unhappy life. It's not that his life was an out-and-out disaster. He had all the trappings of contentment: A good job, a beautiful wife and family, a comfortable home, and a bright future. Still, he wasn't happy.

Truth be told, this was no new phenomena. I had never known him to be happy for terribly long. He didn't suffer from hopelessness, depression, or despair. He simply wanted something better. He was always chasing some utopia created in his mind – the "perfect life" he called it – never recognizing that the life he had was already pretty darn close to perfect.

My friend isn't alone in his quest for a mythical Shangri-La. With places to go, people to see, kingdoms to conquer, mountains to climb, parties to crash, and horizons to reach, any advice resembling "settle down" is quickly disregarded by the strivers and competitors of the world. But settling might be the very path to the life they are seeking.

The person who always wants to be some place better, never lives right where her is. The person who is always looking for Mr. or Ms. Perfect is blind to the remarkable and beautiful persons that surround him. The person who never has enough, never gets around to enjoying much of anything: He never settles in to live, appreciate, or love the life with which he has been richly blessed.

A real, satisfying, happy life can be yours right here, right now, if you will settle down, settle in, and just live it; because at this moment, you are already where you need to be. You might be the only one who doesn't know it yet.

January 29: Hard Of Hearing

A husband and wife had been married for many years when the husband began to fear that his wife was going deaf. Testing his hypothesis, while his wife was in the kitchen cooking dinner, the husband asked from the den, "Honey, what's for dinner?" She didn't answer. So he moved closer to the kitchen and repeated the question; no response.

Then he walked right up to the kitchen door, about ten feet away. "Honey, what's for dinner?" he asked. Nothing. Now he placed himself directly behind her: "Honey, what's for dinner?" The wife whirled around on her heels and shouted, "George, for the hundredth time, I said we are having chicken!" Often, others listen just fine; we are the ones who are hard of hearing.

What a beautiful phrase: Hard of hearing. We don't say "hard of running," if someone has an injured knee, or "hard of seeing" if someone wears glasses. We don't say "hard of chewing" if someone has missing teeth or poorly fitted dentures. But we use "hard of hearing" all the time.

Sometimes the hard of hearing have had an injury, nerve damage, or disease. It's the result of age or overexposure to loud noises. Yes, the teenager that cannot hear you because his earbuds are turned up to excruciating levels, becomes the middle-aged man who cannot hear you when you tell him what's for dinner.

But most of the time we are hard of hearing because we are doing all the talking. We won't stop long enough to realize that a great deal of the noise and drama in our personal world is being self-generated. Stop for one day - one - and really listen. Listen to your family; your coworkers; your neighbors; listen to God.

You might be amazed at what you've been missing.

January 30: The Booger Man

Many of us are afraid of God. We think of him as a merciless, brute who is out to get us. This ghastly, judgmental, angry God that springs up in so many imaginations is a lot like the "Booger Man" my southern grandmother talked about.

The Booger Man was used to keep her grandchildren out of mischief. She would say: "You better behave or the Booger Man is going to get you." Not to be confused with the Bogey Man (a European invention), the Booger Man originated with the Cherokee Nation.

The Cherokee developed a ritual known as the Booger Dance, sometimes called the Ghost Dance by the Europeans, to keep away evil. The tribe would gather for the ritual late at night around a roaring fire, and on cue a group of preselected young men would come storming into the meeting house. They would be dressed in big, furry, grotesque masks.

They would act ferociously, clawing, scratching, and wailing. As the ritual went along, only the proper dance would soothe these savage beasts. Once tamed, each Booger Man would begin to dance with the people and then finally slink back into the darkness. Those who danced out of step would be snatched away, kicking and screaming, and carried into the Appalachian woods.

Is God heaven's Booger Man? Is he a lurking, other-worldly creature waiting to drag away those who fail to stay in step? Is this why we huddle in the corner, praying our prayers as furiously as we can, hoping to placate him?

Yet we cannot make the Booger Man of our imagination reconcile with the God revealed to us in Jesus Christ. For Jesus did not come to frighten us. He came to give us a better way to live. He came to give us life.

January 31: The Wisdom To Wait

Two monks lived together in a monastery. In time one of them died, and within months the other followed. The first monk awoke to discover that he was in heaven, but he realized that his friend wasn't with him.

So off to the lower realms of eternity the celestial monk traveled. That's where he found his friend: He was now a worm, digging in a pile of manure. Immediately the monk commenced to digging, and before long the worm wiggled out and demanded, "Who are you?" The monk answered, "I am your friend, and I'm here to take you to heaven where life is wonderful!"

The worm barked back, "Get lost! I'm staying here!" This was more than the heavenly monk could stand. So he grabbed hold of the worm and started tugging and pulling, begging and pleading the entire time. But the harder he worked at it, the harder that worm clung to his pile of manure. There was no way he was going anywhere.

The above story is an adaptation of a Zen tale meant to communicate an important point: If someone isn't ready to change his or her destructive ways of thinking, acting, and behaving - even guarantees of a happy, blissful life will make no difference whatsoever.

And the more you dig in to "help" that person, to show them the error of their ways, the more tenacious their grip on the manure pile will become. Simply, you can't make someone change. It's not within your power to do so.

We can only wait, hope, and pray that they will reach the end of their rope and "turn their will and life over to a Power greater than themselves." And when this happens, and not a second sooner, we can be there to help dig them out.

FEBRUARY

February 1: Plant A Tree

When the winds of world upheaval begin to blow (they're always blowing), some dooms-daters begin to make predictions about the end of the world. For all their biblical knowledge, they seem to be unaware of Jesus' words: "No one knows the day or the hour." The expiration date set for the universe is knowledge belonging exclusively to God.

Further, as wrong as would-be-prophets are about actual dates, their divination seems to also distract them from the nature of the end of the age. "Look, I am making everything new!" God says in the end. The cosmos doesn't conclude with retribution, but with renewal. The final chapter is not extinction, but transformation. That is our Blessed Hope.

Simply, God believes in and loves his creation in a way that no televangelist or talking-head prophet can ever come close. God has bigger and better plans for his world than just throwing it into the intergalactic trash can. In the words of C.S. Lewis, "We may be tired of this world, but God isn't." He has great things in store, and we get the chance to get in on it and live it beginning today.

A rabbi tells a marvelous story about an old man who planted a tree. When asked if he expected to live long enough to eat fruit from that tree, the old man laughed. "I was born into a world that had fruit ready to eat. My ancestors planted trees for me, and now I plant for my grandchildren."

We can't give up on the world because it's not what we wish it were, or because we think it's all going down the drain anyway; for what we call the "end" will not be the end at all. It will be a renewed beginning.

February 2: Over And Over Again

Today the nation gathers at Gobbler's Knob, Pennsylvania for a uniquely American observance. With bated breath we watch Punxsutawney Phil materialize from his cozy burrow. If he sees his shadow, as the legend goes, there will be six more weeks of winter weather. If he emerges shadowless, then it is the harbinger of an early spring (though since 1886, Phil and his successors have only been correct half the time).

Groundhog Day makes me think not of plump rodents and top-hat-wearing old men, but of Bill Murray. In his now classic comedy film, "Groundhog Day," Murray plays weatherman Phil Connors who gets caught in a time warp and must relive Groundhog Day over and over again. Internet nerds have calculated that Connors stays trapped on Groundhog Day for almost forty years. Why?

The point seems to be personal transformation. Connors must remain where he is until he is a changed man. There is no going forward until that work is done, and had he learned his lessons quicker, the quicker he would have been liberated.

If we review the trajectory of our lives we are likely to find a few common denominators in all we have experienced. That's because there's probably one or two major lessons that God is trying to teach us, a couple of persistent chains he is attempting to break. God allows life to repeat itself, over and over again, until we do the hard, inner work of the soul.

Getting stuck is a necessity and repeating difficult lessons is required, as there are some things that can only be learned in the hard places. But how long we replay and relive the same day is more or less up to us. There comes a time to get it, and to get on with it.

February 3: What About You?

Millard Fuller was a millionaire before age thirty. He gave away his entire fortune before he was forty. He became a friend to world leaders, an advocate for the poor, and a recipient of the Presidential Medal of Freedom.

As founder of Habitat for Humanity and the Fuller Center for Housing, he worked to eliminate substandard housing worldwide. And because of his unfailing vision and tenacity, he was responsible for the sheltering of more than a million people in simple, decent, affordable homes.

Just weeks before he died, on this day in 2009, Millard spoke to my congregation about his life's work. He gushed that morning with all the zeal and energy of a man half his age. He said:

"When I turned seventy people came to me and said, 'Why don't you take it easy now?' But why would I want to do that? I love what I do. I'm not dead yet - I don't even feel bad! I know I don't have much time left, so I've ratcheted up my pace. It is a blessing and privilege to do God's work, to be aggressive doers of good deeds."

In the last book Millard wrote he said: "I am often asked where I get my energy. Well, I believe God loves me and put me on earth for a purpose. I practice good health habits. I like to laugh. And I have been blessed with a wonderful mate.

"All of this contributes to my energy. How long will it last? Who knows? But as long as my energy lasts and as long as I am blessed with a good mind, I intend to stay at it. What about you?"

Indeed, "What about you?" Following Millard's prescription for living may lead to a legacy that will long outlast your life.

February 4: Hammer In Hand

Theologian N.T. Wright uses a powerful example of how our lives fit into the big picture of what God is doing in the world: It is that of a stonemason working on a great cathedral. When these architectural wonders were built during medieval times, the construction process lasted for decades, even centuries. For example, the construction of the Cologne Cathedral in Germany spanned more than 600 years.

For the individual stonemasons, the work began when an architect drew up schematics and then passed his instructions to supervisors, builders, and finally the masons. One mason would shape stones for a particular tower; another carved gargoyles or statues of particular saints. Others labored in the quarry cutting roughhewn blocks.

When the workers were finished with their projects, whatever assignment they had been given, their work was handed over with little knowledge of how it all fit together, or how these pieces contributed to the final product. Since most of the workers would not live to see the building completed, they were forced to trust that the architect would make their work count.

Likewise, we don't know what our life's work will look like in the end. We can only swing our hammer, chisel and trowel in hand, and complete our assignments, trusting God to put all the pieces together. As Wright concludes: "The work we do in the present only gains its full significance somewhere in the future."

We may not live to see that future. We may never know in this lifetime how we have contributed to life's "construction project," but we trust the Architect to make it count, to make it fit together. By God's grace and according to his plan, we will be a part of something more beautiful than anything we can ever build on our own.

February 5: The Only Ones

There's an old joke about a man who arrives at the gates of Heaven. St. Peter asks, "What is your denomination?" The man answers, "Methodist." St. Peter says, "Go to Room 24, but be very quiet as you pass Room 8."

Another man arrives. Peter asks, "What is your denomination?" The man answers, "Catholic." St. Peter says, "Go to Room 18, but be very quiet as you pass Room 8." A third man arrives at the gates. A third time St. Peter asks, "What is your denomination?" The man says, "Baptist."

"Go to Room 11," St. Peter says, "but be very quiet as you pass Room 8." The man said, "I can understand there being different rooms for different denominations, but why must I be quiet when I pass Room 8?" St. Peter said, "Well, the Presbyterians are in Room 8, and they think they're the only ones here."

Of course, in any retelling of this joke, "Presbyterians" can be substituted for any group, because such exclusive, boundary-drawing mindsets are common. These attitudes are not funny, however. They are a severe detriment to God's witness in the world, for God is the one who determines who is "in," and not anyone else.

My friend Landon Saunders says it like this: "Figuring out who is in and who is out is just too much work. It's too heavy of a burden! So I just try to treat every person I meet in this life as if that person will be sitting beside me at the table in eternity."

Such a small change of perspective would do more to advance the kingdom of God on earth than a thousand aggrieved churches that pound their pulpits and point fingers, condemning and excluding others from the love of God and gates of heaven.

February 6: Amen

The word "Amen" means, "Let it be." So at the conclusion of our prayers, we are not saying, "the end." We are actually beginning, for we are confirming and confessing our trust in the God to whom we have just prayed. We are saying "Yes" to God's perspective, and we are saying "No" to all other perspectives.

Therefore, every "Amen" becomes an argument to convince ourselves, over and over again, that God knows us best and knows what is best for us. And since God knows us, he knows we tend to argue with ourselves. We create these stories about how we have failed; how ashamed we should be; how unworthy we are; how useless our lifework has been; how we are a lousy father, mother, parent, or whatever.

I'm convinced that many people can't be quiet and can't still their minds because they can't bear what they say to themselves in the quiet moments. They have to keep the volume of life turned up to ear-bleeding levels and keep the pace of life at breakneck speed.

These people aren't busy, they are suffering. They are attempting to smother the voices in their heads, because a majority of the time the self-guided narrative to which they are listening is erroneous, untrue, and downright destructive.

This, then, is one of the great benefits of prayer: People who pray are reprogramming their software. They are overwriting the faulty components of their thinking. They are experiencing the transformation of their hearts and minds.

In learning to listen to God's voice in prayer they can turn down the cacophony of voices around them and within them. Such praying may not get one everything he or she asks for, but such praying may lead one to getting what he or she really needs.

February 7: To Tell A Story

Hasidic philosopher Martin Buber told the tale of a grandfather who began telling a thrilling story to his grandchildren. The more "into it" the old man got, the more animated he became until unexpectedly he jumped from his wheelchair! In telling the story - and acting it out - it gave new life to the old man. Buber concludes his tale by saying: "Now, that's the way to tell a story!" It's also the way to share your faith.

We often rely on hardened dogma or cascading Scripture references to explain our way of life. This is fine for as far as it goes, but frozen facts and biblical sound bites do very little to invite others to explore faith. These do even less to heal a fractured world.

But if we become so immersed in the story of a gracious God, so connected to his powerful narrative of redemption, so skilled in incarnating Christ that we are animated and enlivened by it, then others just might be attracted to it. Faith just might become a story worth telling; a story worth believing; and a story worth living.

As Paul said to the Corinthians: "Your very lives are a letter that anyone can read by just looking at you. Christ himself wrote it - not with ink, but with God's living Spirit; not chiseled into stone, but carved into human lives!"

This is what Gipsy Smith meant when he spoke of "A Fifth Gospel." He said, "There are five Gospels - Matthew, Mark, Luke, John, and the Christian - but most people never read the first four." It's also what Malcolm Muggeridge was saying with the use of the phrase, "A Third Testament." There is the Old, the New, and you.

As is often said, "You are the only Bible some people will ever read."

February 8: Something By Tolstoy

Tennessee Williams wrote a story about a boy named Jacob and his sweetheart, Lila. Jacob ran the family bookstore, and the couple lived in an apartment above the store - happy married and madly in love.

Over time, however, Lila found the bookstore stifling. She wanted to sing, perform, and see the world. She landed a gig with a vaudeville company and begged Jacob to join her on the road. He couldn't. As the couple parted, Jacob put the bookstore's key in Lila's hand and said, "You will come back some day, and I will be waiting."

Jacob retreated to the bookstore and "took to reading as someone else might have taken to drink...immersed in his books, he waited for his love to return." Fifteen years passed and Lila finally came back. She walked in and Jacob didn't recognize her. "Do you want a book?" he sort of growled.

She answered, "Yes, I do, but I've forgotten the name of it." And she told him a story about two childhood sweethearts; a newlywed couple who lived in an apartment above a bookstore; a young, ambitious wife who left and found her fortune, but could never let go of the key her husband had given her.

Jacob was unfazed. He had forgotten his love for her, forgotten her very face. She pleaded, "You must remember - it is the story of Jacob and Lila!" After a long pause he said, "Yes, there is something familiar about that story; I think it is something written by Tolstoy." He returned to his books and Lila left in tears.

When we immerse ourselves in anything other than God's love, we can forget that love is what life is all about. And if we forget this, we have forgotten everything, for "without love, we are nothing."

February 9: Practice Being God

Some people are impossible to love. You can't dig deep enough, can't try hard enough, can't believe enough, and can't go far enough to make it happen. And I'm not talking about the likes of Adolf Hitler and Charles Manson, either. No, the unlovable are everywhere, and they are fairly normal people.

Bosses, coworkers, in-laws; your rival on the field, in the boardroom, or in the marketplace; your ex-spouse. The guy who cut you off in traffic. The obnoxious mother at your kid's Little League game. There are some real jerks in the world, and they aren't too interested in becoming kinder, gentler, more loving people.

The irony in all of this lack of love is that your personal ability to love others has nothing to do with them. And it has nothing to do with you. See, you can't make yourself love other people, and you can't make them more lovable.

Real love, if it is love, comes from God. So, if the unlovable people we encounter are going to be objects of any level of affection – and I'm not talking about hot, fiery emotion but genuine, gracious concern – then love is something that God must do through us, to us, and for us – and for others. It's not something we can produce on our own.

Instead, we must get to know God better; become more trusting of what God can do, and less confident in our own limited abilities. The more this relationship deepens, the more of God's love we experience; and the more of God's love we experience, then the more loving we become.

This is how, as Clement of Alexandria put it, we "practice being God." For "God is love," and those who know God the best are those who can love the deepest.

February 10: Fixing Life

When my youngest son hopped on an airplane for the first time, he loved it. His favorite part was when the plane would bank steeply to one side. "It's fun when the universe is sideways," he would say, something only a preschooler could appreciate.

Truth is, with the fear, uncertainty, violence, and economic insecurity of this current world, the universe is sideways. Late mortgage payments; no money for tuition; not enough gas in the tank; bill collectors on your constantly ringing cell phone; religious extremism; more reports of more school shootings: In any of these, it's hard to find the "fun." Instead, prayer of the Psalmist comes to mind: "How long O Lord, will you forget about us?"

Some time ago my wife was having a very bad day and had lost her usual cheerfulness. Reduced to tears, I put my arms around her, and said something like, "But honey, I love you." She recoiled, pushed me away and said, "I know. But that don't fix nothing." And she was right.

My love for her didn't change anything about her sideways universe, but we both ultimately agreed that love could give us the strength to go on - fun or not. Because love sustains us, encourages us; it gives us what we really need: The ability to keep going.

If given this choice, which would you take: To have all your problems solved, all your struggles worked out, and all your troubles flushed away; or, would you choose to be deeply, unconditionally, and madly loved? I think I know your answer.

Love is enough, not because it will give us everything we want, but because it gives us the main thing we need. No, love doesn't always "fix" things or our world, but it empowers us, and that makes the difference.

February 11: Love And Marriage

The average wedding now costs tens of thousands of dollars. Flowers, dresses, tuxedoes, pictures, DJs, cakes, catering services, coordinators, and venue rentals: It all adds up to a sizable down payment on a first home - an extremely nice home. But it's more than the money we're talking about. It's also the cavalier attitude that many couples have about getting married.

Young, dreamy-eyed lovers come to the altar with their pockets now empty (or their parents' pockets is more often the case), but with their hearts and heads filled with idealistic hope and romance for the future. This is all good, for these wistful feelings are the necessary fuel that will begin to propel them forward.

Yet, many couples really don't know what they are getting themselves into, being unprepared for the future. They fail to see that an extravagant, black-tie ritual that impresses the neighbors does not a "happily-ever-after" make. And if the actual commitment of the bride and groom is only as substantial as the icing on their wedding cake – sweet and buttery but hardly enduring – then it is no wonder that some ceremonies are still on the Visa card when the divorce attorneys are put on retainer.

Now, I'm no pessimist when it comes to love and marriage. I'm a hopeless, romantic believer, and I believe that some couples know that marriage vows will not insulate them from the trials of life. They enter their joined-together-life prepared; not for every possible contingency. That's impossible.

They are prepared to stick together for much longer than the billing cycle on their wedding expenses. Thus, these are couples who have a real chance to experience the best wedding possible – a wedding that becomes a marriage, for love takes more than a ceremony. It takes commitment.

February 12: More Than Explanation

Recently, I pulled from my bookshelf a few systematic theology books that I had not opened for a long time. The pages were filled with declarations about the attributes and characteristics of God.

God's self-existence, knowability, immutability, infinity, immensity, unity, veracity, holiness, righteousness, omniscience, sovereignty, transcendence – and several other $10 words – with all my handwritten study notes in the margins. This corpus of work was intended to make the theology student feel confident – to demonstrate how right our doctrines are. But as I skimmed the pages I was made freshly aware of how distracted we have become.

For all of Christianity's theoretical words and defenses, the Apostle John was simple and winsome with his definition of God: "God is love." If Christians daily practiced this definition instead of declaring and defending how "right" we are, I imagine the world would be a much different place. With the truth, "God is love," rather than "God is on my side," or "God hates you and your kind," in the hearts of people and animating their actions, it would revolutionize the world.

I know that "love-talk" is the cue to braid our hair with flowers, break out the hookah pipe, drink a little "Free Bubble-Up," and lay back on a bed of unicorns and rainbows. Isn't that about all it is – just talk? But I'm going to take John at his word: Love is God's very nature, and once his love gets planted in our hearts, it spills out to others and changes the world, one person at a time.

God's love must become primary; more crucial than any other belief, creed, or doctrine to which we adhere. Such love will have infinitely more power than any other explanation, because such love is the most important thing in the world.

February 13: Love Saves The World

The late George Carlin said, "Love is incredibly powerful. It is a beautiful thing. But if love had any power to change the world, it would have prevailed by now. Love can't change the world. It's nice. It's pleasant. It's better than hate. But it has no special power." I'm not ready to agree with Carlin just yet.

To that end, there was a rabbi who became friends with a fortuneteller. Every morning the two sat together and watched people head out of the village to work. As a man walked by, the fortuneteller said, "This man will not come back. He will be bitten by a snake and die."

The rabbi answered, "Only God knows such things." They agreed to come together at the end of the day to see if the worker returned. At evening they saw the condemned man enter the village! The fortuneteller ran to him, grabbed his backpack, and emptied it on the ground. An enormous snake spilled out of the bag; a snake very much dead.

So the rabbi asked the man, "What did you do today to avoid misfortune?" The man answered, "I work in the forest. Every day the workers place our food in a common basket and eat together. Today, one of us had no bread and was ashamed. So I told my friends, 'Let me collect the food.' When I came to him I pretended to take bread from him, so that he would not be embarrassed."

To this the rabbi burst out laughing. He said, "Child, today you obeyed God's commandment to love! You saved your coworker and also saved yourself!"

And turning to his fortuneteller friend, the rabbi said, "When one loves from his heart, he changes the fates. Love saves the world from death." Indeed, it does.

February 14: Invisible God, Visible Love

I once visited the Mayan ruins at Tazumal, El Salvador, a place where the ancients gathered to ceremonially soothe their cruel, bloodthirsty deities.

If a severe drought struck the region, then the gods were angry; shed some blood. If the rainy season was monsoonal, or the spring corn crop refused to grow, or if there was sickness, plague, earthquakes, tidal waves, the explanation was always the same: The fickle and nefarious gods had to be appeased.

All ancient religions were built on this foundation: God is angry and humanity stands in constant danger, thus someone has to pay. Much of current religion is likewise anchored to this mooring. It's no wonder then, that the world is filled with hate, bloodshed, panic, and terror. Religious people, the vast majority of the world's population, are afraid of God.

When Christianity succumbs to this type of fear-driven hysteria, it is especially disconcerting. That God is an unpredictable executioner with an itchy, twitchy trigger finger that must somehow be pacified is a gross misrepresentation of our faith, because it is a gross misrepresentation of Jesus Christ.

Jesus "is the visible image of the invisible God," per the Apostle Paul, "And through Christ, God made peace with everything in heaven and earth." Simply, Jesus does not save us from God, but shows us what God is really like. And God is at peace with us. There is no anger to placate and no blood to shed, only his love to receive.

God loves, not because we are good, lovable, or because of what we can do for him. God loves us because he is actually that good. And what we and our world need more than anything – a world up to its collective ears in fear and bloodshed – is that kind of unconditional love.

February 15: The Procession Must Go On

Hans Christian Andersen told the familiar story of an Emperor who loved fine clothes. He easily fell into the trap of two swindlers, who for a large sum of money, claimed they could weave the most magnificent garments imaginable. The Emperor dressed in his "new clothes" and went off in procession through the town, though he was actually naked.

Of course, no one would point out the obvious. Facing the truth was too much, until at last a little child declared boldly: "He hasn't got anything on!" Finally everyone could admit that the Emperor was indeed naked.

The Emperor, however, could not admit the truth. "The procession must go on," he said, and he walked more determined than ever, proudly wearing a costume that wasn't there.

How many people have been ruined by the words, "The procession must go on?" Hiding an addiction; remaining in an abusive relationship; continually apologizing and covering for the failures of a spouse, a parent, or a business partner; maintaining religious beliefs for which they no longer have conviction; propping up a naked life: All because the prospect of being honest is more terrifying than the constantly camouflaging of the charade (when one loses the ability to be honest, that person has lost everything).

Giving up on our processions is not easy. In fact, giving up on our pride is almost impossible. But when the exhaustion of sustaining the sham becomes stronger than our fear of being honest (and what others will say), the foolish procession will end and we can, by grace, be transformed.

The first and basic tenant of change, transformation, recovery, or repentance (you choose your word) is this: One must "admit his powerlessness, and that life is unmanageable." That is the naked truth, and there is no shame in facing it.

February 16: Chains to Change

Centuries ago, those who suffered mental illness were often committed to "madhouses." Patients were subjected to inhumane "interventions" and were generally kept in dark dungeons and chains.

Mercifully, Dr. Samuel Tuke, a Quaker physician and minister building on the work of his grandfather, created one of the first alternative treatment centers. It was a quiet country house where patients were treated, not as wild animals, but as human beings.

Dr. Tuke also broke ground with something he called "moral treatment," and it became the foundation of mental healthcare for the next century. Patients were taught to dress respectably and how to behave socially. The treatment was reinforced by constant monitoring and a system of rewards and punishments.

Outwardly, these patients looked perfectly healthy as their behavior followed the established rules. It was an improvement, but inside the ill remained very much the same, for when the patients' monitors left them alone for any period of time, disaster would strike. The patients could do all the right things when forced from without, but they had no concept of right motivation from within.

"Moral treatment" was a failure and highlighted a limitation as old as the human species: People are not changed by chains – whether these chains be made of iron or be made from rules and coercion. If people are going to change, it is because something happens internally, not because their external behavior has been modified.

Knowing and keeping the rules, even religious rules, is simply not a better way to live. We need a way of life that transcends our chains and changes us from inside; and that is exactly what Christ offers.

Jesus strikes literally at the heart of the issue – our hearts – transforming us from the inside, so that more rules and steeper requirements are not required.

February 17: The Mailroom

Walter went to work for a large corporation. He began his career in the basement - in the mailroom. One day as Walter was sorting the mail, he saw a cockroach on the floor. He was about to step on it, when the roach spoke: "Don't kill me, I'm a magic cockroach! Spare me and I will grant all your wishes."

"Well," Walter said, "Make me an executive of the company and I will let you live." When Walter came to work the next day he found himself greeted as "Mr. Vice-President." It was exactly as the cockroach had promised.

This began a meteoric rise for Walter as he was granted one wish after another. Finally, he was the President of the largest corporation in the world. Then one day Walter heard footsteps on the roof of his penthouse office. Outside he found a small boy praying.

"Are you praying to me," Walter asked. The little boy answered, "Of course not! I am praying to God."

Walter was deeply disturbed. He thought he was at the very top of everything. So after a sleepless night, Walter demanded that the magic cockroach be brought before him once again.

"I have one last wish," Walter said, "then I will set you free, for there will be nothing left to ask. I wish to be like God." The cockroach said, "As you wish."

The next day when Walter came to work he was back in the mailroom.

The New Testament teaches us that Jesus emptied himself of all things to show the length to which God's love will go, and to show us how to love others. He considered serving humanity to be more important than his prestige. He chose the mailroom over the penthouse, and to be like God, so must we.

February 18: Nothing More

When I first became a pastor, I was a green, naïve, ignorant child, full of pep and vinegar, ready to extinguish hell with a water gun. Equipped with a fresh diploma, a newly-inked ordination, and a new red Bible, I worked hard to demonstrate that I knew everything there was to know about leading a congregation. Heck, I thought I knew everything about everything.

The hard work paid off. In proving myself, membership grew, coffers swelled, buildings were built, baptisteries were filled, other congregations were planted, and the church became a sensation.

By the end of my tenure, I had gained a great deal of success. But I also lost a few things along the way: My youthful idealism; my religion; my marriage; my way, and almost my mind.

Most of all, I lost touch with the very reason I had entered the vocation in the first place: The love of Christ. Another hard-striving, pompous, know-it-all once wrote, "Christ has shown me that what I thought I knew is worthless. Nothing else matters but to know Christ and to know that I belong to him" (Philippians 3).

So if I could begin again, I would enjoy Christ more and work less. I would spend less energy on the trivial, and focus more on grace. I would worry less with my image and be "okay" with being ignorant.

This singularity of Christ and his grace, ironically, makes some Christians uncomfortable. They want "more." But there is no more if our first and consuming passion is not to reflect the grace and love of Christ.

After all, "if I speak with the tongues of men and angels, and if I have all faith so as to remove mountains, but I do not have love, it profits me nothing."

February 19: Work It Out

The Apostle Paul wrote to the first generation of Christians, "Work out your salvation with fear and trembling." This is his prescription for living. Life has to be entered as if we are apprentices in need of personal, practical, hands-on experience. This approach might make our hands quiver, but there is no other way to learn than "working it out" - life that is - as we go.

In high school I had a chemistry teacher who took this "work it out" approach to teaching. He moved us from desks to the lab. We were issued safety goggles, rubber gloves, and vinyl aprons. We were introduced to the world of Bunsen burners, Petri dishes, test tubes, formaldehyde-drowned specimens, dissection, and the explosive power of chemical reactions.

He was convinced – and rightfully so – that the best way for someone to learn is to "work it out" and enter the experience and experiment for oneself. To be sure, we set off the fire alarm a few times in the process of working it out.

But when you are learning – either in life or the laboratory – it's not always safe and clean. Sometimes the lab of life fills with smoke and the sparks fly. Sometimes the results we are working toward are much more surprising than we could have ever anticipated. Sometimes our learning is costly and comes with a load of liabilities. But what other option is there?

Given the choice, few of us want to be told about life. We want to actually live – even if it causes our hands and hearts to shake. We don't want the security of notepads and lectures. We want safety goggles and fire extinguishers. Truth told, some things will go wrong; but there is no better way to live and no better way to learn.

February 20: A Dog's Life

My boys were playing in the backyard one day when they called out in unison: "The dog is on the roof!" Indeed, our Shih Tzu – Toby – had inexplicably crawled beneath the deck railing and was two stories off the ground.

I was horrified and my wife was worse. Deranged with panic, she wanted to crawl over the rail to rescue him. So, with the boys ready to exercise their burgeoning football catching skills below and my hand firmly holding my wife by the belt loops at the railing, I gently called: "Toby, come here, boy." Thankfully, he loped over and a family tragedy was averted.

As crazy as this story is, here is the craziest thing of all: While our entire family mobilized to protect and save this precious little dog, Toby was completely, totally, and blissfully unaware of our efforts. Hands were shaking. Tears were forming. Railings were being scaled. Catch nets were being weaved. Meanwhile, he was sniffing leaves, enjoying the view, and inspecting the strange metal floor beneath his feet.

Toby doesn't understand this, but he doesn't have to; he simply lives a dog's life in the loving arms of those who always look out for him. Sometimes I perceive God working the same way.

I sense him hanging in the atmosphere around us; ethereal and intangible. I glimpse him brooding over the circumstances of life, sometimes gently calling, but most of the time just ready to catch us when we fall; or to save us from ourselves when we've crawled too far out on the ledge.

Yes, I believe there is a mysterious, unseen, hovering God in the universe that we cannot always understand, see, or otherwise perceive. But we know he is there, and his enveloping love for us is very real and very good.

February 21: Fish And Fishing

"Give a man a fish and he will eat for a day. Teach a man to fish and he will eat for a lifetime." This proverb falls easily from the lips of politicians, pundits, and policy makers, but it's so much more difficult to practice than to quote. Yet, its ageless wisdom is more needed today than ever.

Some people need a "fish." They need help with their daily bread, a little hand-up to get back on their feet. And there are those who need to "learn to fish." They need a whole new set of life skills; a whole new way of living, or they will be trapped for their entire lives.

Ruby Payne calls this latter challenge "generational poverty." In this case, no living family member "possesses or can transmit the intellectual, social, and cultural skills necessary to change their condition." Thus, if no one in a family knows how to be anything but poor, then the deck is stacked against that family, and they may never see real improvement for generations.

This is not an individual or "troubled neighborhood" problem. This is our entire society's problem, as no culture will survive without addressing systematic, generational poverty and the social injustices and root causes that perpetuate it.

More than 2,000 times in the Hebrew and Christian Scriptures the issues of poverty and injustice are called to the attention of the people of faith. So when we are looking for "somebody to do something about it," we must look to ourselves, for our task is to "bring Good News to the poor. To proclaim that captives will be released, that the blind will see, and that the oppressed will be set free."

We might have to learn a few new fishing skills ourselves, to get this job done.

February 22: Today

The past is a powerful thing. It can trap us, as we constantly look over our shoulders at what "might have been." Looking in the rearview mirror we ask: "Where did my life go off the rails? How could I have made such terrible mistakes? What could I have done differently? Why hasn't God (or my parents or my spouse or my employer) treated me fairly?"

Such questions only end with inadequate replies, proving the axiom true: "There is no future in the past." But there is no future in the future either; not a view of the future that is tainted with fear. Yet, countless people live their lives in a hypothetical time machine, always worrying and fretting over a distant yet to come that might never materialize.

These future-fearing people fill the air with their own questions, questions that usually begin with the words, "What if?" What if I lose my job? What if I am diagnosed with cancer? What if I run out of money? What if the economy collapses?" Again, such questions can't be answered. They only rob worriers of the time they have today.

Then there are those who are preoccupied with the future differently. They aren't worried. They are enthused. They have schemes and plans for tomorrow and say things like: "I'll do it one day... Life will be better some day... Eventually I'll get around to it... In the end I will achieve my goals." But in the end, the end comes and the best-laid plans never materialize.

If we are engrossed with the snarling monsters of our past, obsessed with the fearful uncertainties of tomorrow, or spend our precious few days prepping for an ethereal future, this much is certain: We give away today, and today is all we have.

February 23: Bring It On

The Apostle John had a young apprentice named Polycarp. Tradition says that John ordained him as the Bishop of Smyrna (modern Turkey) where he would pastor for the next 50 years.

When he was 86 years old, Polycarp was arrested and sentenced to die because he would not deny Christ and worship Caesar. His death is the earliest recorded eyewitness account of a Christian martyrdom outside the New Testament:

"The authorities came at suppertime with their weapons, as if coming out against a robber. Polycarp could have escaped but he refused saying, 'God's will be done.' The authorities were amazed at his age and some, ashamed, said, 'Why did we go to such trouble to capture a man like this?' Immediately Polycarp called for food and drink for them.

"When brought to the arena, the judge tried to persuade Polycarp to renounce his faith, saying, 'Have respect for your old age, swear by the fortune of Caesar. Reproach Christ, and I will set you free.' Polycarp answered, 'These 86 years have I served Jesus, and he has done me no wrong. How can I blaspheme my King and my Savior, now? Bring on whatever you want.'

"Thus they collected wood and bundles of sticks and tried to nail Polycarp to the stake to be burned, but he said, 'Leave me as I am, for he that gives me strength to endure the fire, will enable me not to struggle. May I be received this day as an acceptable sacrifice.'"

Today is the Feast of St. Polykarp and anniversary of his death. Reflect upon his courage; he willingly faced severe consequences for his faith. Note his generosity: He gave food and drink to those sent to arrest him. And pray for his determination to be able to say, "Bring it on."

February 24: Our Namesake

I share with my deceased grandfather a deep appreciation for our family's history. I don't run about tracing gravestones or going to reunions, but I do love reading the genealogies.

The first of my family came to this continent thirty years before the American Revolution. They migrated from Ulster, Northern Ireland, after first crossing from Scotland, like so many families known as the "Scott-Irish."

There are the first known McBrayers, lower nobility, who are buried at St. Michael's Church in Dumfriesshire, Scotland; the scrabbling farmers from County Down, Ireland, fiercely loyal to King James (Yes, of Bible translation fame); there is Samuel, the first American McBrayer, born not on American soil, however, but on the boat crossing the Atlantic.

I have ancestors who were captured as POWs in the Civil War, those who owned slaves, and those who liberated slaves. They were artisans, professors, ministers, shysters, and murderers - from every walk of life. In them there is much to admire and much to be ashamed of, but by way of glory or indignity, I carry their name and their blood runs in my veins.

So when I read the old records or visit my historical roots, I have the opportunity to learn, grow, and remember who I am and from where I come. And I'm challenged to think of how my life can shape those who will carry our name in the future.

It's the same with the church. There is much to be proud of, much to be embarrassed over, much to applaud, and much to condemn. While not everyone in our "family tree" of faith is commendable, by way of glory or indignity, we can learn from these to "bear the name of Christ" properly, and to faithfully pass that name to those who will follow us.

February 25: The Arms Of Love

Franciscan priest, Father Richard Rohr, tells a story about eating dinner with a family from his parish. They had a wonderful meal together, and the whole time the toddler in the family, who had just learned to walk, was running about everywhere. As Rohr says, "That little guy could really move, but he had a problem stopping."

He ran to the top of a set of stairs but could not find his "brakes" in time to stop. So he toppled over the edge, banging and careening his way down the stairwell. No one at the table moved; they all sat there, holding their breath in dread.

Four, five, six, seconds passed. Finally, the father leapt from his chair and ran to the stairs. There the youngster was at the bottom of the steps, only bruised a bit, but lying in shock, his eyes bugged out over what had just happened to him. Only when his dad got to him and picked him up did he start crying.

Father Rohr made this appropriate observation: "We can never acknowledge our pain and let the healing begin, until we are taken up in the arms of love. Love allows the crying and the mending to begin."

We all stumble and fall, sometimes spectacularly so. Maybe we ignored the warnings. Maybe we got in over our heads. Maybe we just took a tumble in the dark. Whether by accident or intention, falling flat hurts, and we end up bloodied and blue.

Granted, we are bound to fall; it's our nature as children. But thankfully, God's love is stronger than our failures and his grace will outlast our pain. He will take us up into his forgiving arms, and there we will cry; and there we will heal, until we are ready to run again.

February 26: Break The Kettles

The Chinese have a proverb: "Break the kettles and sink the ships," they say. The saying comes from an ancient military battle almost 2000 years ago. A new tribal king came to power and immediately attacked his neighbor, surrounding the city of Julu.

The king of Julu called for reinforcements from his generals, and the army came marching to save their king. But the rescuing generals dragged their feet. The march to save the king became a quagmire as the generals' incessant strategizing devolved into feasting and drunkenness.

Finally, a junior officer named Xiang Yu took command. He said, roughly translated into English, "When you go to rescue someone, you don't dillydally. You just go do it, like rushing to quench a burning fire." With that, Xiang Yu immediately marched his army across the Yellow River to engage the enemy.

Once on the other side, Xiang Yu gave his men three days' worth of food and supplies and destroyed everything else, including the boats that had brought them across the river, their tents and sleeping mats, their eating utensils, and their cooking kettles. In so doing, Xiang Yu was sending a clear signal to his troops that they had no chance of survival by going backwards.

The way into the future is exactly by this decisive path of "breaking the kettles and sinking the ships." We must do the hard work of feeling the pain of the past so that we might be free from it. Then the future calls us forward, not because we have forgotten the past, but because we have made peace with it.

The only way to make that peace is to quit trying to change what is back there. We can't do anything about the past anyway, so we must learn to let it go.

February 27: Finding Jesus

Jesus said in Matthew 25: "I was hungry, and you fed me. I was thirsty, and you gave me a drink. I was a stranger, and you invited me into your home. I was naked, and you gave me clothing. I was sick, and you cared for me. I was in prison, and you visited me. For when you did this for one of the least of these my brothers and sisters, you were doing it for me!"

Where is Jesus today? In heaven? In a church sanctuary on Sunday morning? Is he locked away in the Vatican or a lofty seminary? No, Jesus is sitting in an emergency room, an uninsured, undocumented immigrant in need of healing. He is behind bars, so far from his parole date he can't think that far into the future.

He is sleeping under a highway overpass. He is an evictee waiting in line at the shelter for a bed and a cup of soup. He is the poor child living in a slum, bearing the stripes of abuse on his body, and with a growl in his stomach. He is an old forgotten woman at the nursing home who no one thinks of anymore, other than as a body taking up space.

He is a refugee in Sudan, an exile from Syria, and a war orphan in Bagdad. He is a mill worker trying to stay ahead of the bill collectors while keeping a roof over his children's heads. Jesus is the poor, the downtrodden, the homeless, the sick, the hungry, the thirsty, the jailed, the lonely, and the overlooked.

As we go to these, the least of these, we go to Jesus. Not figuratively, not symbolically, but literally. To serve those in need - with help, love, and kindness - is to serve Jesus.

February 28: Burdens Lifted

Some have been taught to push through their troubles. "Rub some dirt on it and get back out there," they have been instructed. "Push through the pain," say life's drill sergeants. "If the bone ain't sticking out, then you ain't hurt," comes the call from the sidelines. So they soldier on, dragging their burdens with them.

Others have been taught to ignore their troubles. "Be positive. There's no need to make a mountain out of a molehill. I'm sure things will work out in time. You know, there's always someone worse off than you." Such numbskullery rolls easily off the tongue, but lands like hammer blows on those smothered by their worries.

So caught between comforters who offer no comfort and burdens that cannot be unburdened, those who hurt usually go crazy, get numb, or give up. They suffer in silence, the accumulating pain gathering steadily until they break. Yet, in the breaking is the deliverance.

"Come to me, all who are weary and carry heavy burdens," Jesus said. Obviously, he recognized the human condition, offering far more than harsh motivation or disparaging clichés. He was speaking to burdened, broken people who needed actual relief, so that is what he offered. "You will find rest for your souls," he said.

With this invitation Jesus also recognized that only those who know they are burdened, who are finished with trying to shovel out from beneath their amassed weariness, who are exhausted by their burdens, will be able to hear him.

When one has been sufficiently broken – cracked open as it were by life's experiences – then the relief and redemption they so desperately need will be there waiting for them. As Leonard Cohen wrote, "There's a crack in everything. That's how the light gets in." And that's exactly how burdens get lifted.

MARCH

March 1: Let The Water Settle

A desperate executive who was living a hurried life sought the counsel of an old guru who lived in a mountain cave. The holy man listened to his guest for a while, then retreated deep into his cave, returning shortly with a basin.

He scooped water from the muddy stream passing by the mouth of the cave and offered it to the executive to drink. Of course, it was rejected. The water was far too dirty. After a while he offered the water again, but this time, all the silt had settled to the bottom of the basin and the water was clear and pristine. The man readily drank it. The wise man then asked, "What did you do to make the water clean?" The man answered, "I didn't do anything."

"Exactly!" said the old monk. "Your life is dark and troubled, disturbed and muddy because you are always allowing the water to become agitated. Only when it is calm will you have peace. So do nothing. Be still and let the water settle."

Be still. That's harder than it sounds, no doubt, but it is one of the best things for the health of our souls. As a friend noted recently, the words "listen" and "silent" are spelled with exactly the same letters and mean the same thing. Stillness is the quickest way to listen to God and to find a little peace.

So learn to turn down the noise (and stop contributing to the noise). Learn to cultivate some distance from this clamorous world, because distance is a good thing when it comes to things and people who are harmful.

Learn, by healthy boundaries to keep this raucous, contemporary society at arm and ear's length. You might begin to let the water of your own soul peacefully settle.

March 2: Real Security

There is a single word that has overtaken contemporary US society: Security. From online purchases and porous borders to international terrorism and identity theft, nothing is safe anymore. So much for the days when there was "nothing to fear but fear itself." Now there is everything to fear.

Nowhere is this more evident than when it comes to economics. But to tell you the truth, if you are trusting your money to keep you "secure," you probably should be afraid; it will never give you peace of mind. Don't get me wrong. We all need a few dollars along the way, and money is good for as far as it goes. It just can't go far enough.

Why? Because once you have a little pile of dough you have to go on guard duty. You go into perpetual protection mode, always on the wall, always peering out at the economic boogeymen, always defending, hedging, and securing.

It's as elemental as this: Our level of peace will depend upon what we depend upon, no more and no less. If the source of our security and well-being is this world's economic promises, we should hire better money managers, take more medication, and stuff more gold coins under our mattresses. But if our subsistence is Christ, then no, life will not be easy, but the source of his strength is endless and the peace he offers surpasses all understanding.

Thus, we joyfully live in this world, but recognize it for how fragile it is. We see that ultimately it cannot meet our deepest needs. That responsibility belongs exclusively to God, because in time all our stockpiles will fail us, but he never will. Trusting him to sustain us is not near as dangerous as trusting a system that can never be secured.

March 3: Idiot Compassion

Zen Buddhists use a descriptive phrase that we who are Christian should adopt as our own. The phrase is "Idiot's Compassion." It was first used by Chogyam Trungpa, a controversial Tibetan who helped bring Buddhism to the West in the 1970s. According to Trungpa, "Idiot's Compassion" is this intense desire to help someone who is in need, but this benevolent desire blinds the do-gooder from seeing reality.

The classic example of such behavior is the relationship between the addict and the enabler. Suppose an alcoholic friend comes to you in much suffering. Her body is racked by convulsions and tremors. She begs you for a drink. You are persuaded to offer her a drink - just one drink - to alleviate her immediate pain. You do this, in your own mind, out of mercy.

Yet, in providing the addict another drink, another high, or another hit, you have actually given her more of the poison that will ultimately take her life. This is not mercy. It is foolish cruelty. It is "Idiot's Compassion."

This can be hard wisdom to accept, especially for those who are engineered to "help" others. We want to solve their problems, be a listening friend, or offer a little support while they are down on their luck. In most cases, this is gracious and appropriate intervention, but for some it is disaster, like trying to rescue a drowning man who is still fighting the water. Both the savior and saved will drown in the struggle.

No, I'm not advocating a lack of compassion for those who need some help along life's way. I'm only calling attention to the fact that once you are tangled up with one who refuses to change, that person has a way of making you look and behave like an idiot as well.

March 4: Nothing To Prove

Nikos Kazantzakis was a famed Greek writer and philosopher who wrote the book, *Zorba the Greek*. He is buried on the island of Crete in his ancestral village, a simple headstone marking the spot. The stone reads, translated into English, "I want nothing. I fear nothing. I am free."

This is timeless wisdom, for the things we desire, the things we want, the things we think we need, and the things we chase imprison us. The pursuit, the game of acquisition - and we're usually chasing emotional rather than material things - actually steals our happiness. The pursuit is a dead-end, and only when we have given up, given out, and given over, can we ever be happy and free.

Now, if a Greek philosopher's epitaph is too highbrow for your tastes, then maybe you will be better served by the words of Kris Kristofferson as sung by Janis Joplin: "Freedom is just another word for nothing left to lose." And usually the last thing we lose is our wretched insecurity that has us forever chasing after fool's gold, playing for the fickle crowd's applause, or trying to climb some insurmountable mountain to showcase our strength.

There's nothing wrong with ambition, for it has its place. There's no shame in having God-given abilities; be thankful for them. The problem is when we go scrambling for accolades and approval, when we become something of stage actors trying to obtain that elusive appreciation, recognition, and validation.

The problem is when we feel we have something to prove to others - that we are capable or lovable. Then, we have imprisoned ourselves, and only when the striving ends can we be free.

It's only when we have let everything go, when we have nothing left to prove, that we will begin to truly live.

March 5: Keep The Basket

A 92-year-old Georgia woman was expelled from her church where she had been a member of for 50 years. The notification she received read: "You are no longer a member of this church as you have shown non-support towards the church in the areas of constant and consistent financial and physical participation."

The woman admitted that she had not been giving as she once had. She also admitted that she had not attended church recently - since she was an invalid - a fact evidently ignored by the pastor and congregation before they excommunicated her.

Rather than coming to a decades-long member and helping her, praying for her, supporting her - the church excommunicated her. "If you can't participate, and more importantly can't put your dollars in the plate, then good riddance" - was the mentality. Of course, if she were to show up some Sunday and drop a fat check into the collection basket, I'm sure all would be forgiven.

And speaking of baskets, here's an old story I would like to bring to the attention of that church: A farmer got so old that he could no longer work. His son, now in command of the farm, would look at his father doing nothing and say to himself, "He's of no use any more.".

So one day the son brought home a large basket and told his father to get in. The son then dragged the basket to a high cliff. As he approached the edge from which he would throw his father, his father called from inside the basket.

Looking inside, his father smiled and said, "I know you are going to throw me over the cliff, but before you do, may I suggest that you save this basket. Eventually, your son will need it for you."

March 6: Be Holy

The words "holy" and "sacred" are sometimes used interchangeably, but there is a huge difference between the two. Sacred comes from the Latin, "sacrum." You might recognize that "sacrum" is the name of the bones in your pelvis. The Romans called this part of the human body "sacred," as it houses the reproductive organs, and as such, it is from where life springs.

Thus, the sacred was recognized as something that had to be protected and secured. That is an excellent picture, actually, of how we employ sacredness. Human beings create sacred rituals (along with church furniture and traditions) that build barriers and mark territory. This allows us to keep everything and everybody perceived as a threat on the outside.

The sacred is the ritualistic space, community, and people-dividing behavior of human beings. But this is not God's way, a God who is holy - not sacred. Holy is something that is "whole." The root word is "health." Holiness is something that is complete, unbroken, intact, and secure. No additional policies or procedures are necessary to make it so.

Therefore, what is holy is strong and accepting, defined less by unapproachability and more by openness. The holy doesn't alienate, it invites. The holy doesn't separate, it welcomes. The holy doesn't divide, it embraces.

Whereas what is sacred is a small restricted space that must be sheltered and guarded, the old Norse word for "holy" means "a large living room," where people are made to feel very much at home.

I pray that God will make us holy: Whole, healthy, welcoming people who can hardly be made to feel insecure. I also pray that he never allow us to become a sacred people, for when we lose our ability to welcome others, we have lost our unique place in the world.

March 7: The End Of The World

Researchers say that Earth is headed toward an apocalypse. Our sun is becoming a "Red Giant." Its core will intensify and expand on a gargantuan scale. Eventually, the sun will become so large that it will suck our planet in and everything will be vaporized. The good news is this catastrophe isn't going to happen for another seven million years.

Of course, life on this planet will likely end long before our sun reaches critical mass. Outside of being obliterated by an asteroid, atmospheric destruction by a super volcanic eruption, there is always the prospect of pandemic, famine, and the exhaustion of the earth's fresh water supply.

And then there is the biggest danger for future humanity: Ourselves. We could easily destroy one another with our nuclear arsenals. Our technology we now so love, could run amok. Some unforeseen disaster involving genetic mutation or yet to be invented scientific advancement could be our undoing.

Ray Kurzweil believes that humanity has "about even chances of making it through this next century." But then he adds the caveat that he has "always been accused of being optimistic."

While the survival of life on Earth appears grim from a scientific perspective (and definitely from some religious perspectives), it doesn't appear to be so from God's perspective. God believes in life, and he is not planning a cosmic funeral.

"Behold, I make all things new," is his mantra, and the final scene he gives us in the Scriptures is not one of planetary destruction. It is a "new heaven and a new earth" where there will "be no more death, sorrow, crying, or pain."

Human life on this planet will indeed reach a terminus and we will all die. But that won't be the end of the world; it will be a new beginning.

March 8: Vulnerability

On Jesus' last night before his crucifixion, he gathered his disciples and gave them the commandment to love and serve one another. Then he showed them how.

He rolled up his sleeves, threw a towel over his shoulder, and with a basin of water, squatted down to wash the filthy feet of his disciples. Jesus took the position of a slave and honored those who had not the slightest indication of how holy his act was.

Walter Brueggemann describes this scene: "To kneel in the presence of another is to be totally vulnerable, because you are in an excellent posture to have your face or your groin kicked in. Our Lord made himself vulnerable precisely in that way! He knelt, not in humility or in fear, but in strength and confidence, opening himself to others."

This was a demonstration course for how to live, for Jesus never maintained feelings of superiority over others; he eagerly gave up his rights and privileges; he didn't defend himself with angry tirades or theological manifestos; he taught - and showed - vulnerability.

A follower of Jesus testifies to and celebrates the truth he has come to know, but knows in equal measure that the truth has been washed through and through with a foot wash basin. The power of the disciple of Christ is a power wielded, not by force or fist, but by a holy hand towel.

He who would be like Jesus does not lord over others. He gets down on the ground, down on his face, down in the dust, the mire, and the mud. He makes himself completely and totally exposed. Even if those whom he serves kick him in the face; even if they stone him to death; even if they crucify him on a cross: Vulnerability is a holy exercise.

March 9: Walk On

In ancient Jerusalem there was a pool of water called Bethesda. It was a common belief that an angel came from heaven at certain times and "stirred up the water" of Bethesda's pool, resulting in miraculous healing for anyone who could get in the water.

Jesus once made a visit to Bethesda and healed a lame man he found there. Then, he gave the newly made-well man practical instructions: "Pick up your mat and walk." This wasn't to get the man's bed out of the way. Jesus was saying, "Get it out of here so that you won't come back to it!"

This former invalid had been coming to Bethesda for the better part of four decades. That is a long time to waste lying alongside a bubbling brook. And now that he was empowered to live a better, healthier life, it would be easy for him to fall back into old habits. Jesus wanted this stretcher removed so that the man would not have the temptation to return to it.

This olden story of faith predates today's advances in neuroscience, but Jesus already knew what researches have confirmed: Routines – good or bad – cause neurons in the brain to alter their patterns. So in the process of breaking a habit, the brain must also be "rewired" to change a person's behavior. This means placing barriers in the way that lead back to old habits.

If we want sustained change for our lives, there must be a grace-infused commitment, not to return to those ways, persons, lifestyles, and behaviors that will only take us back to the unhealthy way of life we knew before. If we are going to remain well, we must put away our "mats and walk" on, never returning to who and what we once were.

March 10: You Will Be Free

During the Civil War thousands of slaves made their way out of slavery on what was nicknamed the Underground Railroad. It was a secret escape route that took slaves from the Deep South across the Mason-Dixon line.

The slaves were assisted by people known as "conductors" who transported their cargo by clandestine means, all the dangerous miles to freedom. And it was Ms. Harriet Tubman who was the greatest single conductor in the history of the Underground Railroad.

An escaped slave herself, and often referred to as "Moses" for her chain-breaking efforts, Tubman was responsible for leading nearly a thousand people to freedom, including her siblings, parents, and numerous nieces and nephews. And though she journeyed deep into slave territories many times with a huge bounty on her head, she was never caught.

She credited her success to the fact that once a slave came into her custody, no matter how afraid or demoralized that person might become on the journey, she never let them return to their chains. She would say to them, with all the resolve her tiny, five-foot frame could muster, "You will be free... Or you will die."

Freedom was a favorite term of the Apostle Paul in the New Testament, for in his day, slavery was as common as in the American South in the 1800s. But a slave could be freed by means of a "ransom." Ransom is a term straight from the slave trader's auction block and means, "To remove from the marketplace."

What God has lovingly planned and what Jesus has dramatically accomplished is the actual rescue from slavery – in all its varied forms: Spiritual, emotional, psychological, and physical. We are truly free, our captivity is eradicated by Christ. Let us never return to our chains, no matter what.

March 11: Paying For Your Raising

Have you heard the phrase: "Paying for your raising"? It is something like the parental cycle of karma. All the sins of your youth and all the ways you hurt your parents, come home to roost in your own children. So you suffer, as this saying goes, as your parents suffered, but there is no way to "pay for your raising."

A child born into a middle-income family, excluding the cost of college, will cost his or her parents nearly $250,000 to get that child to high school graduation. Now, if you think you can go to your adult parents' home, and with one fell swoop stroke them a check for a quarter of million dollars and call it even, then you are insane.

You can't pump the serotonin back inside their brains. You can't undo all their gray hair, crow's feet, and high blood pressure that you caused. For you, they had weight gain, counseling sessions, hormone therapy, and sleepless nights. You imposed upon them impossible decisions, private fights, monetary sacrifice, and countless tears.

Your parents experienced existential guilt, law enforcement interventions, miserable teacher conferences, and gastroesophageal reflux disease: You did this to your parents! We all did - your kids will do it to you - and there's no way to repay any of it. But there's no expectation to do so, because most would endure all these heartaches again and again for the sake of those to whom we gave life.

How else can you explain why perfectly sane, highly functioning adults keep having children? It isn't craziness, it is love (though, if you have ever been in love, you know how close it appears to madness).

Parenthood is an act of steady, secure, unshakable, unearned, uncaused, and sometimes unappreciated love. That's nothing that anyone can pay back.

March 12: A "Yes" Face

There is an story from early America that found Thomas Jefferson and a number of his companions attempting to cross a flooded river while on horseback. Each rider plunged into the raging current, man and animal fighting to get across.

Another traveler - one on foot - watched the group closely. Finally, needing to get to the other side himself, he asked Jefferson to take him across. The President agreed and the two made it safely to the other side.

Once across, a man in Jefferson's party asked the traveler why he had selected the President to carry him across. The traveler was stunned. He had no idea it was the President who had carried him through the flooded river. He simply answered: "All I know is on some of your faces was written the answer 'No,' and on some of your faces was the answer 'Yes.' His was a 'Yes' face."

I believe God has a "Yes" face. "Every good and perfect gift is from above," the Apostle James said, "coming down from the Father." He indulges his children with goodness and grace. But his propensity to say "Yes" doesn't mean he is overindulgent. He isn't afraid to say "No." God may sometimes refuse to give us what we ask for because in his love for us he wants to give us something better.

That something better might be patience. It might be spiritual growth and maturity. It might be a change or improvement of character. It might be the good fruit of love, joy, peace, kindness, or self-control. Two things are certain: These gifts are better for us than the lesser things we crave.

God still has a "Yes" face even when he doesn't give us what we want. In those times, he often gives us what we need.

March 13: "I Am"

One of the great British writers of the last century was Gilbert Keith Chesterton, known by his initials, G.K. He was a three-hundred-pound mountain of a man whose intellect, honesty, sense of humor, and savvy were even larger. He authored thousands of literary works from newspaper articles and short stories to complex novels and poetry.

A committed follower of Jesus, he often faced skeptics, agnostics, or atheists in public debate. He would proceed to dismantle them with his jokes and brains, and then with civility invite his vanquished foes to the pub, treating them as his friends.

He was a master of the one-line zinger, long before television sound bites. He once said, "The Christian ideal has not been tried and found wanting. It has been found difficult; and left untried." Another favorite barb of his was, "A dead thing can go with the stream, but only a living thing can go against it." And one more: "I owe my success to having listened to the very best advice, and then going away and doing the exact opposite."

When Chesterton was at his peak of popularity and wit, a London paper, The Times, solicited responses from its readership by asking this question: "What is wrong with the world?" You can imagine the result as hundreds of long, detailed letters poured in to the editor.

Then The Times asked a number of distinguished authors and leading thinkers of the day to respond to the question. Again, the essays poured in, verbose and long-winded. The shortest and most powerful response came from Chesterton.

Here is Chesterton's answer to what is wrong with the world. He wrote: "Dear Sirs, I am." That kind of honest humility would go a long way in making the world a better place.

March 14: The Illusion Of Control

Ellen Langer wrote the book on control, literally. Her work is entitled, The Illusion of Control, and in it she shows that we are delusional, thinking that we can influence the outcomes of certain events, even those events over which we have no command.

My favorite of her research examples sites drivers who feel that they are much more likely to be in an accident when they are not at the steering wheel. Sitting in the passenger seat feels too unsafe. But move that passenger to the back of the automobile, and his feelings of anxiety completely skyrocket. In fact, the further removed from the driver's seat he was moved, the more the test subject felt that an accident was inevitable. Why? He was not the one in control.

This is one reason why I recoil from the banality of the bumper sticker, "God Is My Co-Pilot." No phrase is more descriptive of our neurotic need to be in control, and yet, keep God on standby should we get into a situation that is just a bit too much for us.

Yet, critics of faith often argue that belief in God is an irrational mindset at best, or serious derangement at worst as God's existence cannot be "proven." Faith, as the argument goes, is simply "anxiety management." I understand and appreciate this argument. Yet, I counter that we all have confidence in something, in some foundational truth or principle that guides our lives.

For me belief in God is a far safer bet than trusting humanity. Not because I believe God will do things my way, but because surrendering my life to a Higher Power makes a lot of sense when there is so little I can control anyway. Besides, control is an illusion, and the evidence is irrefutable.

March 15: Quiet Time

I don't have to work very hard to convince you that this world is a noisy place. Talking heads, radio shows, 24-hour news, analysis on every hand, opinions like armpits: Court is always being held, comments are always being made, and there is the constant eagerness to share the oh-so-correct perspective. There's always someone babbling about something, and the air becomes so saturated with pandemonium, it seeps into our souls.

Jesus understood this and once instructed his disciples: "When you pray, close the door and pray to your Father who is unseen...do not keep on babbling like pagans, for they think they will be heard because of their many words." Even in prayer, the "fewer the words the better," it seems, instructions to remember when we have a daily "quiet time:" We would be better served by actual quiet time.

There's no need to imitate the ear-splitting world that thinks the loudest opinions will actually be heard. It's useless to go on yammering. Instead, settle down. Be still. Get quiet.

It's not unlike the familiar story from Lyndon B. Johnson's administration as told by Skip Heitzig. At a special dinner, Johnson called upon one of his staffers to say grace. The man, named Jim, began praying and President Johnson, in his brash way, interrupted. "Speak up, Jim, I can't hear you," the President said. Jim answered, "With all due respect, Mr. President, I wasn't talking to you."

That's exactly what Jesus is teaching his disciples. Too often, far too often, prayer is not an invitation to stillness and humility before God. It is an invitation to commotion. It is "babble," as the King James Version translated Jesus' instructions. It is foolish rambling that is about as far from a "quiet time" as one can get.

March 16: Nothing To Fear

In the 1870s a menacing bandit began burglarizing the Wells Fargo stage coaches in northern California. Over a decade he succeeded in almost thirty robberies. He would wait for the coach at a narrow pass, emerge dressed in black with a hood over his head, and would be carrying a double-barreled shotgun.

To match his appearance, he had a deep baritone voice, and would point his gun at the driver and kindly say, "Sir, will you please throw down your treasure box?" This terrifying gentleman bandit was nicknamed "Black Bart."

Eventually the authorities tracked Bart down. But when they arrested him, they couldn't believe what they found. "Black Bart" was actually a man named Charles Boles. He was not seven feet tall, young and rugged. He was an older, handsome, delicate man who never fired a single shot at his robberies because he never even loaded his gun.

Bart/Boles used the most crippling weapon in his arsenal: Fear. Through dread he made a good living, but when unmasked, he was nothing people said he was. He was just a deep, shadowy voice behind a dark mask and empty suit.

I'm not naive; the world around us is dangerous. But the living Christ has shown this world for what it is: Powerless against those who are in him. This doesn't mean the world will not hurt us or that some of the things we fear won't take place. It simply means that nothing in this world can finally or completely destroy us.

In these perilous times we don't have to lose our heads or our confidence. The power we have been given and the love we have been shown flows from the Providence who is larger than our fears, and when we live in Him, we can live unafraid.

March 17: Where They Are

The year was 387. The place was ancient Scotland. A baby boy was born and named, Maewyn. He grew up as most children of his day, at the edge of the known world, but ended up in the wrong place at the wrong time. A roving band of Irish pirates captured young Maewyn as he played along the coastline. He was carried back to Ireland and enslaved.

After many years Maewyn escaped captivity and returned home to Scotland, but his time in Irish slavery had changed him. He had come to faith and sensed that God wanted him to return to Ireland as a missionary. So Maewyn completed his training and was sent as the first Christian missionary to Ireland. At his ordination he took the Gaelic name, Padraig. In English we know him as Patrick.

Patrick might be the most beloved saint the church has. Drinking Guinness or Jameson may be a part of his appeal, but that is hardly the beginning. Patrick, more than most, meets people where they are – and that is why we love him.

When Patrick arrived in Ireland, most missionaries converted "heathens" by force. But rather than imposing his faith on the Irish people, Patrick simply invited them to know Jesus. He did not overpower, he obliged. He did not attack, he adapted. He came in humility and simplicity, attempting to foster faith, not force it.

On this, his day, we still have much to learn from Patrick, for his way of sharing faith could heal today's world. Vulnerability. Service. Humility. Meeting people where they are. Treating neighbors with dignity and respect. Honoring the lives and stories of those we encounter – plain civility – might be the best way to keep our society from devouring itself, and it was Patrick's way of changing his world.

March 18: More Than Words

Frederick and Elizabeth Noble got married on New Year's Day, 1941. It was a quick ceremony, as Frederick was on a 48-hour leave from his British Tank Regiment. Between military assignments, Frederick took time to write hundreds of love letters to Elizabeth while he was away.

In fact, the two exchanged love letters long after the war was over, for decades, even after they had retired to the English countryside in their 90s. After the Nobles died, their children discovered a tea chest that contained every love letter Frederick and Elizabeth had exchanged. It is an extraordinary collection of love notes spanning more than seven decades.

Yet, the collection, in and of itself, is just that - a collection, an assemblage of words. What gives the collection power, is what gives all such things their power: The love behind the words. Indeed, Frederick and Elizabeth were so bound by love that they could not live apart. They died in December, 2011 – just hours apart.

You too have received an extraordinary collection of love notes. It's that best-selling book of all time; that leather-bound volume shoved into the nightstand drawer or sitting ragged and dog-eared on the kitchen table (Or it's downloaded as an app on your mobile device). It's the Bible, and yes, it is a love letter written to you.

"A love letter?" you ask. "I thought the Bible was a book of religious laws, a book full of condemnation, genocide, hard to pronounce surnames, and the occasional children's story. Isn't it just a bunch of words?"

Might you look deeper and read closer, for the Bible is enlivened by God's Spirit and constructed by divine affection. It is much more than words. It is a love story from the One who can't live without you.

March 19: Hauntings

Sometimes we have to go backward in order to finally move forward. We must face our sordid personal history, confront our deepest pains, and acknowledge our foolishness. This is necessary to "getting on with the future." Yet, most of us will never go back on our own. We must be forced to do so.

Someone or something has to take us by the collar, as it were, and push us backward to resurrect our past mistakes, failed relationships, and boneheaded decisions, so that keeping everything all nice and tidy in the attic of our memory no longer works. But in that confrontation, there is a pathway to a better future.

"The past is the past! Let bygones be bygones," we say to avoid the pain of yesterday. Yet, the past is only the past if we have learned from it. We can let bygones be bygones only if we have let those days break our hearts. We can let yesterday go only if we have properly grieved over those things we can do nothing about. If we haven't finished this hard work of the soul, then the past will continue to haunt us like some terrible phantom.

When will we know that we have properly faced the past? I think it is when we no longer have anyone left to blame. We stop blaming those who harmed us, as they were prisoners in their own hell. We stop blaming God for not doing what we wanted or expected. And we stop blaming ourselves for being foolish.

For if the past could have been different, it would have been. It was what it was, and it now is what it is. When we realize this, we might begin to put the hauntings of our past where they belong: In the past.

March 20: The Ones Jesus Loves

"Just who do you think you are?" Now there's a question that has been posed more than a few times. Usually it is a weaponized question of sorts, laden with accusation; or it is a declaration aimed at someone's preposterous behavior. Nevertheless, I think it is an essential question.

Consider the writer of the New Testament book commonly known as "John." Tradition holds that this Gospel was written by the disciple John, one of Jesus' closest associates, though the writer, mysteriously, never identifies himself by name.

If I had written a book that was an eyewitness account of the life and times of Jesus of Nazareth, I would have signed it - as gigantic as a billboard - but John did not. He used the pen name instead: "The one Jesus loved."

Why such an alias? I think John was forcing his readers to take hold of the core meaning of what it means to be in relationship with Jesus. He was asking the question, "Just who do you think you are?" for John understood that his core identity was directly connected to the love Christ had for him.

So much so, that he did not think of himself as a fisherman, a disciple, an apostle, or a Gospel writer. He was simply one who was supremely loved. That's who he was, and the exact identity he wanted us to embrace.

We are no longer just names or faces. We are not defined by occupations, labels, race, nationality, failure, our family of origin, culture, popularity, or the ancillary chorus of the voices around us. We are simply the Ones Jesus Loves. This is our identity and who we really are. Is this too much to understand? Probably, but we don't have to understand it to accept it, embrace it, and live it.

March 21: Like Your Underwear

The word "hypocrite," in its original context, came right from the Greek and Roman theaters of ancient times. It means "play-actor." A hypocrite was a person who played multiple roles on the stage. In one scene he or she played one character. Later, the actor would don a mask or a costume and play another character - maybe three or four different personalities in a single performance.

Over time a hypocrite came to mean a person who changed his or her mask depending on the crowd. As Jesus used the word, a hypocrite was one who performed for the audience, and as he said, hypocrites "receive all the reward they will ever get." If you play for the crowd, he inferred, if your ambition is to draw attention to yourself, then when you get it, you earned your pay. There is no further reward from God but an empty hand.

So, Jesus offered a better way: "When you give," he said, "don't let your left hand know what your right hand is doing. When you pray, go to a closet and shut the door. When you sacrifice for a cause, don't broadcast it." In other words, keep your religious activities on the quiet side; as much as possible, keep it between you and God. Otherwise, you risk corrupting what would be a good deed.

No matter what it is: Missions, teaching, preaching, giving, praying, singing, organizing, helping - if it is done to impress or draw the attention of others, no matter how noble the act, it is wrong - for if it is not driven by love for God and neighbor, it becomes driven by pride and ego.

My friend Landon Saunders said it superlatively: "Wear your religion like you wear your underwear; make it rarely visible." That's good advice, indeed.

March 22: Take It Outside

Pastor Kyle, fresh and green out of the seminary, invited a young African missionary to share about his work. But there was a problem: No person of color had ever stood in the pulpit of his Texas Baptist church.

On the appointed day the young African arrived and spoke with deep love for his continent. He was received well, but a couple of folks couldn't tolerate this "mixing of the races." At church a few nights later, a man stood and said, "I'm tired of this preacher talking about race, and I'm fixin' to whip his ass."

Pastor Kyle said, "The people got more upset that he said 'ass' in church, than the fact that he was going to whip me!" But here the guy came, climbing over the pews. Four big men intervened and said, "If you're going to whip the preacher...take it outside."

The entire congregation spilt outside. Kyle had no idea what to do. He was strong, but he didn't think it was right to fight a parishioner. Just as the first punch was about to be thrown, those same men intervened: "If you're going to whip the preacher," they said, "you'll have to start with us." The man left, never to return.

Kyle visited that church decades later. To his astonishment, half the congregation was African-American! He was told: "Preacher, the neighborhood changed, and thanks to what you taught us, we opened our doors." Kyle's time at that church in the Texas pines had really made a difference.

There are times when we must fight fiercely for what is right. Not with clenched fists and angry words, taking up the weapons of the hateful. Instead, we fight with love, humility, patience, grace, and justice. Otherwise, we will be defeated before the fighting ever begins.

March 23: Fight On

Every few days my friend goes to an "infusion laboratory" for her chemotherapy treatments. The "lab" is a simple room with comfortable, leather chairs lining the walls, each chair with a pump that pushes what everyone prays is cancer-killing compounds through the body.

Competent, smiling nurses respond to the needs of the patients and the beeping machinery. Doctors float into the room as needed. Faces grimace over the prospects of yet another needle stick; cancer war stories are told and retold; and blankets are handed out with sips of ginger ale and nibbles of saltine crackers to ease the nausea.

These fighters are all held together by the solidarity of their battle. Through the blood, sweat, and tears they fight; they fight like gladiators in the arena. And gladiators they are, for they are desperately fighting for their lives. More so, they are fighting for what it means to be human.

They are marshaling all their grit and resilience (and something that borders on elegance), not just to stay alive physically, but to guard their very souls.

This reminds me of legendary pacifist Pastor A.J. Muste who during the Vietnam War stood in front of the White House night after night with a lit candle. A reporter asked him, "Do you really think that standing here with a candle can change the world?" He answered, "I don't stand here with my candle to change the world. I stand here to keep the world from changing me."

Those in the arena understand that physical life may be taken from them, but by God's grace, no disease will ever rob them of their innate worth as unique creations of the Almighty. They understand that the fight may not change their prognosis, but the fight prevents the disease from changing them.

March 24: Twinkle, Twinkle Little Stars

If credit could be earned for hours spent in a Sunday School, I would have had a PhD before turning ten. In the pre-hyper-technological age of flannel boards, chalk drawings, and construction paper, I learned the stories and doctrines of the Bible (in King James English of course); and I learned to ferociously compete with my classmates.

On the wall of my childhood Sunday School class was a giant, gridline poster with a place for each child's name, and then all of these vacant boxes running to the right, eager to be filled with gold stars. Bring an offering? Put a gilded check in the box! Are you staying for worship? A trophy is yours. Read your Bible every day this week? Another star blesses you from heaven.

Obviously, those with more stars were more dedicated, spiritual, committed, and obviously more beloved by God. Those with fewer stars had a lackluster faith, reflecting their inability to "measure up."

When we engrain a competitive spirit into faith - a culture of public shame and reward - is it any wonder we end up with some really faith-damaged adults? Adults that give up on faith all together; adults that hold God responsible for the way religious systems treated them; adults that grow anxious at even the prospect of darkening the door of a church.

There is plenty of competition in this world, plenty of winners and losers. But Christianity is not of this arena. Spiritual formation is not a competition, and faith is not an instrument to humiliate those who can't shine as brightly as others.

I'm all for spiritual instruction; but we would be better served by approaching faith with a non-compete clause squarely in place. The stars shine brighter in the sky than on the Sunday School wall.

March 25: A Prescription For Misery

Here is an ironclad prescription for personal misery: Attempt to keep every thing, person, detail, and moving part of your life, family, job, health, or schedule in precise working order as you would have it, without modification. Demand total compliance without flexibility, adjustment, or concession and you can be assured of never having a minute of peace for the rest of your life.

Understandably, it is good to have a place for everything and everything in its place. But things don't stay in place. That's why there is no peace in trying to master other people or things. If we can't learn to live with the chaotic reality around us, then life becomes a constant exercise in finding only those things, people, and situations that will comply with our will.

Such an approach to living reduces life to a tiny space, space not much bigger than a coffin. For the sake of easing our anxiety (mistakenly thinking that control equals peace), we drive away, alienate, and distance ourselves from some of life and love's greatest experiences. Obviously, peace must be accomplished some other way.

In the New Testament both Jesus and the Apostle Paul forbid Christians from being anxious. Neither Paul nor Jesus take the view, "don't ever worry about anything under any conditions." The focus is on self-obsession, the fidgeting anxiety created within us when things aren't going our way, when things feel out of place, and we can't control the circumstances/people around us.

This is anxiety created by our efforts to fix, manage, and shape life to our unyielding standards. This is why every great spiritual tradition speaks of letting go, denying self, surrendering, and detaching. For when we outreach our capabilities, we are left with uneasiness, not contentment, the very opposite of what we seek.

March 26: Multitasking Madness

Neuroscientist Earl Miller says, "People can't multitask very well, and when people say they can, they're deluding themselves." As a test, try to write an in-depth email and have a detailed conversation on the phone at the same time. Or try to study for an algebra test while playing a video game. It's impossible. The tasks will compete one against the other until there is a numb paralysis within the struggling brain.

The stupefying effect of multitasking may have been first observed in felines, not humans. But scientists did not make this breakthrough. Lion tamers did. Some still remember the sensational lion tamers of the great circuses, men who would strut into a steel cage with little more than a cracking whip in one hand, and a chair in the other.

They knew that a dining chair wouldn't keep the lions from devouring them (nor would the whip). What they knew was that the four points of the chair's legs, bobbing about as they were, tangled the lion's mind. In an attempt to focus on multiple points at once, the animal was rendered more or less powerless.

What an apropos parallel for those of us living in a world gone mad with multifarious activity. Our energy is so entirely defused and our attention so thoroughly diverted, that we are essentially incapacitated. We would do well to hear the words of Jesus who gently but categorically rebuked multitasking by saying, "You are so worried and distracted by many things, when only a few things are needed."

We aren't super-sized computers built and equipped with hulking CPUs. We are human beings, born to laugh and love; born to take life slowly and deeply as it comes to us; and born to be uncaged, set free from the madness of multitasking.

March 27: A Special Welcome

I hope to aspire to the courage and clarity of Our Lady of Lourdes Church in Daytona Beach, Florida. Author Jon Acuff got his hands on a copy of a bookmark that the Florida church hands out to all Sunday newcomers. And while opinions on the following words have ranged far and wide, for my part, I love it, and recommend it. In part it reads:

"We extend a special welcome to those who are single, married, divorced, gay, filthy rich, dirt poor, and 'yo no hablo ingles'...You're welcome here if you're 'just browsing,' just woke up or just got out of jail. We don't care if you're more Catholic than the Pope, or haven't been in church since little Joey's Baptism. We extend a special welcome to those who are over 60 but not grown up yet, and to teenagers who are growing up too fast.

"We welcome soccer moms, NASCAR dads, starving artists, tree-huggers, latte-sippers, vegetarians, and junk-food eaters. We welcome those who are in recovery or still addicted. We welcome you if you're having problems or if you're down in the dumps or if you don't like 'organized religion,' we've been there too.

"If you blew all your offering money at the dog track, you're welcome here. We offer a special welcome to those who think the earth is flat, work too hard, don't work, can't spell, or because grandma is in town and she wanted to go to church. We welcome those who are inked, pierced or both.

"We offer a special welcome to those who could use a prayer right now, had religion shoved down your throat as a kid or got lost in traffic and wound up here by mistake. We welcome tourists, seekers and doubters, bleeding hearts...and you!"

March 28: Come On, Get Happy

According to the Legatum Institute, which gauges the happiness level of the world's countries, the Scandinavian countries comprise the happiest region of the world. The United States is no longer in the top ten, as we have been sliding downward for some time. I don't think this comes as much of a surprise.

Happiness is affected by many things: Environment, genetics, and economics to begin with. But ultimately, barring emotional or mental dysfunction, happiness is a choice we make. No, we don't live in Scandinavia or have control over our chromosomes. We can't do anything about our age and very little to change our personal economics. But there are other things we can do.

We can choose to live near our friends. We can decide to practice gratitude. We can do work we find fulfilling. We can opt out of the blame game, and quit holding God, life, circumstances, past lovers, ex-wives, former business partners, parents, and reality responsible for doing us in.

We can make choices that will lead us toward becoming happy, joyful people or we can make choices that will result in us becoming chronically unhappy people. Regardless, that choice belongs to each and every one of us.

It was Viktor Frankl, famed Jewish Holocaust survivor and brilliant Austrian psychiatrist, who best articulated the power of choice in personal happiness. Reflecting upon his time in the concentration camps he wrote, "Everything can be taken from a man but one thing: the last of human freedoms - to choose one's attitude in any given set of circumstances."

If you want to be happy you don't have to move to Northern Europe or wait for science to alter your genetics. But you do have to choose to be happy, and no one else can make that choice for you.

March 29: Shattering Simplicity

In the living of our faith, complication and baggage just seem to naturally collect like barnacles attaching themselves to a ship. It requires vigilance – the closest and most careful attention – to keep faith simple, to stick with the lifestyle Jesus taught: "Love God and love your neighbor."

In this regard I like a story told by Jim Wallis. When he was a teenager he picked up a girlfriend to take to a movie, an act strictly forbidden by the church of his youth. He was reared as a Plymouth Brethren (They make Lutherans look like Unitarians, by the way). Everything was wrong - everything. If something was the least bit stimulating or did not directly and sufficiently honor Jesus, it was considered a sin, and movie-going was one of their many prohibitions.

As Jim and his date prepared to leave the house, the girl's father stood in the doorway blocking their exit. He said to the couple, tears in his eyes, "If you go to this film, you'll be trampling on everything that we've taught you to believe." While the Plymouth Brethren shaming was over the top, the man's conviction was honorable, in a curious sort of way. He was begging those he loved to stay true to the path.

I have similar convictions when it comes to simplicity. Thus, I have lost count of the times over the years when people wanted "more" - more words, more dogma, more doctrine, more rules, more command and control. At such times, I firmly grip the doorframe and say, "No, let's keep it simple."

If we can learn to love God and love our neighbors (No easy task), it will be enough. It will be more than enough; for "shattering and disarming simplicity," said the great C.S. Lewis, "is the real answer."

March 30: Face First

When a giraffe gives birth, she does so standing. Thus, her newborn's first act is to fall six feet to the ground, crash-landing on his face. Then the youngling's mother spends the next hour knocking him down when he attempts to stand. Only when completely exhausted will she allow him to stagger to his feet.

This isn't cruelty. It is the youngster's first and most necessary lesson: If you are going to stay alive in a world of apex predators, you better learn to stand on your own feet.

Yes, this is a dangerous, predatory world and we need to learn our lessons well. But since none of our mothers hatched us in the Serengeti, immediately kicked us in the head, or thumped us like a drum in the hospital nursery, we can't rely upon nature's classroom. We have to find a different way. That way is wisdom.

Wisdom is more than intelligence. It's knowing what, when, and how to live skillfully; and wisdom is in short supply in today's world. But beyond dropping all the idiots of the world on their heads, what can we do on a planet with so little wisdom? As simplistic as it sounds, we can pray.

James said: "If you need wisdom," and heaven knows we do, "ask God, and he will give it to you." Wisdom is there for the taking, if – and this is a colossal "if" – we will ask for it and trust him. And that's the rub. We want to trust ourselves, not realizing we will land in the dust over and over again.

Yes, it's hard to "let go and let God," show the way. But his way is the only path to true wisdom, and it's a path far less painful than constantly falling on your face.

March 31: The Life Of Surrender

Life always comes down to a choice. We will do things our way or do things God's way. We will trust what we can do, what we can see, what we can predict, how far we can go - or we will trust God, and what he can do. There is nothing else.

This is what Jesus was getting after when he said, "Deny yourself, take up his cross and follow me." He wasn't talking about self-inflicted punishment or depriving oneself of anything that is the least bit joyful. He was saying, "Don't trust yourself. Live the surrendered, sacrificed life."

Elsewhere Jesus summarized the life of faith in a single phrase. And if we could just once in life utter this prayer with sincerity, it will likely be enough: "Thy Will Be Done."

Sure, we can be "the masters of your fate and the captains of your souls." It is invigorating to face the storms alone, to navigate the waters solo, and to call our own shots (though eventually it is exhausting). Or we can hand the heavy responsibility for life over to God and allow him to do with it as he pleases.

Humanity has been trying to manage its own destiny for more than a few millennia now, and while our knowledge and technical proficiency continue to grow, our ability to relinquish the clutching grasp we have on our perceived destiny has not. We are as self-centered and selfish as ever, managing only to hurt others, our planet, ourselves, and our future.

So the decision, a choice made daily, must be made: To continue with our self-centered, destructive ways or entrust God with all of life's outcomes. Orienting our lives in his direction requires a life of surrender, but it is the only life worth living.

APRIL

April 1: Save Your Words

There was a time when a "fool" described an entertainer. Fools were common in the palaces of kings and queens, court jesters who made monarchs laugh. It was not the most secure job, as the fool could easily be beheaded for the offense of a bad joke.

Thus, a fool was someone who not only had the job of being laughed at, but was one idiotic enough to take such a job. As the word and its use evolved over time, a fool became someone who "lacks good judgment." Maybe it is immaturity. Maybe it is ignorance. Maybe it is inexperience. It's a person not capable of making good choices.

The book of Proverbs goes further, describing a fool a hundred or so times. The word means "fat," "heavy," or "thick." It is someone who is immovable, stuck, unyielding, and stubborn. It is the person who refuses to "get it," who refuses to learn, and refuses to accept correction or critique.

A fool cannot be taught - not by people or by his or her circumstances. In the words of Hebrew scholar William Wilson, "The fool has a weak mind but confident expectations," so it's damn the torpedoes, full speed ahead, and nothing you say or do will make a bit of difference to the fool.

If you don't believe me, go into business with a fool, marry a fool, move in with a fool, work for a fool, hire a fool, and you will discover it to be one of the most maddening experiences of your life.

The better part of wisdom is to keep some distance, for a fool is as toxic as poison, and will suck you into never-ending insanity. In the words of the old Greek proverb, "Talking sense to a fool only makes you foolish."

April 2: A Secured Identity

I received a mystery package recently and inside discovered an appetite suppressant - but I didn't order it. Shortly thereafter I received a second package. This time it was a set of audio CDs to learn "Quick and Simple Japanese." Then, a third package arrived at my door. It was a box of those super-absorbent hand towels sold on late night infomercials.

Then I knew what was going on. Someone had stolen my credit card information and was having his way with my account. I called my bank and oh yes, a cyber-thief had been very busy. Dietary supplements, Japanese CDs, airline tickets to Bangladesh, car wax, hundreds and hundreds of dollars of charges.

We have a unique 21st century name for this type of crime: Identity theft. What a strange phrase that is; as if a person's humanness can be reduced to the digits on a piece of magnetic plastic, the nine numbers individually assigned by the US government, or an email password. Surely there is much more to personal identity than what can be hijacked over the internet?

Absolutely, but most times we are content with shallowness, because most of us have no real sense of who we genuinely are. We are made to be as Christ, but we have settled for much less. As Paul put it in his letter to the Galatians, "I have been crucified with Christ so I no longer exist. It is Christ who lives in and through me."

The "Christian life" is a wondrous exchange of identity. You swap your individuality for the person Christ is forming and constructing within you. Christ is now the animating force of your person, the center and ground of your being. Jesus will make you the real you, and that identity can never be stolen.

April 3: Good News

Sharing Christian faith is known as "evangelism." This is the English rendering of a Greek word meaning "to proclaim the good news." But sometimes our news doesn't sound so good.

There is a subtext to some evangelization methods that go something like this: "God is really ticked off with you, and if you don't pray this prayer, believe the way I believe, and don't hurry to the baptismal waters as quickly as possible, then he will strike you dead."

There isn't much good news in such confrontations, because there is no sharing of God's love. God appears hateful, never inviting, but demanding. God doesn't plead, he prosecutes. God doesn't pursue wayward children as a heartbroken parent; God dogs hardened criminals like a trigger-happy bounty hunter, with a ready execution order.

I can no longer speak to others about an angry, perpetually irritated God who only wishes to stamp out humanity because I no longer believe in such a deity - not in light of Jesus, and the love of God he came to reveal to the world. We are now "compelled by love," to employ Paul's phrase.

We share our faith not to coerce, force, intimidate, or to instill terror. We share our faith because of and for love's sake - the only worthy compulsion. We have learned that God loves us, remarkably so, and loves our neighbors with equal measure. This love changes us; cures our dysfunction; and gives us new life.

It would be a good idea not to speak a word about faith, God, or the gospel until love is the means, message, and motivation for everything we say. When we can share the love of God by speaking of the ever-loving Christ, while loving those to whom we speak, then we are sharing good news indeed.

April 4: The Word Of God

On Sunday mornings untold numbers of worship leaders will read the Bible and conclude: "The Word of God for the People of God." The shocker is this: Nowhere in the 66 individual books of the collected Old and New Testaments does the Bible take the title, "The Word of God" for itself.

It speaks of the Word of God, to be sure. It gives dramatic accounts of people hearing God's voice. The Scriptures give instructions to God's people, but the self-elevating inscription of "The Word of God" is conspicuously absent.

Still, the Word of God is an essential phrase in the Christian dictionary, and by affirming the words of Scripture, we are declaring our willingness to hear God's voice and follow where he leads. For the "Word of God" is not a dead, static reading in an echoey, stone chamber. It is a dynamic invitation to grow in love, to expand one's faith, and to follow Jesus.

John wrote, "In the beginning was the Word. The Word was with God and was God. That Word became flesh and dwelt among us." The true Word of God, by the Bible's own testimony, is not a written document. It is a Person. It is the Christ, the one we call Jesus. Thus, the Bible is always pointing to him as the supreme power and authority for faith, and nothing else. He is "The Word of God for the People of God."

It is right to be called "People of the Book," that is, lovers of the Bible. But let us remember that we are not Biblicists, because the Bible itself isn't the end of our convictions. We are Christians, followers of Jesus who are always heeding his voice and moving in his direction, the author, sustainer, and perfecter of our faith.

April 5: Our Father

"Our Father." Only two words, and yet, if we learned to pray these words as Jesus instructed, our lives would be radically transformed. In Jesus' day it was not uncommon to address God as Father; this wasn't new. But Jesus made this way of speaking to and thinking about God, normative. "Father," in Jesus' view, should be the customary interpretation of God.

Jesus went so far as to call God "Abba." This was an affectionate Aramaic title used by the smallest of children, a term of tenderness. To think of God as "Papa" or "Dad" was a total upheaval in terms of God language.

The pietistic Jews of Jesus' day wouldn't even say God's name, nor would they write it down, all in an effort to maintain reverence. And a common Jewish prayer of Jesus' day began with sixteen different adjectives to describe God, but the prayer never called his name.

What a contrast, as Jesus began his prayers with the simple, audacious word "Father." God is neither a distant, ambivalent, unapproachable deity, nor a vindictive titan who has to be constantly placated. Instead, he is a loving parent, and consequently, we are his beloved children.

This unconditional, parental love of God was the driving force behind Jesus' ministry. Jesus didn't come to earth to change God's attitude toward us – as if God hated us all along and Jesus had to prevent our destruction – that is absolutely preposterous.

No, Jesus came to change our attitude about God, revealing him to be a benevolent Father wooing us into his welcoming arms. This God can be trusted. He can be revered. He can be loved, because he loves us. Embracing God as Father is nothing short of a spiritual shake-up, correcting the many misrepresented images that have been put before us.

April 6: Like A Rolling Stone

In Greek mythology there was a king named Sisyphus. He was a treacherous man, so much so that the gods banished him to hell. He was condemned to an eternity of rolling a huge boulder to the top of a hill. Then, the rock would roll back down to the bottom, and Sisyphus would be forced to start over again.

Many Christians are like Sisyphus, always pushing that rock up the hill only to see it slip away just as they "arrive" at the top. Proof of this effort is betrayed by words like: "I have got to do better...I must try harder...I need to give more...I should pray longer...I'm not good enough...I ought to read the Bible more." Faith becomes a terribly heavy burden that we are pushing up the hill.

This concept is completely foreign to the spirituality of Jesus. Matthew 11 frames the contrast best: "Are you tired? Worn out? Burned out on religion? Come to me. Get away with me and you'll recover your life. I'll show you how to take a real rest" (The Message).

We think that our spirituality depends upon all that we can do, and many of us live with the old Protestant work ethic hanging around our necks like a yoke. Boiled down to a bumper sticker mantra we think: "If it's going to be, then it's up to me." That's nothing short of sacrilege, even if it sounds resolute and brave.

There will always be another stone to push up a hill, another mile to run, another burden to bear. But faith should not be one of these. Trusting Christ is not a ball-and-chain, holding us down in a slave's hell. It is the very means to live a light and free life.

April 7: Do What You Please

The Old Testament Law contains 613 commandments. The majority of these are negative: "Thou shalt not" type commandments. These prohibit activities ranging from coveting your neighbor's cow to wearing pants made from two different materials (seriously, look it up). The remaining commandments are positive: "Thou shalt." These order adherents to perform in determined ways and means.

Such a legal code is incredibly lengthy, yet it's just the beginning. The oral tradition that supplements the Law (as commentary and explanation) is also extensive. Translated into English, it is a multi-volume set of more than seven thousand pages (For perspective, the largest dictionary at the local library has only about fifteen hundred pages).

So it's no surprise that Jesus was once asked this pertinent question: "Which is the most important commandment in the Law?" The questioner was looking for Jesus to throw him a bone. With so much material to sift through, where should obedience begin?

Jesus' answer was legendary: "Love the Lord your God with all your heart, soul, and mind," he said. "This is the first and greatest commandment." He then added, "The second most important is similar: Love your neighbor as much as you love yourself."

This caused Augustine to say later, "Love God and do whatever you please. For the soul trained in love will do nothing to offend the Beloved." If only practical faith could stay on this level of holy simplicity.

Christians are a verbose group. We always have something to say, prove, defend, attack, clarify, protect, or explain. As if the massive religious codex that came before us is not enough; as if centuries of creeds, confessions, and commentaries haven't rounded out the picture, yet. We would do well to stick to simplicity, acknowledging that no one can improve upon our Founder's humble words.

April 8: Clear Communication

A poor fellow's vehicle conked out on the side of the road. Finally he convinced a speeding motorist to stop and help. "If you could just push my car at 40 miles per hour," the stranded motorist said, "I'm convinced it will start."

Sliding back behind the wheel of his car, the driver waited for that gentle nudge on the rear bumper that would move him down the road. It never came. But then the driver saw his rescuer in the rearview mirror. He was a quarter of a mile away and bearing down on the broken-down car at 40 miles per hour - just as he had been instructed.

Doubtless, most Christians want to see serious change in the world. We would love to see less violence, greater compassion, a moratorium on our limitless consumerism, and fewer public displays of vulgarity. But the solution is not to meet these challenges with being judgmental, taking revenge, waging cultural warfare, and condemning every person who doesn't agree with us.

If, in our passion to communicate something we feel very strongly about, said communication becomes hateful, as Christians we have wrecked our message. The path of Christ is to love those whom we consider our opponents. The way of Jesus is to engage and pray for our enemies, not to kill them.

As Mahatma Gandhi famously said, "We must become the change we wish to see in the world." That is, if I want a less violent society, I must become less violent. If I want to experience more compassion, I must become compassionate. If I want less consumerism, I should pull my own leg out of the commercialistic trap.

That is clear communication: Becoming the redemptive message that can change the world. To do less, is a wreck waiting to happen.

April 9: Unleashed

When I was a bit younger and braver, a group of friends and I shot the rapids of the Ocoee River. The Ocoee is one of the South's great adventures, a torrent of whitewater fun. At least it was fun to watch. Once in the water, the power of those rapids was incredible.

We couldn't dictate to the river with our little paddles and rubber dinghy any more than we could stop the sun from rising. We had to go where the water pushed us.

Living the life of faith is a lot like that. We have our raft, paddle, and are in this boat with our friends on the same journey. What began as a joyful, fun adventure somehow turns into an unstoppable flood. We are paddling along best we can, moved by the unleashed Spirit of God.

And sometimes we are more than moved. The journey of faith becomes a bone-jarring exercise in survival, crashing over the rocks and through the rapids. We are jostled from the security of our raft, forced to scream out of desperation for a lifeline. We struggle just to keep our noses above the water.

We may get the relieved opportunity to list in quiet pools, catching our breath and resting our muscles from time to time. But then, the water will pick up and we are on our way again.

Sure, there are things we can and should do along the way: Pray, hang on, watch out for our friends, and paddle like our hair is on fire. But ultimately we are riding the wave of God as he does his good will and purpose. His power has been turned loose in our lives, and all we have to do is hang on and let it take us where it will.

April 10: Check Your Pockets

It's not uncommon to hear someone in the heat of an argument to paraphrase the words of Jesus: "Judge not!" It's true, Jesus did say this, but these words are probably misapplied as much as anything he ever said.

The better translation of Jesus' words is, "Do not condemn others." This changes the whole equation, as Jesus doesn't ban "judgment" in the sense of discernment, making honorable choices, or being an informed person. Rather, Jesus is forbidding the condemnation of others, calling the disciple to focus on his or her own life, not what other people are doing.

To this end, there is a story from Rabbi Mendel Futerfas who survived years in the Soviet Gulags. In the Gulag, one of the activities that was prohibited was playing cards. Still, some of the inmates managed to smuggle in a deck of cards, and enjoyed playing as often as they could.

The guards knew this, and would storm in with surprise inspections looking for the cards, though they could never find them. They checked every inch of the barracks including strip searches of the inmates, but the result was always the same: Nothing. Yet, as soon as the guards left, the cards would reappear and the games continued. Eventually the card players let Futerfas in on their secret.

"As soon as the guards enter the barracks," they said, "we slip the cards into their pockets. Right before they leave, we slip them back out again. It never occurs to the guards to check their own pockets."

"Judging" does not prevent us from having and sharing opinions. But it does mean we refuse – absolutely refuse – to condemn others. We leave "room in our hearts for God's grace," and that room is made possible by looking in and emptying our own pockets first.

April 11: Some Assembly Required

The three most frightening words in the English language are: "Some assembly required." You order something online; a toy or a bicycle for your children. Or you go to a big box store to get a grill or patio furniture.

When UPS brings it to your door or you find the item you're looking for in the store, it's not ready to go like you saw in the online catalog or the advertisement in Sunday's paper. "Some assembly required," the box says.

So, you lug this box the size of a mattress out to the garage and open it. There are buckets of screws, connectors, rods and unidentifiable small pieces of plastic that you will never use no matter what the directions say. And for the next six weeks you attempt to put this thing together.

"Some assembly required," or as the Apostle Paul said: "Continue to work out your salvation." We have been given this wonderful gift of grace and salvation. This gift is like getting a bicycle in a box or a swing set bound by straps and smothered in Styrofoam peanuts. You've got to put it all together.

You can't ride the bike if it stays in the box. You can't play on the swing set if it remains disassembled. You can't enjoy your furniture if you don't connect the pieces. And faith will not be what it is intended to be if you don't work it out.

Maybe faith has become such a burden for some of us because we're lugging around on our backs the box full of assorted spiritual materials, but we haven't figured out how to put it all together. So, find your work gloves and break out the tool chest. Call your neighbor to lend a hand, and start working it out.

April 12: A Saint Goes Marching In

On April 12, 2013 a true saint left this world: A self-proclaimed "ragamuffin," named Brennan Manning. As a young man Brennan entered seminary and became a priest. He would go on to become a theologian, campus minister, spiritual director, defender of the poor, and the author of dozens of books.

If Manning's story had ended there, there would be little doubt about his sainthood. But Manning's life disintegrated into horrific alcoholism. He became homeless, busted, wretchedly living on a quart of vodka a day.

It took him months to get sober, but he did, only to relapse. When sober again he began writing in earnest, left the priesthood, married, and moved to New Orleans (he was an avid Saints fan), where his marriage would end in divorce, and again he would land in rehab.

Manning said that the greatest regret of his life was not his alcoholism. It was "The time wasted in shame, guilt, remorse, and self-condemnation. Not the appropriate guilt one ought to feel after committing a sin, but wallowing in guilt, almost indulging in it, which is basically a kind of idolatry where I am the center of my focus and concern.

"Thus, I can waste no more time being shocked or horrified that I have failed. There's nothing else I can do now but help sinners journey from self-hatred to God's love."

This blessed, bumbling drunk; this muddled mix of failure and faithfulness; this holy, blue-eyed and blue-jean-wearing champion of grace did exactly that for untold thousands – he helped them find the love of God in spite of personal shame.

And while I only knew him through his words, he did the same for me. So from one ragamuffin to another, "Thank you, Brennan. A saint truly is marching in."

April 13: Get Out!

The most heated arguments I have ever witnessed in church were not over theology, leadership, or future plans. The worst controversies I have endured were over worship styles.

Should we use hymnals or modern worship music? Should drums be allowed in the sanctuary? Can the pulpit be moved to accommodate the children's choir? Is it okay for someone to clap their hands after the solo?

Additionally, I've led worship with robed choirs and pipe organs. I've tapped my foot and clapped my hands to the cranking riffs of old hippies with electric guitars. I've listened closely to the tight four-part harmony of southern gospel.

I've worn a suit and tie to church; I've worn shorts and sandals. I've delivered three-point sermons with a poem and a prayer; and I've preached with the technological assistance of multimedia, projectors, videos and fog machines. I've witnessed the traditional Easter cantata; and I've seen a few interpretive dance steps across the church podium.

Which of these styles is "right?" Really, that's the wrong question. The better question is, "What happens when the worship service is over?"

To that point, the final words of the old Latin mass were, Ite missa est – "Get out!" This gets to worship's purpose: When the last song is sung, the last prayer offered, and the last homily delivered, the goal of worship is to leave the sanctuary to go serve others.

So, take your pick: Sermons or liturgy; southern gospel or anthems; drums or pipe organs; corporate prayer or contemplation; kneeling benches or mosh pits. But if these things do not translate into loving action in the community, if these things do not force us out of the building in service to others, then we have more issues with the substance of our worship than the style.

April 14: The Attraction Of Love

According to a Pew Research Center report, a full one-fifth of Americans are now unattached to religion, and the Protestant majority is no longer that; Protestant Christians now make up less than 50% of the population.

The Pew Report goes on to say that the religiously unaffiliated think that religious organizations are "too concerned with money and power, too focused on rules, and too involved in politics." Combine this study with the respected statistics of the Barna Research Group. According to Barna, those unaffiliated with religion use several primary words to describe Christians, words that include: "Judgmental, hypocritical, and insensitive."

I know not every Christian behaves harshly toward others. The most gracious, caring, and welcoming people I have ever met are Christians. But the most obnoxious, hateful, and critical individuals I have ever met are also religious people. And this has to change.

I feel strongly that the last thing most communities need is just another religious institution: An institution that pounds the pulpit and its parishioners with unyielding dogma; that points fingers, condemns, and excludes others from the love of God; that can never confess its shortcomings, admit when it has been wrong, or meet people where they are rather than demanding that people come to it.

No, communities don't need more hardened, inflexible places like these; but every community needs simple, uncomplicated, receptive places of grace. Every community needs a communion of friendship, freedom, and faith that will build bridges to the world, not boundaries of separation and marginalization. Simply, every community needs a place of radical hospitality and attraction that welcomes all to know a loving God.

I call these places "church," and I hope that where hardened institutionalism ends, love can begin, for the love of God is the most attractive force in the universe.

April 15: The Real Thing

There is a story about St. Augustine who was writing his book on the Trinity. He was walking along the seashore, deep in thought, when he noticed a little boy pouring seawater into a hole that had been dug in the sand.

Augustine smiled, and then said to the boy, "Young man, you will never get all the sea into that one little hole." To which the boy responded, "Well, you will never get all of God into that one little book."

Indeed, God is bigger than our books, our doctrines, our belief statements, and our theories about him - far bigger. He is a mystery that can never be explained. The best we can do is use the tools at our disposal: Words, metaphors, stories, and pictures.

And even then, we are attempting to express the inexpressible. In some ways, every time we open our mouths to describe God, we commit something akin to heresy; because whatever we say will be wrong - or at least incomplete.

C.S. Lewis explained it like this: Suppose a man looks out at the Atlantic Ocean. Then he goes and looks at a map of the Atlantic Ocean. When he does that, he has turned from something real to something less real. He has turned from actual waves and salty air to "a bit of colored paper." The map is important, but it's not the real thing.

We are skilled at knowing the ins-and-outs of all our religious charts, but God wants us to know him. After all, we cannot have a relationship with a map. We cannot commune with a theology. We cannot experience creed or doctrine. But we can commune with and experience God, a God that is an ever unfolding enigma of wonder and grace, larger than the universe.

April 16: How Far Is Heaven?

Morris awoke one morning disgusted with his life. "My wife never gives me a moment's peace. My children are foolish. I can barely make a living, and my house is falling in," he said. "I'll never be happy."

Then Morris remembered what his rabbi said: "Someday we will go to heaven where everyone will be happy." Morris said, "I will go find heaven!" and he started off in the direction his rabbi pointed whenever he talked about paradise.

As night fell, Morris took off his boots and pointed them in the direction he was walking, so he would know which direction to go in the morning. He then fell quickly asleep. While Morris slept, an angel came along the trail. The angel noticed Morris' boots pointing toward heaven and realized Morris' intentions. Mischievously, the angel turned Morris' boots back toward home, and with a chuckle journeyed on.

Morris awoke at sunrise, put on his boots and started off in the direction they were pointing. He noticed that the path looked oddly familiar, especially when he came to an old wooden gate that seemed to be the entrance to heaven.

He entered the house and sat down at the table, the smells of heavenly food making his mouth water and his stomach rumble. A beautiful woman, like his wife when she was younger, served him a delicious meal and he gladly ate. Meanwhile, two young children danced happily into the kitchen, heavenly children who were so joyful and friendly that Morris had to sigh with happiness.

"Yes," he thought, "it's exactly as the rabbi said. Heaven is simply wonderful."

This old Yiddish tale is the truth of the gospel. For when we ask the question, "How far is heaven?" we never have to look beyond the world in which we live.

April 17: For The Long Haul

Those of us who grew up in the revivalistic tradition were often asked the question, "What if Jesus came back today?" That's a good question. But here is a question that might be better: "What if he doesn't?"

What if Jesus does not come back today... Or tomorrow... Or next year... Or next decade... Or next century? If we aren't prepared for the long haul, prepared to persevere into a distant future, then are we actually living out the blessed hope we profess?

We who are Christian could take a lesson from "The Long Now Foundation." It has one essential goal: To reverse the trend in our culture of short-term thinking. The founders believe that our "accelerating technology, the short-horizon perspective of market-driven economics, the next-election perspective of democracies, and the distractions of personal multi-tasking" have given us "a pathologically short attention span."

They want to provide some sort of corrective balance to our short-sightedness, and encourage "the long view and the taking of long-term responsibility, where 'long-term' is measured in centuries, not months or years."

Illustrating this long-term thinking, Long Now is building a massive clock that will tick for the next 10,000 years. The point of the clock is not to mark time; it is to rekindle our hope in the future.

The church, allegedly the most hopeful community in the world, could use some of that thinking, because Jesus will probably not return before you finish reading this article. He'll probably not return today, and likely not return in your lifetime.

"God is not slow about keeping his promises," but we must know that God works on a timetable that is all his own. We have to be prepared to faithfully persevere no matter how long the wait.

April 18: More Than A Hero

On April 18, 1938, a true American hero was born: Superman. At least that is the date that he first appeared in Action Comics. Superman is the creation of Jerry Siegel and Joe Shuster, children of Jewish immigrants. Teenagers during the Great Depression, the two began drawing cartoons to create a hero, a hero that would give the world hope.

This hero would have the strength of Samson, the liberating power of Moses, and the majesty of David. They named their character Kal-El, which means "the voice of God."

As his story has evolved, Superman has moved from being an Old Testament hero, to a messianic figure. A father sends his only son to save the Earth. His father tells Kal-El, "The people of Earth can be a great people. They only lack the light to show the way. For this reason I have sent them you, my only son."

On earth Kal-El is raised by adoptive parents, travels to the arctic wilderness to commune with his father, and at age 30, begins his work fighting for truth and justice. Meanwhile, he keeps his superpowers hidden, appearing as Clark Kent, a "mild-mannered reporter" that most everyone ignores. The similarities to Jesus are obvious, of course, and not accidental.

Granted, Jesus isn't Superman. He's not a cheesy, clandestine, comic book hero who wears horn-rimmed glasses for his day job. He is the "Lord of Lords" before whom "every knee will one day bow." Yet, Siegel and Shuster's creation might help us better visualize just how extraordinary Jesus is.

"Faster than a speeding bullet, more powerful than a locomotive, able to leap tall buildings in a single bound?" Leave these lesser feats to Superman. Because we don't need a hero as much as we need a Savior.

April 19: Full In The Face

Not long ago the world was combating the largest Ebola epidemic in history. Ebola is a fearful illness with a dreadful mortality rate, and scientists know precious little about it. This has not, however, kept courageous health workers from battling the disease, unselfishly submitting themselves to incredible risk in the process.

I heard one of these workers, a nurse, interviewed on radio when the Ebola outbreak was peaking. The interviewer asked: "What materials are needed to improve your work?" I waited to hear her speak of more money, hospital beds, or IVs. But the nurse gave a surprising, most beautiful answer.

She said, "What we need are new biohazard suits; ones with full, clear screens so the patients can see our faces." She spoke of how patients were scared, sick with this gruesome disease, afraid of dying, isolated from their family and friends, and were being cared for by "foreigners" who didn't necessarily speak their language.

She concluded: "We need the new suits so they can see our faces... so they can see us smile at them, and be less afraid."

This nurse is a skilled caregiver, regardless of her technical proficiency, for she understands that the healing process requires kindness, warmth, and clarity as much as it requires antibiotics and oxygen tanks. "So they can see our faces," is simply, good medicine.

Her words reminded me of the great Aaronic blessing from the Hebrew Bible. It goes something like this: "May God bless you and keep you. May God smile on you, look you full in the face and give you peace."

It's all that anyone could ask for, good medicine for sure: To have a life that flourishes, for God to grant peace and grace, and for Providence to smile in our direction - that is good medicine indeed.

111

April 20: Stop And Listen

One autumn afternoon my sister and I were ripping up the soil in my grandmother's fallow garden. My sister, in her clod-crushing zeal, whacked me on top of the head with a garden hoe.

I was whisked away for stitches in my bleeding scalp, but the treatment was about as bad as the ailment. I was separated from my parents. The doctor never spoke to me. Two nurses silently but forcibly held me down.

All along I twisted and turned, convulsed and screamed, begging for an explanation of what was happening. Finally, I screamed at the top of my lungs, "Will someone please talk to me!"

That was the magic phrase. The team of tormentors stopped, told me what they were trying to do, how long it would take, and how much it would hurt. I then lay perfectly still until the procedure was complete.

Listening is largely a lost art. Medical professionals run us through their offices like cattle through a chute. Politicians stubbornly ignore our voices. Our children discount our counsel. Our spouses cannot recall the conversation we had just this morning. Trusted friends won't lift a gaze from their glowing capacitive screens to look us in the eyes.

I understand more and more why Jesus often said, "He who has ears let him hear," because for the most part, we do not use the two fleshy instruments attached to the sides of our heads.

If we took the time to actually listen, we just might begin to appreciate, rather than vilify, others. We just might find that the world would grow a little quieter, more peaceful. We just might find that those we have long ignored actually have something worth saying. We just might discover the greatest tool in human communication - listening to what others say.

April 21: Who He Really Is

A.W. Tozer wrote, "What comes into our minds when we think about God is the most important thing about us." I can hardly disagree with his conclusion, and if Tozer is correct, then our perception of God shapes our character and actions like little else.

So it's no wonder that some faithful people are the way they are: Loving, helpful, sacrificial, kind, and giving. They think of God this way. But on the other hand, some religious people are angry, suspicious, unforgiving, and even murderous. These folks, in turn, think of God in these terms as well, and it shows.

Personally, this is why Christ is so important to my faith. He offered a revolutionary vision of God, a new way to think about who God is, and how God relates to creation. Jesus showed us a God best described as an affectionate parent. This God really does love, accept, treasure, and cherish us - as a "Father has compassion on his children." This was the driving force behind all Jesus said and did.

It becomes clear, when diving into the words of Christ, that he came not to change God's thinking about us - he came to change our thinking about God. In light of Jesus, we must let go of all understandings of God that are less than loving or less than gracious. This will reorient our entire lives and correct so many of the misguided and misrepresented divine images that have been put before us.

Thus, the moral and spiritual authority for our lives is no erratic, cold-hearted tyrant. Such a God is unworthy of worship, incapable of being trusted, and impossible to love. Thankfully, such a God doesn't exist, for Jesus has shown us who God really is, and that God is a God of love.

April 22: The Empty Spaces

In her book *Gravity and Grace*, the late Simone Weil wrote, "Grace fills empty spaces, but it can only enter where there is a void to receive it." With those words she emphasizes a truth that has been lost on most of us.

Somewhere along the line we forgot that Jesus taught and modeled emptiness, showing us that egotism, pride, and ambition are the real enemies of spirituality. Because when our hands, heads, and hearts are full, we are simply unable to accept what God offers.

I remember a story about a scholar who climbed the mountain to meet the Zen Master and learn from him. This scholar had an extensive academic background and was a wealth of knowledge.

The two sat together and the scholar began talking about all he had done, studied, and all his endeavors. The Master listened patiently as he also began to brew tea.

When the tea was ready, the Master began pouring it in the scholar's cup. He poured until it filled the cup, ran over into the saucer, into the scholar's lap and onto the floor. The scholar jumped up shouting, "Stop! Stop! The cup is full!"

The Master stopped and said: "Yes, and you are just like this cup. You are so full of yourself that nothing else can get in! You can be taught nothing else until your cup is empty."

None of us will receive God's good grace or experience genuine transformation so long as we remain full of ourselves. The gospel is completely unappealing – it is downright repulsive – to those of us who feel that we can manage our lives with our own abilities, resources, accomplishments, or on own terms.

As long as this self-reliance reigns supreme, the transformational reign of God cannot take hold in our lives.

April 23: In The Mix

Years ago I wrote a column that a newspaper editor entitled, "The Beautiful, Blended Family of God." It was a delightful little piece; upbeat, optimistic, and buoyed by idealism. My "blended family" sounded like a sweet swirled coffee that you might enjoy at a corner cafe.

I'm still filled with hopeful joy for my family, but now our blendedness sometimes sounds and feels more like what pours out of a concrete mixer than what flows from an espresso machine. The rocks and mortar clang around in a sloppy soup, but like concrete, we are sticking together the best we can.

The truth is, "family" is a messy business, and it doesn't really matter much whose family it is. They are all dysfunctional - all of them - and the dysfunction is measured only by degrees. Some are a little healthier, some not so much, but all of them have their quota of tears, struggles, gut-punches, and general banging about in the mixer of life.

It encourages me, in a twisted kind of way, to read the Bible and note the fouled-up families that I find there. None of these families provide very much ammunition in the "defense of the biblical family" that we hear so much about these days. Rather, these train wrecks that are the real "biblical" families are exactly that: Real. And they make my little slice of life a harmonious walk in the park by comparison. Yet God somehow accomplished marvelous things in spite of all the dysfunction.

This divine mercy gives me great solace, especially when I get torqued over how my family should be, ought to be, or is supposed to be. These families help me to see how family actually is, and to find God's grace in the midst and mix of it all.

April 24: Holy Harley

When I was a young college student I had the opportunity to go with a friend to a "revival." It was a week-long gathering when people of the community crammed their families into the pews to sing rousing gospel songs, to hear the pleadings, exhortations, and condemnations of the best visiting evangelist the church could afford, and for everyone to have an annual time of repentance whether they needed it or not.

As I made my way to the front door I passed by a long line of Harley Davidson motorcycles, and just inside the church, occupying the back pew, there sat the motorcycle gang. Leather, vests, ponytails, tattooed flesh: It was the complete Hell's Angels package.

Being a young, eager revivalist myself, I said to my friend, "Good. Maybe these heathen will get saved tonight." And I meant it. I sat several pews away from them and found myself piously praying for their salvation because I just knew they were seconds from splitting hell wide open.

After the service got started, the pastor called on one of the deacons of the church to come forward and offer a prayer. One of those wicked bikers rose from his seat and started down the aisle. This chaps-wearing biker with a beard to his waist was not only a church deacon, but a self-financed missionary to the road houses, biker bars, strip clubs, and truck stops of America.

I left that revival thinking that it would have been better to give the revival budget to this biker's ministry rather than spending it on some flamboyant evangelist. And certainly I left with a lesson scorched deep in my conscience: Never point a finger or a prayer at those you consider sinners. They may be more holy than you can imagine.

April 25: When I See It

Supreme Court Justice Potter Stewart famously said of pornography: "I could never succeed in defining it, but I know it when I see it." Such a characterization applies to forgiveness.

I first "saw" forgiveness in a woman named Corrie Ten Boom. I never met her, but as a child I heard about her. She and her family were Dutch Christians who hid Jews in their home during the Second World War.

Eventually the Nazis discovered the family's secret and they were arrested and sent to concentration camps. Only Corrie survived. Later, she began traveling Europe speaking to churches about her experiences. At one such meeting she recognized a man in the crowd: He had been a guard at her concentration camp.

The man walked up to Corrie and said, "I know that God has forgiven me for the cruel things I have done, but I would like to hear it from your lips as well. Will you forgive me?"

Corrie wrote, "While only seconds, it seemed like hours passed as I wrestled with the most difficult thing I had ever had to do. 'Jesus, help me!' I prayed silently. This healing warmth seemed to flood my whole being, bringing tears to my eyes. 'I forgive you, my brother!' I cried. I had never known God's love as intensely as I did then."

What Corrie Ten Boom did that day cannot be explained. It can only be witnessed, marveled at, and experienced. When one suffers an incalculable loss and is able to respond with grace rather than revenge, it is a miracle performed by God himself.

Thus, forgiveness is not achieved by trying harder. It's achieved by God – sometimes in spite of us. I can't explain it; I can't always understand it; but I certainly know it when I see it.

April 26: More Like Jesus

Dorothy Sayers was fond of saying that Jesus endured three great humiliations: The Incarnation, the cross, and the church. Jesus has subjected himself to a spastic, debilitated, malfunctioning body; a body called the church. And the church - we - can misrepresent his message.

We angrily thump the Bible. We hurl condemnation at all the people who disagree with us. We use our faith as a weapon against our opponents. But, even as we use Scripture to back our actions, this seems entirely inconsistent with what Jesus would do.

Maybe we don't need to aggressively quote Bible passages as much as we need to meekly surrender to the way of Jesus, following his trajectory, becoming and living more like him. He was humble and compassionate; full of grace and truth; the epitome of sacrificial love; forgiving toward all, welcoming to the most repugnant among us; filled with the Spirit that gives love, joy, peace, patience, kindness, goodness, faithfulness, gentleness, and self-control.

If our reading and living of the Bible isn't making us more like that - more like Jesus - then, simply, we are doing something wrong. If, in reciting our favorite verses, and memorizing the text, and proclaiming the truth, we only get more angry; more suspicious of others; more judgmental and fixed in our self-righteousness; more indifferent and apathetic toward the world; more greedy and egocentric - then we might know some religious quotes, but we haven't yet submitted to Jesus.

Thus, the real challenge for people of faith is not defending a holy book or a "biblical worldview" against those who don't believe it. The challenge is to "grow in every way more and more like Christ, so that the whole body is healthy and growing and full of his love." For when we love, we are never more like Jesus.

April 27: The Choice Is Yours

Your small, toddling child is in a room with you. She is at point A. You want her to be with you at point B. You have two options to make this happen.

Option 1: Go get her. You can physically carry her to where you want her to be. This is the quickest, easiest, most efficient way for you. She may kick and scream. She may cry out. You may have to resort to forceful, unkind measures, but it will get the job done.

Option 2: Invite her to walk to you. This option is replete with risk and danger. She may wander off; she might fall down and hurt herself; she might get terribly distracted; she might not come to you until she has exhausted herself otherwise.

All kinds of possibilities unfold - for good or for bad - with this second option, but for me life is more like this. If God has picked up his creation under his arm and is now dragging it toward some predetermined, unalterable point, then life is an unchangeable, torturous racket. But if he is calling us to where he is, inviting us, all while giving us space to accept or reject his invitation, that gives us opportunity to write (or un-write) our future in partnership with the leading of the Spirit.

And that's the thing about the future; it is not yet carved in stone, not as long as we have the power of choice. We can make choices that bring about better tomorrows, or we can make choices that are utterly destructive, dooming our future. God has made allowance for either outcome, vesting us with this responsibility that makes us human beings.

So if you think your tomorrows are already determined, think again. Your future has yet to be written.

April 28: Electricity In The Air

My aunt and uncle lived in an old house with low ceilings, yellow, shag carpet as deep as a wheat field, and in the center of the living area, a massive upright gas heater.

The combination of these things caused the house to be so sufficiently charged with static, it could set off an electroscope. I would walk around the house in my tube socks, sliding like I was wearing snowshoes, building up a monumental electrical charge. Then I would wait for my sister or brother to walk by while I held a straightened paperclip.

If I touched a sensitive part of their body, say the bottom of an earlobe, with my homemade electrical probe, it was like reaching out and taking hold of the hem of Jesus' garment. The power surged through with three inches of blue flame.

I wish church was more like that. No, I'm not talking about the mischievousness of children, though some of the more stoic congregations I have encountered could stand a good dose of levity. Nor am I talking about yellow shag carpet. A few congregations need to be told that "Harvest Gold" went out of style decades ago.

I'm talking about the spark; the sense and knowledge that there is a power in the room, a power that animates, moves, and stirs us. It is something far more than emotionalism, histrionics, or religious sentiment. It is the Living Presence that will not allow us to sit still or remain where we are.

It is no wonder why some people won't go to church; it is because they have already been, and have found it to be as lifeless and dead as a dodo. There is no passion in the pew or in the pulpit. A little spark might make all the difference.

April 29: You Are Stuck With You

On a visit to my hometown I took time to drive by my childhood home. It was the first time I had seen the place in decades. It was largely unchanged except that it seemed so much smaller.

The neighborhood itself had gone to seed. Homes were completely abandoned. Once beautiful yards were overgrown. Everywhere I looked I saw dilapidated, deteriorating, run-down homes. What happened? It was a failure of vigilance. Everyone moved out or moved on, and homes that aren't lived in break down.

The same can be said for our hearts. By "heart," I mean the mysterious, inner person. It's tempting to run away from who you are, moving out and moving on, but at the end of the day you have to come home to yourself. And home will not be a very pleasant place if you haven't taken care of the space, if you have no center - no core - if you haven't taken care of where you live.

Put bluntly, you are stuck with you; and if you have let your heart go to seed, how can you ever be happy occupying a place like that? If your heart has been given over to the wilderness, if the dust and mold are a foot deep, and if cockroaches and critters have taken over the joint, why would anyone else want to share that space with you?

Yet, an abandoned heart can be revived. Trim the hedgerows with prayer. Cut the grass, that is, keep bitterness nipped in the bud. Repair those broken places of the past, long ignored. This kind of sweat equity will clear the cobwebs and clean the windows, and you just might learn to love the person God has made you to be and the life he has given you to live.

April 30: Changing The World

Leo Tolstoy said, "Everyone thinks of changing the world; but no one thinks of changing himself." Everything we see in the larger world - the good, the bad, and the ugly - is a reflection of the individual, human heart. You can't maintain a sane world when everyone in it is crazy. So we can't begin with the world. We have to begin with ourselves.

If anything about this world is going to change, it will be you (It's worth re-reading that line), and the change cannot be cosmetic, superficial, or an artificial cover-up. Change must be deep within, where our darkness lurks, our transgressions take shelter, and where all our spiritual neurosis is born.

One of Jesus' more interesting parables is about a person who gets free of an evil spirit. Some time later, the spirit returns and finds the person's life swept clean and in order. The spirit moves back in with all his malicious friends, and the person's condition is worse in the end than in the beginning.

It's plain what Jesus is saying. Surface changes don't work. Clean the junk out of your heart. Wash the windows of your soul. Change the drapes and the sheets. But if you don't allow God's Spirit to take up transformative residence in that now orderly space you have created, then all the rubbish you sent to the curb will be back in spades. Ask any recovering addict if this isn't true.

People want to change their lives (at least some people), but they don't "put the question marks deep enough" in searching for their answers. They don't dive into the depths of their hearts to open those locked closets and cast light on shadowy basements. They refuse to do the work of the soul, and thusly, refuse to change.

MAY

May 1: The Last Straw

"The straw that broke the camel's back" is an old, familiar proverb with which we all have had some experience.

For instance, someone manages her work, household, and usual routine with ease, until her father is diagnosed with cancer. She is devastated, but marshals her strength and carries on. Next, her teenage son is expelled from school; and her husband loses his job; and her oldest child drops out of college. Miraculously, she holds it all together.

In the midst of all this, she maintains her leadership of the homeowner's association, the PTA, her tennis club, and church board. But then she comes home one evening, and finding the washing machine broken, she loses her mind and has to be hospitalized. Only the most obtuse observer would say her breakdown was the result of a broken appliance.

Back-breaking strain is rarely, if ever, the result of a single event or trauma. It is cumulative. The last straw lands on our backs, and the weight of it all cascades down. No amount of soldiering on, doubling up, or internal pep talk can stop the avalanche.

At such junctures, while sitting broken and overwhelmed by the life we have accumulated on our shoulders, it's a good time to learn the necessity of off-loading some unnecessary burdens. Granted, much of what we carry can't be mitigated. But many of our heaviest burdens we willingly picked up ourselves.

An often quoted verse from Scripture says, "Cast all your cares on God, because he cares for you." It's true. This is exactly where those concerns we can do nothing about should be placed, but as to the burdens we have picked up on our own, those don't need to be cast on the Lord so much as they need to be cast aside.

May 2: For Overachievers

Scientists have a name for it: Ergomania. "Ergo," meaning work, and "mania," which means passion. Ergomania is a "passion for work." In contemporary society we use a different term for an individual suffering from this condition: The "workaholic." And the condition thrives in houses of worship.

We religious people work very hard, often killing ourselves for God. Why? I believe it is because we do not believe that God really loves us. Most of us are working like slaves to earn his love, unaware, it seems, that his love is already ours in abundance.

And why should we believe it? Our parents never accepted us without conditions. This merciless culture is constantly judging us and our level of success. Our spouse left us for someone younger, better looking, or richer. Our coach tells us we'll never make the team, and yes, even the church gets in on it too.

Yet, Jesus' invitation is for us to get off of the spiritual hamster wheel and to crawl out from beneath the choking yoke of religious workaholicism, and dance freely to the easy tempo of grace. Grace will teach us to serve God, not to make him like us, but because he already adores us. It will teach us to give up our overachieving and slaving ways, and find peaceful rest for our souls.

Now, if work is your passion, and time spent on the treadmill suits you just fine, then disregard all I have said as useless drivel and carry on.

But if you have had it; if you are sick and tired of being sick and tired; if you're looking for a way out; if you are finally at the end of yourself and need a rest, have I got good news for you: That is exactly what Jesus offers.

May 3: Let Go Or Be Dragged

A friend who has some experience with horses sent me a most picturesque proverb: "Let go or be dragged." It is the unmistakable truth.

Take my friend's horses as an example. Training such animals requires a great deal of lassoing, roping, and "breaking." But sometimes, as the proverb goes, the breaker becomes the broken. A tipping point is reached where the trainer must regroup, or risk being ground into the corral's dust. Let go or be dragged.

Think of the little one who refuses to leave the playground. Haven't you seen mothers and fathers, quite literally, hauling the kicking and screaming child to the car? Let go or be dragged. It's the single handler left holding a giant Macy's Day Parade balloon. He's no match for 10,000 cubic feet of helium! If he hangs on, he will be pummeled against lamp posts, battered along 42nd Street, and become a spectacle in front of 40 million children watching on Thanksgiving morning. Let go or be dragged.

We all will face situations, diseases, circumstances, relationships, people, challenges and conditions that are larger, stronger, and longer-lasting than we are. We have two options and only two options in such encounters. We can keep fighting an unwinnable war, and whatever we have dug our claws into will drag us into a bloody pulp.

Or, we can accept our limitations and admit that we are not omnipotent. We can accept life for how it is, even when life isn't fair. We can let go. And in this surrender – this little act of dying – we stop our suffering. We get to live again.

For this is the counterintuitive way of the cross; the paradoxical power of Christ: We only live once we have died. We only win if we surrender. Let go or be dragged.

May 4: Boundaries

There is an ancient story from the Cherokee Nation that was used to illustrate the danger of getting too close to something dangerous. A young boy was making a journey through the forest when he came across a rattlesnake. The rattlesnake spoke to the boy: "I am very old. Please, take me to the top of the mountain so I can see the sunset one last time."

The boy responded: "Mr. Rattlesnake, this I cannot do. If I pick you up, you will bite me and I will die." The rattlesnake answered: "No, I promise I will not bite you." The young man relented and carefully picked up the old rattlesnake. After a while, he was able to hold the snake confidently to his chest as he carried it up to the top of the mountain.

They watched the sun set together. Afterward the rattlesnake turned to the young man and said, "Take me home. I am very tired, and very old." The young Cherokee carefully picked up the rattlesnake once again and took it to his chest, tightly and safely. Just before he laid the rattlesnake down, the snake turned and bit the boy in the chest. The boy cried out in shock and pain.

"Mr. Rattlesnake, what have you done? You promised not to harm me! Now I will surely die!" he cried. The rattlesnake could only offer a sly grin with this slithering answer: "Ah, but you knew what I was when you first picked me up."

How much trouble would most of us stay out of, if we simply avoided what we know is dangerous. Certain people. Certain places. Certain situations. Throwing healthy boundaries to the wind, we fail to learn the most obvious lesson: The most poisonous things are best resisted by leaving them alone.

May 5: Sacred Cows

In their book, *The Starfish and the Spider*, Ori Brafman and Rod Beckstrom take a detailed look at the native Apache tribe of what is now the Southwestern United States. The Spanish were unsuccessful in subduing this wild band. The Mexicans likewise failed. At first, the Americans fared no better.

Adaptable, decentralized, as fluid as the wind that blew across their deserts, the Apache would not yield. Then, the American government gave the Apache tribal leaders cows, and everything changed. Once in possession of this rare resource, and with the buffalo population hunted to extinction, wealth in the form of walking, bawling bovines became the virus that ate away Apache society from the inside out.

The tribal leaders used the cow as a form of reward and punishment to control rather than lead their society. To be an Apache no longer meant being a part of the land, being owned by creation. Now the Apache had wealth – cows – and according to Brafman and Beckstrom, it broke their society.

Wealth is not inherently evil, but it is dangerous. Wealth can blind us to the distress of others. It can make us controlling and greedy. It can make us reliant upon softer lifestyles.

The solution is to push our wealth away from us and out into the world where it can serve God. For neither the Christian nor the church are ends unto themselves – spiritually or materially – but we are called, as the people of God and imitators of Jesus Christ, to bless and serve the world.

For it is when we serve, we find our true identity; when we are generous, we are inoculated against greed. And when we sacrifice our "sacred cows," we free ourselves from the tyranny of this self-absorbed, selfish world to be people of genuine faith.

May 6: Like A Rock

Bob Seger is a legendary song writer and performer. My personal Seger favorite is the tune "Like a Rock." In the refrain Seger screams into the microphone, a refrain about himself as a younger man: "Like a rock, I was strong as I could be; like a rock, nothin' ever got to me; like a rock, I was something to see; like a rock."

Seger captures the years of youth perfectly. It is a time of unbridled optimism, strength, and arrogance. A young man or woman can do anything, be anything, try anything, and overcome anything. Honestly, a young person needs this kind of bravado when life is just getting started. But he or she will also learn that the do-everything, dare-anybody, defy-anything ability of youth doesn't last.

We live a little while and experience a few disappointments. We bury loved ones, lose a job, marriage, house, career, or a fortune. We are betrayed by a friend, a business partner, or a lover. We suffer, hurt, age, have our hearts broken, or muddle through a couple decades of muted frustration. Then we learn, and this learning is as absolutely necessary as youthful strength, that we really aren't "like a rock" at all. Life, like erosion, has a way of reducing the hardest stone into sand.

Admittedly, this realization might cause you to hit the booze or pills and collapse into a hopeless stupor – many past the prime of youth do exactly that. But the recognition of personal limitation is not cause for despair. It is liberation.

It is deliverance from the "try-harder-and-do-more" life. It is freedom from the totalitarianism of "If it's going to be, it is up to me." In short, it is surrender, and surrender is true faith and true life.

May 7: The Wall

Many people begin their walk of faith, and everything goes as they expected. But somewhere along the way things go terribly wrong. The orderly, stalwart faith that used to "work" for these true believers becomes a muddled mess. Faith splinters into a million tiny pieces.

It is more than a crisis of faith, more than a theological bump in the road. It is an unraveling. The once unshakable believer descends into the blackness, what Saint John of the Cross called "the Dark Night of the Soul."

This is what Janet Hagberg calls "The Wall." I've lived through such an experience, but it was Hagberg who so eloquently described it. Those who hit "The Wall" feel so lost, adrift, and dismantled at their very core, that to keep doing what they were doing is impossible. "The Wall" breaks faith and people apart.

Here's the only question: "What will come out of the splintered and scattered pieces?" Well, one can harden his heart and sweep the shards of faith into the dustpan, giving up on faith completely; or one can pick up the broken pieces, with bloodied hands and heart, and reassemble faith on the other side of doubt.

No, it won't be the same faith he once had. It won't be an improved or updated version of the beliefs he formerly held. No, it will be a new construction altogether. Faith on the other side of "The Wall" will not take a person back to where he was; it will move him to where he must be.

So if you find yourself crushed against what feels like the concrete and steel of disbelief, with not a drop of faith left in you, don't throw it all away just yet. In the breaking, you might find that faith has a new beginning.

May 8: Just Paper

A late friend of mine was a World War 2 veteran who fought for General Patton. He helped liberate a number of concentration camps, was in Germany when the unconditional surrender was tendered on this day in 1945, and on those rare moments when he spoke of the war, he told mind-bending stories.

One such story involved his tank unit, late in the war, after it had crossed the Rhine River and was deep into Germany. Patton was moving at blazing speed, as was his style, so US forces had to forage from the land around them, as they were often without basic supplies. One severe shortage was paper goods, and war or not, this was a crisis.

So the servicemen began using German Reichsmarks, the German currency, as toilet paper. Twenties, fifties, thousands - it didn't matter the denomination - it was just paper. The currency that had driven the finances of Europe, that had financed the effort for world domination was now worthless, useful only for the latrines and as kindling to start fires. When all of life's accounting is complete, that's about as useful as our fortunes will be.

This is not because money is inherently evil, but because it is not made to last. Gold. Silver. Bonds. Savings accounts. Offshore accounts. They will all pass away, just as certain as all currency and markets passed before them.

So what do we do in this temporary world to "store up" eternal treasures in the world to come? John Wesley had an answer. He said, "It is the duty of every man to work as hard as he can, to make as much money as he can, to spend as little as he can, so as to give away all that he can."

Such is the kingdom of God.

May 9: For Boo-Boos

"Religion is the opiate of the people," Karl Marx said. He believed that faith kept believers incapacitated, preventing them from experiencing real, personal, substantial change. In short, Marx criticized the false relief that faith can bring – false because nothing ever really changes.

Honestly, much of what is called "faith" is little more than a sedative. It helps people to forget their pain and suffering, helps them sleep at night, and keeps them hanging on for next week's dose of tranquility; but it does very little to move people to a place of growing, spiritual health.

Consequently, faith can become a first-aid kit, what we turn to only when something hurts, and leaving it in the cabinet otherwise. Yes, when life hurts I want relief. Yet, the real power of faith is not its ability to magically stop our pain or to provide a fix to get us through a rough spot. Faith simply doesn't remove our troubles and worries, offering bubble-gum-flavored baby aspirin and cartooned band-aids.

Rather, faith does more than medicate our boo-boos or make us happy when we have been made sad. On the contrary, faith has the power to transform us, to shape and fit us for life, making us whole and well. It would do us and Marx well to hear the words of the Apostle James. He said, "Faith that does not lead to change is a faith that is dead."

It is possible to find great inspiration in our faith; to be comforted and reassured. Yet, if such beliefs do not have transformative power in our lives, then we do not have faith. Instead, we are addicted to spiritual tranquilizers that blind us to the reality of our world and the renewal God seeks to produce in our lives.

May 10: Less Is More

Paul wrote: "I can do all things through Christ who gives me strength." There's no way he could have anticipated how those words would be used centuries later. Printed on bumper stickers for aspiring marathoners; a benediction for victors at the end of a football game; inscribed on the t-shirt of a middle-aged man attempting to reclaim his lost youth: I don't think this is what the Apostle had in mind.

Paul was not offering an "I Can Do" attitude. It was a "He Can Do" submission. No, this isn't about overcoming, but accepting. It's not a call to heroic-like effort, rather, it is positioning oneself to receive the strength that Christ offers. Contentment is not the result of trying harder - no matter what overachievers or iron-pumping athletes might say - it is the result of relying upon a Power greater than yourself.

And this is why Paul's words are often so grotesquely misappropriated. They are used as a form of defiance against the odds, used to magically conjure up our personal strength when we have none left, making us try harder, go farther, endure longer, and never surrender until we are victorious.

This is the exact opposite of what Paul was saying. It is only in surrender, the surrender of our own power, that the power of Christ can be ours. Words from legendary gospel singer Larnelle Harris fit the bill perfectly: "It's not in trying; but in trusting. It's not in running; but in resting. It's not in wondering, but in waiting, that we find the strength of the Lord."

Determined, tireless self-sufficiency will take you far in life, but not quite far enough. To be genuinely content, and genuinely powerful, it won't take more - but less - less of yourself and more of Jesus.

May 11: Forgiveness

Four-hundred and ninety times. That was Jesus' answer to the question, "How many times should I forgive someone?" I don't think Jesus was being literal; how I wish he were! Then there would at least be a boundary. No, Jesus was saying, "Stop keeping score.

To forgive every single time you are hurt, harmed, offended, cheated on, ripped off, mistreated, abused, wrongly accused, verbally assaulted – every time – sounds like lunacy. Why would Jesus say such a thing?

The answer: When we forgive others without limit, we are treating others as God treats the world. God loves and forgives without restraint or limitation. So when Jesus teaches us to forgive without limit, he is calling us to bear the loving image of God in the world. We forgive because that's what God does.

I don't think profound, God-like forgiveness is something we humans can accomplish on our own or within our own power. I don't think it is something we conjure up with gritted teeth and by trying harder. No, forgiveness is something God does through us. Our only responsibility is to be a conduit, a passage through which God's love can flow; and the better we understand God's love, the more that love will spill out to others.

Consequently, forgiveness is not so much something we do, as it is something we discover. It is the discovery of God's inexhaustible, inconceivable, insuppressible grace – for ourselves – and for those who have hurt us. It is this discovery of forgiveness that can change us and change the world.

If we do not believe that forgiveness can change the world, then as clearly as I know how to say it, we do not believe the gospel. If forgiveness has given us a future, it can do the same for everyone else.

May 12: Un-Crucified

Few of us know the Christ-shaped self, the real person that Jesus would create in each of us. Instead, we have this edifice, this outer image we portray to others and protect at almost any cost; this shell that we have constructed around us for years (or what has been imposed upon us by others). But it's just that – a shell.

It is bark on the tree, protecting what is inside. And when that bark gets peeled back, and life will surely peel it back, then most of us discover that we are pretty hollow on the inside. We lack substance. We are just names and numbers without any real identity. We haven't let the Christ-life be fashioned within us, thus we have no self except the false, egotistical one that we have carefully manicured.

The short of it is this: We are un-crucified (if that word exists). When the nails of Providence painfully pierce our self-centeredness, we choose to jump down from our crucifixion. When the fires of God's grace rise to burn away the shoddy lives we have constructed from bits of straw and chaff, we leap from the altar as quickly as possible.

When the weight of the cross, the cross that would crush and remake us, falls heavy on our shoulders, we crawl from beneath the load before it finishes its work. Yet, the forging of faith and the making of lasting Christ-centered identity is only accomplished by an execution. By loss. By the death of the false self.

So as long as we protect what we think is ours, so long as we struggle to avoid all necessary suffering, so long as we refuse to relinquish the identity we have constructed, we will never become who Christ would make us.

May 13: Social Networking

"Social networking" sites have created an effect now known as "online dis-inhibition." That is, we lose our restraint, our better judgment – sometimes we lose our minds completely – and say and do things we would never do if not hiding behind the pseudo-invisibility of the Internet.

A congressperson posts racy online pictures and scuttles his career; a middle-aged husband explores a "cheating" site and ends up in divorce court; a high school football star loses his promised scholarship because of his Twitter rantings; a young woman can't land a job because prospective employers Google her and deem her a liability: These are the realities of today's world.

I don't want to sound like some crazed Luddite who hates technology. I love WI-FI, streaming video, GPS, downloadable audio, and satellites. I'm not ready to give up these things. But neither am I ready to accept all of these technologies without some critique and discernment.

While I now recognize the countless alternative ways we can connect with others, I also recognize that we are lonelier and more disconnected than ever. I can see that we are more aware of the world around us than any previous generation, and yet I see that we may be the most narcissistic generation to ever live in North America.

We must guard against real communication disintegrating, and the constant undermining of real, human connection. Technologies aside, we still need flesh-and-blood relationships, connections that are built upon mutual respect, actual time together, shared interests, and face-to-face conversation.

People of faith may have more at stake in this issue than most, because faith only flourishes in the environs of an authentic, unselfish community, not a virtual imitation where people hide behind their avatars. Real friendships require actual presence, not page counts.

135

May 14: Home Sweet Home

Jesus said, "Abide in me, and I will abide in you." With this invitation Jesus was welcoming his disciples to remain connected with him. Eugene Peterson gets right to it when he translated Jesus words like this, "Make your home in me just as I do in you."

Home is where each day begins and where each day ends. Home is where we eat, rest, relax, take shelter, play, and love. Home is where we go when there is no other place left, and where we always return. Home is that glorious place where we can walk around in our socks and underwear, scratch our backsides without worrying about who is looking, and lounge around on the weekend without showering or shaving if we so choose. Home is where we can drop all our burdens, barriers and coping mechanisms.

Home is sweet, it is where the heart is, and it is our castle. It is where we bring the bacon and where we wait for the cows to arrive. Home is like no other place in the world, and no matter where or how far we travel, home is where we always call, well, home. It is where we feel safe, secure, and ultimately, where we can be ourselves.

We can set aside our anxieties and fears, and curl up on the couch and collapse in contentment, at home with Christ. As Jesus said, "Make your home" – relax and be yourself – "with me."

European mystic, Francois de Fenelon, wrote to one of his students who had finally figured out a bit of this "abiding" business. He said, "Nothing makes me happier than seeing you peaceful and simple. Isn't it just like paradise?"

I don't know much about paradise, but this sure is a lot like coming home - home, sweet, home.

May 15: The Gospel According To Jesus

When Jesus began preaching his gospel in the Galilean hills, his message was clear and singular: "The Kingdom of God is at hand. It is here and now," he said. "It is today."

Jesus' intention, it seems, was not to rescue people from earth, per se, transporting them to a far removed heaven. His intention was to put heaven inside of people. A gospel that ignores this fact – and this current world – because our status in the next world has been properly secured, is a distortion of Jesus' redeeming message.

Thus, the gospel according to Jesus, is not just about a harp-playing, cloud-riding, hymn-singing, glory-praising, pie-in-the-sky heaven. It is holistic, all-encompassing deliverance, now. I'm not denying the existence of the afterlife; but I do not believe that we have to die to personally experience the life God has for us.

Jesus' first disciples did not have the benefit of two-thousand years of Christian tradition and theology. All those disciples had were Jesus' words: "Follow me, for the Kingdom of God is at hand." They had no promises of a big heavenly payoff. No fluttering angels' wings, no crossing over the River Jordan to the Hallelujah Shore, no promises of golden streets or pearly gates, no "full assurance that you will go to heaven when you die." All they had was the invitation of Jesus to "Follow me." For them, that was enough.

I believe that how Jesus taught us to live and the life he has to give, is the greatest hope for the present. He offers redemption, in all its magnificent and diverse manifestations, as more than the blessed hope of heaven. He offers it as the blessed hope for today, because today – not tomorrow – is the day of salvation.

May 16: Come On In

"Always be prepared to give an answer to everyone who asks you to give the reason for your hope." These are the words of Simon Peter, written to some of the first Christians. And like most words, these instructions have not always honored the intent of the author.

Peter wrote this when Christianity was new, unheard of in most places, and very often viewed with suspicion. Thus, a graceful and thoughtful explanation "for the hope that you have" was absolutely required. Thousands of years later, Christianity is still handled with suspicion by many. Not because it is a novel invention, but because a large core of its adherents have misapplied Simon Peter's good words.

Having a "prepared answer" – that is a ready opportunity to interact, dialogue, and discuss beliefs with others – has been replaced with defensiveness, anger, and out-and-out hostility toward those who see things differently. Many have forgotten to read the second half of old St. Pete's instructions: "But do this in a gentle and respectful way," he said.

My beliefs, as important as they are, do not give me the right to be belligerent toward others who do not share my beliefs. Our convictions need not – should not – can not – must not – be used to hurt or harm others.

Jesus didn't create an "in" group, an assembly of privileged elitists who have all the answers. He came to create a "come on in" group, a crowd of fellow-journeyers who come to love God, experience grace, live life, and serve others together.

Even if this group had all the answers to all the questions in the world (and humility should caution anyone from making such a claim), the attraction would not be how "right" they were. It would be the gracious, respectful, gentle way they lived.

May 17: Check Your Reflexes

Centuries ago there was a group of European Christians known as the Anabaptists. They were "anti-baptizers," scorning infant baptism and a heap of other cherished church doctrines. As a result, they were violently persecuted by Catholics and Protestants alike.

One such persecution broke out in 1569. A bailiff was sent to arrest Anabaptist Dirk Willems for holding secret religious meetings. Dirk ran for his life with the bailiff right on his heels, throwing himself across a small ice-covered lake. He crossed safely to the other side, but the bailiff crashed into the freezing water.

Willems immediately turned back and rescued his pursuer. For his kindness, Dirk was arrested, and after refusing to renounce his faith, was burned at the stake. Here is the question asked by today's Anabaptists: "Why did Dirk Willems turn back?"

Joseph Liechty answers, "It was not a rational choice. It was an intuitive response. The only force strong enough to take Dirk back across the ice was an extraordinary outpouring of love, and the only love I know like that is the love of Jesus."

Can we reach a place in our walk with Christ, that when we encounter hate, suffering, injustice, or frustration that our immediate and reflexive response will be Christ responding through us; a place where we don't have to think about it, we don't have to plan a response, but supernaturally and instinctively - like a reflex - Jesus comes alive in our hearts.

Dirk Willems acted as he did because he had been so spiritually shaped by Jesus that his response was the only response he was capable of making. Dirk's life and identity had been swallowed up in the person of Jesus, and it was Christ who now lived through him - the same Christ that lives in each of us.

May 18: Freedom From Fear

In Madison, Florida, you will find a striking sculpture of four angels, their wings unfurled in the wind. It is the "Four Freedoms Monument," based on a speech by President Franklin D. Roosevelt.

Roosevelt said, "We look forward to a world founded upon four essential human freedoms: Freedom of speech, freedom of every person to worship God in his own way, freedom from want, and freedom from fear."

As idealistic as all these freedoms are, that last one is the hardest: The freedom from fear. Fear is the currency of the world in which we live, but as citizens of a kingdom "not of this world," we have access to a peace that displaces fear; a peace that "surpasses human understanding."

From where does this peace come? Better fiscal policy? More powerful weapons? A stockpile of canned food, bottled water, and ammunition? No. The only source of peace is love. When you know you are perfectly and completely loved, there is nothing left to fear, for perfect love dispels fear.

Paul once asked a rhetorical but significant question: "Can anything ever separate us from Christ's love?" In other words, will God's love for us really last? Can we count on it in face of multifarious threats and dangers? The answer is an emphatic "yes!"

Paul concludes, "Nothing in all creation will ever be able to separate us from the love of God that is revealed in Christ Jesus our Lord." His love is sure. It is strong. It is eternal. It is ageless. It is the one unvarying element in the cosmos, able to overcome everything.

So, if the created universe can contain it, God's love can overcome it. Fill in the blank – whatever it is - nothing can separate you from God's love. And certainly, that includes our deepest fears.

May 19: The "Uns"

There is a lot I don't understand. I don't understand the science of how the sun can be 93 million miles away, provide life-giving light and heat to this planet, and keep our solar system from devolving into chaos, but I believe it, and I experience its light and heat every day.

I don't understand Newton's Law of Gravitation or Einstein's later Theory of Relativity, but I know these things keep my feet grounded on terra firma every day, and anchor me within this time and space.

I don't understand how oxygen is processed by the bronchial tubes in my lungs, but my lack of understanding doesn't keep me from breathing! I don't understand the strange affection I have for puppies, the passion I feel for football, the satisfaction that comes from being with those whom I care about, or the serenity produced by sitting on top of a high mountain or seeing the Gulf of Mexico on a cold, winter day.

I understand very little about these things. But I still experience all of these richly and deeply, and these experiences make me alive.

Can't God's love work the same way? As a shining light, a grounding force, a sustaining atmosphere; an affection, passion, and serenity that gives us life and meaning? No, I can only understand bits and pieces of it all, but my lack of complete knowledge should not prevent me from believing and living this fact: I - like you - am unconditionally and eternally adored by God.

We may be unworthy, undeserving, unprepared, undone, unnoticed, unthankful, unjust, unfair, uneasy, and unaccepted. We have been unknown, unapologetic, unhinged, unraveled, undesirable, unbearable, unclean, unethical, underhanded, uninterested, unkind, and untouchable.

We have been unwanted, unlucky, unnerved, unpopular, unpredictable, unqualified, and unstable. But understand this: We have never been unloved.

May 20: Lighten Up

Do you want to be happy? Or do you at least want to have a better chance at being happy? Then lighten your load. Simplify your life. Give up on a few assignments. Write a few resignation letters.

The most deeply spiritual thing that some of us could do is have a garage sale. Or purge our calendars. Or quit participating in a few of our many activities.

This is because the source of our unhappiness isn't related to a poor prayer life, the lack of reading the Scriptures, or going to church too little. We are carrying too much baggage. We are trying to manage too much stuff. We have too many possessions, too many obligations, and too many batons juggling in the air. This is an unqualified recipe for misery.

All of these weights and concerns of life – most of which we have assumed and they haven't been put upon us by anyone else – are choking out any real chance at being happy, as we simply cannot carry our self-loaded burdens; we can't enjoy the simplicity of life; and we haven't the time to lift our heads to see the beauty around us.

None of us can live our lives, worship our God, enjoy our world, or take care of those who have been given to us to love, if we are constantly looking at our own shoelaces, burdened with ourselves and our many concerns.

Thus, when we simplify, we are doing much more than getting rid of physical possessions or conserving our precious time. We are sharpening our emotional focus; we are making spiritual space. We are choosing to be happy.

Happiness, after all, is a choice. It is your choice, and you are the only one who can make it. Choose wisely, and lighten up.

May 21: Put Out The Fire

Lal Shahbaz Qalandar was a holy man and scholar born in the 1100s whose ancient travels and mythological stories are legendary. In one story, Lal Shabaz was wandering through the desert with a friend as evening began to fall. The desert was terribly cold and the two realized they had no way of igniting a fire.

Shahbaz's friend suggested that he transform himself into a great bird (the meaning of "Shahbaz") and fly down to hell to collect coals for a fire. Shahbaz considered this a wise suggestion.

After many hours Shahbaz returned to his friend empty-handed. Puzzled, he asked why he had not returned with fire. Shahbaz replied, "There is no fire in hell. Everyone who goes there brings their own fire, their own pain, from this world."

There is a great deal of truth in this story. Anyone suffering from the results of their own hard-hearted decisions or by his own hand is truly suffering hell. He has hurt himself, and nothing hurts worse than a self-inflicted wound.

By Jesus' definition, the most "burning torture to bear" is resentment and unforgiveness. When we refuse to forgive others, we sentence ourselves to hell. Our future depends upon our willingness to extinguish the burning inferno in our souls by forgiving those who have harmed us.

Dr. Fred Luskin said: "To forgive is to give up all hope for a better past. Forgiveness clears things. You can then say that this awful thing happened to me. It hurt like hell, yet I'm not going to allow it to take over my life."

To acknowledge that something "hurt like hell" is not the same as staying trapped in hell. This admission forges a firebreak and says, "It ends here!" Forgiveness is the first step in putting out the fire.

May 22: The Kudzu Conspiracy

"The kingdom of God is like kudzu." Would Jesus have said such a thing? Yes, I think so, as he compared God's work to a growing "mustard seed" and like "yeast mixed in with dough." I don't know much about mustard seeds or yeast, but as a Southerner, I know a little bit about kudzu.

Kudzu was introduced to the United States on the nation's hundredth birthday. The Asian plant was quickly loved by gardeners, with its large green leaves and purple blooms, and nurseries began selling mail-order seedlings.

But it was the Dust Bowl years that really rooted kudzu in the American soil. The vine was touted as a "wonder plant," and the USDA distributed the plant and seeds everywhere – especially the South - to stop the erosion of topsoil. Little did anyone know that the Southeastern United States was the perfect environment for kudzu to grow, and grow and grow and grow.

Kudzu overtakes the environments into which it is introduced. From just a few seedlings, a few sprouting vines, it explodes and cannot be stopped. Such is the kingdom of God.

Let it have its start – in people's hearts, in people's lives, in the midst of this planet's pain and suffering – and the world will in fact, change. It will be redeemed, as slowly and steadily the God Movement invades this world.

Certainly, people are still hungry. Wars are still fought. There is suffering, injustice, and evil. But we believe that love is growing, inch by inch. This causes us to throw ourselves into a fractured world, not only because we care, but because we believe God isn't finished yet.

He is making all things new, and he has chosen to do this through you and me as we join God's loving plot to revolutionize the world.

May 23: Free To Be Free

Mennonites use the term "non-violent evangelism." It describes a way of sharing faith that does not harm those with whom they share. It is built on mutual respect, love for others, and a commitment to the other person's freedom. People are treated as seekers, not potential converts, without pressure, arm-twisting or coercion.

Seekers are simply invited into radical hospitality where questions and exploration are not only tolerated, but welcomed. These non-violent evangelists share their faith with a "come and see" attitude, opening their hearts to others, leaving the results to God.

Many of us, overtly and subtly, have taken a very militant approach in sharing our faith with others. We corner people. We demand immediate decisions. We use emotionally charged environments to wrangle decisions. Should we share and live our faith? Absolutely! But I believe every person is capable of relating directly to God without coercion or interference by others.

In the words of Herschel Hobbs: "The Church cannot fasten its iron grip upon anyone's soul. This is the worst of all tyrannies. And it is made worse by its claim to be in the name of God who created men and women to be free."

Every person should be given the right of free choice in his or her relationship with God (or without God). Every individual should be given the dignity as image-bearing creations of God to arrive at his or her own spiritual conclusions, choosing to be Catholic or Coptic, Methodist or Muslim, Buddhist or Baptist, Jew or Jainist, Anglican or Atheist, without any heavy-handedness.

No, not everyone will "convert" to our way of thinking or adopt our ideas about faith. But faith isn't about force; it is about being set free. God entrusted people with that freedom. Let's do the same.

May 24: Blowing In The Wind

It was September 1997, and Pope John Paul II was presiding over the Italian Eucharistic Congress. The Harlem Gospel singers had just finished performing, when who should walk out on the Vatican stage but none other than Bob Dylan.

Sporting a cowboy hat and playing a Les Paul electric guitar, he sang three songs for worshippers: "Knocking on Heaven's Door" (appropriate); "A Hard Rain's A Gonna Fall" (vintage); and a salute to the aging pope, "Forever Young" (classy).

Not everyone was happy about the iconic face of rock-and-roll showing up for church. Cardinal Ratzinger, (who would become Pope Benedict) hated it. In his opinion, it was all wrong. Rock music? Wrong! Guitars in worship? Wrong! Bob Dylan before the Pope? Wrong! Wrong! Wrong!

Pope John Paul II seemed to have enjoyed it. He delivered a short homily after Dylan's concert that included lyrics from Bob's "Blowin' in the Wind." He said: "You've asked, 'How many roads must a man walk down before he becomes a man?' I answer: One! There is only one road and it is Christ, who said, 'I am the life.'"

Pope John Paul's words had echoes of another Paul, the Apostle Paul, who once said that all his spiritual accomplishments, all his religious fanfare, all his ceremonial ballyhoo, all his pompous credentials, and all his ceremonious posturing were now considered garbage. They were trash. Junk. Rubbish. Literally, it was all manure. The only thing that mattered to his faith was Jesus Christ.

It's easy to get hot and bothered over what is right, wrong, appropriate, inappropriate, proper and improper in regards to church and worship. Most of this bluster is just junk; opinions and stylistic differences. But if the focus of life is right - on Christ - then I hardly think we can go wrong.

May 25: Rooted in Love

Near Mpumalanga, South Africa, are the marvelous and mysterious Echo Caves. These caverns are home to a remarkable ecosystem, and one of the more amazing species found there are the famous and unique wild fig trees.

As far as plant life goes, these fig trees appear to be normal run-of-the-mill fruit bushes. What makes them so famous is the unseen: Their roots. Researchers and spelunking scientists have followed the roots of these trees deep into Echo Caves – 400 feet deep to be precise – the deepest known root system in the world.

These trees have survived and thrived in an arid climate for decades, employing an unparalleled root system to wring hydration from the deep, rocky soil. This is more than a science lesson; it's a lesson for life, as you probably know a person (or a few people if you are really lucky) not unlike the wild fig trees of Echo Caves.

Their environment is harsh. They have endured the drought of loss, injustice, and suffering. Their circumstances have been fiery, downright oppressive. The soil that life has given them is rocky and as hard as concrete. Yet, somehow, they survive and thrive. Their roots must be incredibly deep.

But deep into what? Maybe the Apostle Paul gives the best answer in a beautiful first century prayer: "I pray your roots will grow down deep into God's love and keep you strong." Or as Viktor Frankl said it, "The salvation of man is through love and in love."

Those who endure, even flourish, in the worst of conditions are those who have a very real connection to God's goodness and grace, and refuse to blame God for every wrong that life dishes out. They have rooted themselves deeply in his love, rather than in bitterness or resentment.

May 26: Don't Pray For Rain

I heard an Amish farmer say about the will of God, "We don't pray for rain. But we are thankful to God when the rain arrives." This is a unique perspective, as many of us have been taught that "God's will," if discovered, can end all the angst and indecision of life.

So we fret over what God wants us to do, thinking there will be complete and total disaster if we miss the secret plan he has for us. We writhe in the anguish of our decisions, never feeling good about any choice we make until we finally conjure up our bravado or foolishness, smile through gritted teeth, and give a direction a whirl.

If it all works out, we praise God for his magnificent direction. If it is a belly-flopping disaster we feel terribly ashamed, question God, or blame our weak faith for the calamity.

The truth is, most Christians really want to do "God's will." Equally as true, however, is there is no exact formula for finding his will. It is as much about trial and error as it is about praying and seeking.

Maybe we can take a cue from the Amish farmer and neutralize the mystery of finding and doing God's will. Maybe we can learn to simply trust God with our circumstances - whatever they are. Maybe, rather than trusting an exact path and direction for our lives, we can learn to trust God with our lives. After all, God is stronger than our failures, and he never fails to reward those who seek him.

Meister Eckhart, a medieval mystic and predecessor of the German Amish, wrote: "God wants no more from you than for you to let God be God in you." If that's not God's will, then I don't know what is.

May 27: The Safety Net

The Golden Gate Bridge is a California icon that has withstood the elements for decades now, and there are few living Americans who remember the San Francisco skyline without that bridge.

The roadway of the bridge is extremely high, some 250 feet above the water. But the suspension towers, at their peak, are even higher at 750 feet. Construction at this altitude, along with contrary winds, icy fog, unpredictable weather, and occasional seismic tremors from below, made for one of the most dangerous places to work in the world.

The bridge's chief engineer, Joseph Strauss, finally installed a gigantic safety net beneath the bridge. By giving the workers an increased sense of security, they progressed far more quickly and efficiently than before. They were so efficient that the project came in at more than $1 million under budget – that's in Depression era dollars – an outrageous pile of cash for the time.

But the greatest savings wasn't the money. It was the men working on the iron high in the air. Nineteen workers fell into that net during the construction of the Golden Gate Bridge and every one of them walked away without a scratch. Having cheated death, these workers proclaimed themselves "The Halfway-To-Hell Club," saved by that miraculous web of safety.

Grace, the beautiful but ethereal cornerstone of the Christian faith, at its basic definition is a safety net. When we slip and fall we are caught by the soft, loving hands of God. No fall is too far and no loss of grip is too irresponsible because God's grace never loses its bounce.

Does this make grace too easy? I'll stick with Charles Spurgeon's counsel on the matter. "If people do not like the doctrine of grace," he said, "then give them all the more of it."

May 28: Underfoot

Years ago my youngest son and I rescued a frog from our garage. We talked about the frog's warts, his strong legs, and bulging eyes. After the brief science lesson, we set him free. My son followed his new friend around the yard trying to catch and pet it. But the frog wouldn't oblige.

In frustration the boy lurched forward and crushed the frog beneath his foot. I was horrified. "Why did you do that?" I demanded. His answer was as telling as it was simple: "Because he wouldn't listen to me."

Some of us think that God is a lot like that. He's just itching to crush us for the slightest offense. Maybe it is the result of an anxious childhood or bad religious experiences, but we often see God as some kind of irritated, old, school-master keeping a ledger of our sins; a neurotic bully who cannot wait to rub us out. But this is not the God revealed to us by Jesus.

Jesus reveals a God who loves us so much that he was willing to die for us - not kill us. That's what the cross is about. On the cross God wasn't saying, "Look what you made me do to my Son," launching a cosmic guilt trip.

No, the cross was Jesus revealing, not God's anger, but his love. The cross, and the passion that orchestrated it, was not designed to shame us for our failures or to crush us in judgment.

No, it was an intentional unveiling of God's heart. God was showing us how far his love would go, inviting us to flush away these horrible misconceptions about who he is. In the process he was calling us to himself; to a God worth believing, a God worth worshipping, a God worth loving.

May 29: Here I Stand

"Here I stand! I can do no other," Martin Luther reportedly said as he stood before the Pope who was investigating his radical beliefs. Taking a "stand" has been the Protestant rage ever since.

Getting to our feet, it doesn't take long for words like doctrine, creed, and orthodoxy to get thrown around. Or, we use the opposite of these: Error, heresy, and sacrilege. We take our "stand" and if you believe "this, this, and this" then you can "stand" with us. If you believe something else, well, stand aside.

But the older I get, I find there are fewer things I'm willing to stand and fight over. It's not because I don't believe anything any longer, but because with age, the more I see God's love and grace as the only non-negotiable.

Not all my friends agree with me. They are made uncomfortable by an abundance of "love talk," and want me to quit overemphasizing a gracious God. They want me to declare a more "responsible position." They want me to "take a stand" on the "pertinent moral and social issues of our day."

Okay, I can do that. On so many of the hard and troublesome issues of our times, I take this stand: I stand for grace and love. For if Jesus came, not to condemn the world, but to redeem it, how can we who bear the name respond any differently?

Yes, my theological beliefs are important. Yes, what I believe about all the moral and social issues of the 21st century mean something. But "if I speak with the tongues of men and of angels, and if I have all faith so as to remove mountains, but I do not have love, it profits me nothing." Here I stand. I can do no other.

May 30: Moving

When I was packing my family and belongings for a move out of state, a Czech friend shared a proverb from her country: "The best move is a fire," she said. So true, especially when the amount of junk we have to carry with us is enough to break our backs.

Our attics are filled with stowed away anger, resentment, and unforgiveness, kept in mothballs because we aren't ready to let go. Into the basements of our hearts we have shoved our hate, fear, and distrust toward God, and we have locked the door, never wishing to handle these things again.

Our cupboards and closets are running over with unresolved regrets, personal disappointments, and the tyranny of "what-might-have-been." The moving truck into your future is plainly not able to hold all your stuff.

To move on, all of these stores and stocks have to be dealt with. Yes, I think we would all prefer a fire. That would be easier. Just start life fresh and clean, without all the boxes, baggage, disassembly and disorder. But a do-over is not one of our options.

I wish there were a different way, but there isn't. If we are going to move (or you can substitute the words, "mature, grow," or "develop"), we have to sort through what is worth keeping, and what must be dropped at the curb - maybe this is why it is so hard - naturally we are hoarders and want to keep everything.

But the quicker we make this decision, the quicker we can get a little further down the road. Let's begin where we are, with who we are, and with what circumstances we have been blessed or cursed, and from there move into the future. It's not easy, but it is the only way.

May 31: Hula-Hoops

Here is a vividly illustrated description that should be seared into your memory banks. It's originally from Jean McLendon, a long-time therapist in North Carolina, but a phrase now used in 12-step work, organizational management, and family counseling. I'd like to apply it to all facets of life – especially spirituality. The phrase is: "Stay inside your own hula-hoop."

McLendon suggests that we are all working through life with a hula-hoop; round and round it goes, representing our life's labor; the work and calling that only we can fulfill. We are certain to let it all fall to the ground if we attempt to leave our space and hula-hoop to invade someone else's.

We see their ring slip off their hips and fall to the ground. We want to fix it, so we go intervene. Someone else is hula-hooping far too fast, so we go to slow them down. Another person has her hoop up dangling around her head – completely unacceptable – so we attempt to put it in its proper place.

What happens? McLendon says, "You can't hula someone else's hoop without messing up your own efforts. You can observe, advise, cheer, and offer support, but as soon as you try to do it for someone else, you get into trouble yourself."

This is much more than "minding our own business," though that is a helpful, albeit rarely followed, piece of advice in its own right. This is actually a healthier, far more peaceful way to live.

Peace is not accomplished by the proper arrangement of our circumstances, as if we could impose our personal will on the people and things in our orbit. Peace is a path we follow, a discipline we practice, and a restful space we maintain – inside our own hula-hoop.

JUNE

June 1: The Teachers

"No more pencils, no more books, no more teachers' dirty looks." With summer upon us, our children will soon be set free from school once again. It is sweet release, but none more so than for teachers who will be dancing with joy.

It's been said that if teachers were paid like professional athletes, and if athletes were paid like teachers, our society would be a much better place. Amen to that. But money is not the reason these men and women give themselves to the classroom.

Sure, teachers would take a raise (or two), but they teach for other reasons: They teach because they love working with children. They teach because they are drawn to a particular subject. Or they teach because, as a student, they themselves were greatly influenced by a teacher. In fact, influence seems to be the real reason teachers teach.

Only parents and close family members have the kind of unparalleled impact on youngsters as teachers. The influence is incalculable. The Apostle James said, "My brothers and sisters, most of you shouldn't want to be teachers. You know that those of us who teach will be held more accountable."

Why this higher standard? Because teachers have an extra responsibility, not only as adults that little ones observe, but also as ones who encode and train our children. Teachers are the architects and designers of the future. That is indeed, a great responsibility and theirs is nothing less than a divine calling.

Sure, there are a few bad apples in the educational barrel (these can be found in any field), but all in all, teachers are a heroic lot who deserve our support, admiration, and even our prayers. God knows if I were matched daily against twenty-five second graders, I'd want someone praying for me.

June 2: Growing Up

The Hebrew word for anger literally means to "blow out your nostrils" or to "smoke." That's apropos, for we all know what it is like to get that fire burning and boiling on the inside, only to have it explode out the chimney of our mouths, minds, and fists.

How much pain has anger caused each of us by fueling words that can never be recalled, actions that can never be undone, and memories that can never be erased? How many divorces, wars, irreconcilable differences, failed business partnerships, murders, errant texts and assaults have been the result of primal, fully vented rage?

Now, is there such a thing as justifiable anger? Yes. Is there anger that is right and just? Absolutely. But genuine "righteous indignation" is a rarity. The anger that most often consumes us is the anger of offense. We feel insulted, disrespected, or that our rights have been violated. Our rage is self-centered, the result of others not doing what we want them to do.

A great deal of this anger stems from a lack of maturity, as our emotional growth is stunted. Like small children - or worse, raging teenagers - we are stuck in an adolescent selfishness. We want everything and everybody to orbit around us, to do as we command. Frankly, this is a formula for frustration, as it demands of others and the world what cannot be given.

How do we calm the burning fire within us? Well, we can control everything and everybody around us, forcing them to comply with our will (Let me know how that works out, okay?), or we can grow up. Francois de Fenelon said it simply: "The moment you stop wanting everything your way, you will be mature. Until then, your life will be full of trouble and agitation."

June 3: People Get Ready

Curtis Mayfield's song, "People Get Ready," is a rarity. It has a clear, redemptive, gospel message, but is accepted as vintage rock and roll, always counted among the greatest rock songs of all time. But Mayfield wrote it as gospel.

Mayfield started singing when he was kid at his grandmother's church. He learned to play guitar, piano, and most every instrument he could get his hands on. He joined the Impressions when he was a teenager, and entering adulthood, got involved in the Civil Rights movement, becoming close to Dr. Martin Luther King, Jr.

Dr. King was scheduled to come to Chicago and Mayfield was part of the delegation to meet King at the train station. "People Get Ready" came out of that wait. He was writing about a real train, but also about a symbolic train; the train of salvation and redemption; that train "bound for glory" (per Woody Guthrie); a train bringing transformation and change; a train that turns the world upside down.

Mayfield said this song was knocking around in his subconscious, the product of "all that preaching of my grandmother and those Sunday ministers. It's about a train that changes the world... that takes everyone to the promised land."

Curtis Mayfield is right about the gospel; the life of faith is a life of waiting. Waiting at the station; looking down the tracks; listening for the rumble of those diesels; that lonesome whistle in the distance. But faith is also "getting ready."

As Peter said, we are "looking for the day of God, but we are also hurrying it along." We hurry it along by living in such a way that the kingdom of God comes within us first. We get ready by staying ready, and becoming "the change we wish to see in the world."

June 4: Worth It

"If your hand causes you to sin," Jesus said, "cut it off and throw it away." That's a pretty tough surgical intervention if you ask me, and he doesn't stop there. He goes on to name other body parts as well. "Cut off your foot. Gouge out your eye."

We could debate for the next few decades how literal or metaphorical Jesus was being. Such a debate would serve to only distract us from putting into practice the spirit of what he said. No, I don't think Jesus was endorsing personal dismemberment. Rather, he was emphasizing, in rather dramatic fashion, the need for life-saving, future-salvaging initiative.

Better to lose an arm than lose your whole life. Better to throw away something you consider incredibly valuable, than to throw away your future. It seems best to accept Jesus' words as a simile for "Desperate times call for desperate measures." At times, drastic steps have to be taken to save the one and only life you have been given.

You will probably never have to lose a limb to save your life, but you might face an addiction, a dependence, a poisonous relationship, or a business arrangement that robs you of life. There are some people, places, and things that are no good for us, and we have to make the hard, brave decision to "cut off our arm," if it means saving our lives and our futures.

It will be painful. It will hurt. It will bleed, but you have so much life in you, so much future joy to experience, so much living to do, you must do what you must do.

These are strong words; difficult words; hard words to hear and practice. But these are words that lead to life, and your life is worth it.

June 5: Don't Be Afraid

The Apostle Paul said, "God has not given us a spirit of fear and timidity, but of power, love, and a sound mind." He summarizes the most often repeated command in the Scriptures: "Don't be afraid."

Over three hundred times in the Hebrew and Christian Testaments the Bible speaks to us with the simple words, "Fear not." The most repeated command is not "Love thy neighbor," or "Repent of your sins," or "Do not kill," as important as these things are. The most repeated instruction is to not be afraid.

What an appropriate reminder for us - that we don't have to be afraid. For we have been given the power to face uncertain days; the love to overcome the hatred and bitterness that surround us; and soundness of mind when everything else seems so out of control.

Our security is not dependent upon the strength of our military or foreign policy. Our future is not guaranteed by the performance of the stock market. Rising energy prices, inflation, and the never-ending economic upheaval may cramp our portfolios. Elevated terror threats may cause us to alter our travel plans, but these should not take away our peace of mind. For this is a peace that comes from above, and it surpasses all human understanding.

Dr. E. Stanley Jones said it superbly: "I am so made that in anxiety and worry, my being is gasping for breath. These are not my native air. But in faith and confidence, I breathe freely. We are inwardly constructed in nerve and tissue, brain cell and soul, for faith and not for fear. God made us that way. To live by worry is to live against reality."

During these perilous days, we can still choose to live within the reality of God; a place without fear.

June 6: An Act of God

It happens every time a major natural disaster strikes. Some Christian "leader" begins pointing fingers, blaming the victims, and speaking of God's raging vengeance. Even insurance companies get in on the fault-finding, referring to otherwise inexplicable disasters as "acts of God."

I do not believe that God causes destruction. Rather, it is God who enters sorrow and comes to those victimized. It is not God, who with a cosmic breath, causes earthquakes, tsunamis, tornadoes, or hurricanes. Rather, it is God who weeps with those left to bury the dead. How does God join those who suffer? Through you and me.

As a Christian, I believe that the greatest divine revelation is the appearance of Christ, who showed us in the flesh what God is really like. Sent from God on a truly earth-shaking mission of grace, he now sends his followers to do the same. "As the Father sent me," Jesus said, "I am sending you."

Walt DeNero, former Director of the University of Georgia's Fanning Leadership Center, used to tell a story about two log-sitting turtles, discussing world events. One turtle said, "I wonder why God allows so much suffering in the world? I'd like to ask him 'why' when he could do something about it."

The other turtle said, "Why don't you ask God that question?" And the first one responded, "No. I'm afraid God might ask me the same thing."

We should probably quit analyzing the weather looking for the judgment of God. Instead, we could see times of disaster as the time to give, help, love, and be the hands, feet, heart, and compassion of God to those who hurt. An "act of God," is not a cataclysmic disaster. It is a deed of love and grace toward those who need it most.

June 7: Too Much Of A Good Thing

When my wife decided to clean our aquarium with a dose of anti-fungus agent, I thought that was a good idea. But when she medicated the water with ten times the recommended dose, things didn't go as well as she had hoped.

We didn't know there was a problem until the next morning when we found four goldfish half-scuttled at the top of the tank begging for air. My wife's zeal was a prime example of how too much of a good thing can become toxic rather than being helpful; not unlike religion.

It is like a pharmaceutical. Within it, there is the power to heal and restore, or there is the power to consume and destroy. It can be a remedy for the soul's ills, or it can be deadly poison.

Maybe this was what Jesus was getting at when he warned his disciples about the religious zeal of those consumed with rituals, sacred protocols, and proper ceremonies. Certainly these people had good and worthy intentions: They wanted to please God and see others do the same.

Yet, their application of the product was over the top. They "crush people with unbearable religious demands and never lift a finger to ease the burden. They shut the door of the Kingdom of Heaven in people's faces" All their passion and enthusiasm leaves those around them over-treated, floating belly-up begging for air and mercy.

Agreed, people would be healthier, more whole, and more spiritually sound if they had a little less goop in their lives. But let's make sure we don't overdose those around us with zealous inflexibility. They need grace-filled air more than they need the rites of purification. And what we think will help them, might actually send them belly-up to the surface.

June 8: The Entire Bible

I once came upon a little church named the "Entire Bible Baptist Church." Obviously, they intend to practice the "whole counsel of God" and do everything the Bible commands. But nobody practices the unabridged Bible. This is a good thing, because there are parts of the Bible that are nothing short of confounding.

Consider that owning slaves, selling your children into servitude, and executing adulterers are all permitted in the Bible. Further, eating shrimp and pork chops, or wearing clothes blended from two different fabrics (so much for my favorite pants) are not allowed. Does the Entire Bible Baptist Church keep all these commandments? I doubt it.

What then do we who love the Bible do with these conflicting texts? This will be an overly simplistic answer to some, but for me, I have come to read the Bible through the lens of Jesus of Nazareth. In other words, I take a "What Would Jesus Do" approach and use him, his words, and his way to better understand.

So when I come to these inexplicable and sometimes bizarre passages, I look to Jesus to make sense of them. And I discover that most of the time Jesus is silent on these issues, and when he does speak, it is speech seasoned with love, grace, and course-correcting freedom. That's why for me, the "entire Bible" is not the foundation of faith; Jesus is.

Answer this question: When you first came to faith, did you believe and practice everything in the Bible? Of course not! Most of us couldn't quote much more than "Jesus wept," could name only a handful of the individual biblical books, and were blissfully ignorant of the theology that churches fight over.

But we knew Jesus loved us, and that was enough. I believe it still is.

June 9: When You Say Nothing At All

God gets blamed for a whole lot of the kookiness in this world. Someone says "God spoke to me," or "I heard God's voice," and religious movements begin when the person actually needed a mental health examination. And let's be honest; sometimes the stories are more tragic than religious. Some of history's greatest atrocities have been committed because someone "heard God speak" to them.

Yet, I believe that God speaks to us. Now, I don't believe God's instructions ever include harming others or committing any type of violence. Such voices are patently inconsistent with the way and person of Christ. And no, I don't think God's voice arrives in our inboxes as an unalterable blueprint for life.

Besides, if God did speak that clearly (and maybe he does), most of us would miss it anyway (maybe we have), for it seems God prefers communicating through stillness rather than through the brilliance of signs and wonders.

It's summed up by Dan Rather's interview of Mother Teresa from decades ago. Paraphrasing, he famously asked her, "What do you say to God when you pray?" She answered, "Nothing. I just listen." Rather then asked the follow-up question: "What does God say?" Mother Teresa said, "Nothing. He just listens."

In a relationship of love and trust, being together is enough, and more is understood in the silence than when using all the words in the world. God only requires the quiet and silent heart to quietly and silently speak.

A great deal of religion is built upon the desire for divine fireworks; megaphoned, crystal clear answers; God showing up in flamboyant and undeniable style. But that's not his manner, not very often anyway. Getting quiet will do more to sharpen one's heart to God's voice than all the religious pyrotechnics in the world.

June 10: Forgiving Not Forgetting

Researchers have found a few people who can remember almost everything about their lives; and I mean almost everything. These people can recall every single day of their lives down to every meal ever eaten, the exact clothes worn on any given day, and when asked about a specific date, they can even tell you what the weather was like on that day.

It's a phenomena called, "Superior Autobiographical Memory." I hope we learn a great deal about the human brain from them, maybe even make some advances in the treatment of Alzheimer's or dementia because of them; but I do not envy them. I have a hard enough time trying to forget some of the things from my past as it is.

The things that lodge like splinters in our brains the deepest are those times and occasions when others have hurt us badly; when we have been wronged; or when we have been violated, mistreated, cheated or harmed.

It is impossible to forget these things no matter how many times we are told that "time heals all wounds" and no matter how many times we are told to "forgive and forget." No amount of counseling, therapy, hospitalization, or medication – nothing short of a lobotomy – could erase the pain from our memory.

The answer to the pain is not in the forgetting; it is in the forgiving. Forgiveness is the only thing that heals our deep, bleeding, unforgettable hurts. How so? By facing the painful memories head-on and feeling all their agony, injustice, and rage, we also begin to diffuse these memories of their power - because they hold power only so long as we desire vengeance.

Once we no longer feel the need to retaliate, so many of our painful memories begin to hurt us so much less.

June 11: The Host

Artist Andy Gray wrote a parable about a little boy who stumbled upon a mysterious door. He entered to discover a beautiful garden inside, and in the midst of the garden, a great table heavy with a feast. Joyful people were there eating together.

The child saw a Man standing at the head of the table with a warm smile and inviting eyes. The boy wondered aloud, "Who is He?" The nearest attendant answered, "He is the Host of this feast. He opened the door and invited us in. He loves us."

The boy's eyes brightened and he moved toward the Host. But the attendant stopped him and said, "If you do not know His name or the story of how He opened this door, you cannot be here. You must leave."

But the child was undeterred. He failed to hear the attendant's prohibition because he was drawn overwhelmingly to the feast table and the Man of the garden. He moved forward and extended his hand and his eyes met the Host's. There was an immediate, joyful recognition. Meanwhile, the attendant stayed where he was to stand guard by the open door.

Isn't it obvious what this story is about? And isn't it just as obvious which one of the two people best knew the Host? The more we understand Jesus, the more we must realize that people encounter him all the time, and all over the place, even before they realize who he is or how to call his name.

People hunger for that moment of recognition and connection with the Host, and we who have already stumbled into the party, might remember that we are servers at His table, not guards at the door. Then we can rejoice when Christ welcomes another child who has come diligently seeking.

June 12: Who's There?

A salesman had a flat tire on a lonely road late at night. It was dark, cold, raining, and without a cell signal or spare tire, he was stranded. He saw the light of a farmhouse across a field, and with no other options, started walking.

"Surely," he thought, "this farmer will have a telephone." But then he started doubting: "What if the farmer refuses to come to the door? What if he comes to the door with a shotgun and shoots me? What if he gets angry at being bothered and refuses to help me?"

These thoughts stuck in his mind so that the longer he walked, the angrier and more distrustful he became. "Why, that selfish old farmer," he said aloud, "how dare he not help someone in need? How could he leave me out here in the cold and the rain?"

Finally on the porch, the salesman began banging on the door angrily, frustrated and drenched. The farmer called out from inside, "Who's there?"

The salesman answered: "You know good and well who this is! It's me! You can keep your stinking phone! I wouldn't use it if it was the last one in the county!" And back to his car the salesman trudged in the rain.

Most of us aren't atheists. We believe in God, but we don't know what God is like. We don't believe that God wants to help us, as we have convinced ourselves that he would never answer if we called on him while in trouble. But, God is on our side. He wants to help us if we will let him.

So give him that chance; to be your friend and an "ever present help in time of trouble." It's dark, cold, and wet out there. Where else can we go?

June 13: Taking A Sabbath

Things tend to pile up. Laundry. Dishes. Inboxes. The hours we put in at work. It all gets higher and heavier, and the breathing space we used to enjoy becomes a mountain of accumulation and responsibility.

The demands placed on us by our volunteerism, our families, our children's schedules, our schooling, these become too much. Our personal, emotional, and spiritual lives begin to look like an episode from "The Hoarders".

Because our lives can quickly be suffocated by all we have and do (and by all we have to do), regular rest is crucial. The biblical word is "Sabbath." Sabbath is more than a day of the week, it is a way of life. Rooted in Creation, God established weekly rest whereby we might regain our easily betrayed balance and sanity.

Healthy Sabbath observance is still a large part of the Jewish faith tradition, but we Christians, especially those of us reared with the good-old-Protestant-work-ethic, we view Sabbath-rest more as a sin, than a privilege. But busyness is not a virtue. It is a vice, a vice corrected only by vigilance.

You will have to be intentional about resting. You will have to say "no" to some obligations. You may have to relinquish some of the junk piles in your life to make more space. You'll have to pass on those commitments that you do not feel absolutely passionate about.

Take a nap. Use all of your vacation days. Get away. Get alone. Leave the unwashed dishes till tomorrow. Take a Sabbath. It won't be easy, but it is vital, for if you do not put in some rest and expunge your heaps of accrued junk, you may wake one day to find the air smothered out of the life you thought you were living.

June 14: Pickled Pain

Missionary physician Dr. Paul Brand was called to a patient who had suffered extreme leg pain for years but would not consider amputation. Finally, the pain became too much: "Take this leg off!" the patient demanded.

The patient, however, made one morbid condition before submitting to surgery. The amputated leg had to be preserved in a massive jar of formaldehyde. The patient wanted to sit it on a shelf and jeer at it: "You can't hurt me any longer, leg!" he planned to squawk each day.

But, the amputee developed phantom pain; it's the feeling of real pain from a limb no longer there. For Brand's patient, he had struggled with that leg for so long that the throbbing sensation lodged in his brain.

We all keep a collection of pickled limbs on the shelves of our minds. And the pain these produce is no shadowy phantom; the suffering is all too real. Bad decisions, former relationships, an ill-fated rendezvous, bygone injustices and defeats: These things still hurt.

Much of the pain and regret we carry around (or what mocks us from the shelves) is the result of not accepting this truth about ourselves: We are not irredeemable and damaged goods. We are the objects of God's undying, unending affection.

Sure, we've all heard that "God loves the world," but it is so much more personal than that. God loves more than the world, he loves you. He does so with such profoundness, that none of your failings, baggage, hang-ups, or preserved and pickled attachments will ever separate you from God's love.

If your past and memory banks can contain it, God's love can overcome it, and it is that kind of individual love – deep, abiding, and unshakable – that changes us, eases our pain, and sets us free.

June 15: Trusting

"But they that wait upon the LORD shall renew their strength; they shall mount up with wings as eagles," said the prophet Isaiah by way of the King James Bible. Modern translations translate the verse, "But those who trust in the Lord shall renew their strength." The latter is the better wording, as trusting and waiting can be two very different things.

Waiting is not enough. The challenge is trusting, placing our confidence in the right place. What is needed is trust in God while we wait. This is what leads us to a sense of peace, perseverance and strength.

Isaiah's example is the eagle. Eagles are able to cover incredible distances, rising thousands of feet into the sky, reaching speeds of sixty miles per hour. But these beautiful birds may flap their wings only once or twice over the course of hours. Conserving their energy, eagles have one of the longest, healthiest life spans of any bird in the sky, some living up to fifty years.

Compare that to the smallest bird species: The hummingbird. They too can reach speeds of sixty miles per hour. They too can cover great distances, some migrating five hundred miles across the Gulf of Mexico. But that is where the similarities end.

Humming birds beat their wings 80 times a second and their hearts beat more than 1,200 times a minute. And for all their amazing speed and effort, this does not lead to a life of longevity. The majority of hummingbirds die within a year, their strength exhausted and their little hearts having given out.

So which species will you be? A busy hummingbird, buzzing, constantly on the move, torn apart by anxiety; or will you be more like the eagle who rests, letting the wind of God's strength carry you along?

June 16: A Few Things

A long-time resident of Florida, I have learned that we only have three seasons: The hot season, the hotter season, and hurricane season.

To that point, I despise hurricane evacuation. The hurricane evacuation process for where I live is one of the longest in the country, and my experience with it has been one great exercise in frustration: Gridlocked traffic, frustrated drivers, tired children, and me needing a Valium.

After our last evacuation I was so exasperated that I vowed to never do it again. That was a lie. I'm not one to shake my fist in the face of Mother Nature. If a huge, ugly, buzz saw of a storm is barreling down on the coast, I'm going to get me and mine out of the way.

So we talk about hurricane evacuation around our house, and what we would take with us if we had to leave our house behind. The "must-have" list is fairly short, because honestly, we don't need a whole lot to be content and satisfied in this world.

Most of what we possess and strive for could be washed away, and quickly we would realize how valueless all of it is compared to those things that really matter. Having those we love with us, a few creature comforts, and the intangibles of love, peace of mind, and the faith and hope that things will work out even if the storm comes – these will be sufficient.

When the evacuation is on, and you can cling to a few things, pick the right things. These will be enough to get you through the storm. Thankfully, I get reminded of this every season. It's a reminder I need - we all need - because we don't need as much as we think we do to be happy.

June 17: Why?

In many ways, faith helps make meaning of life. It interprets this senseless world so that it has some kind of purpose. What we see, hear, feel, and experience has to be arranged and interpreted in such a way that life doesn't devolve into hopelessness.

Yet, all explanations fail when forced to interpret the horror of meaningless violence, like what happened on this date in 2015: The horrific shooting at Emanuel AME Church in Charleston. Tidy, digestible solutions to all of life's problems are not forthcoming.

In an iconic photo taken outside of Emanuel, a group of mourners held a giant sign with one word on it: "Why?" That's the word that asks it all, but there is no answer to this question, not in this lifetime.

We don't know why God allows or tolerates the evil that invades our lives or why he offers so little explanation for suffering. But we do know that God goes with us through it all because his Son, Jesus, when he was dying on the cross, aimed this exact question at God: "Why?"

Jesus, we believe, was God's anointed one, and even with such a privileged position, still he was found in the fashion of a man and subjected to injustice. As such, he was forced to ask questions from within suffering, but questions never undermine faith.

Belief in God is not an insulator from tragedy. Following Christ does not guarantee a trouble-free life. Nor will having "more faith" lead to less difficulty in this unfair world or meaningful explanation for every sorrow.

God may not always rescue us, may never explain things to us, but he always identifies with us and goes with us, for in Jesus he knows what it is like to be haunted by the question of "Why?"

June 18: The Missing Piece

Shel Silverstein's two most famous works are on opposite ends of the creative spectrum. One is a Grammy-winning song made famous by Johnny Cash in 1970, a song entitled "A Boy Named Sue." The other work is a picture book entitled, *The Giving Tree*.

But my favorite Silverstein work is a children's book named, *The Missing Piece*. It's a masterpiece about a rolling circle with a huge missing wedge. And since the circle has this missing piece, he can't roll very fast. But his pace allows him to enjoy the scenery around him, to talk to butterflies, and enjoy a quiet life.

After many miles, he finally finds his missing piece, and begins to zip along at speeds he could only imagine before. But while rolling through life at breakneck speed, the circle realizes he can't do the things he used to do. So he removes that once missing piece and goes back to the life he had, a life where his weakness was obvious, but it was the life he lived best.

All of us have these missing pieces that force us to slowly shuffle along. These gaping holes are there to slow us down, so that God can get to us. He may not fill in the missing piece, but he will give us himself, for the grace of God fills human emptiness.

When we are weak, he is strong. When we decrease, he will increase. When we feel like our life is one huge, colossal malfunction, that is the cry to heaven for God's grace to pierce our darkness and somehow to give us life.

Claim those broken places and missing pieces; don't try to fill them in so quickly. Those are the doorways and the windows for God's grace to shine through, so let it.

June 19: Faith To Fall

Somehow I found myself on a climbing wall. You know the behemoth: A slick, black wall with colorful rubberized grips peppered across its face. The climber gets fitted with a harness and hard hat, and off he or she goes to the top. I tried - but I couldn't do it.

Climbing wasn't the problem. It was the height. I have a morbid case of acrophobia, and what made it all the more challenging were the last words of the attendant: "When you get to the top, you have to let go." There was no climbing down (because of the tension on the safety rope), and there was no backing out.

I learned a few things about faith while clutching to that wall. Like, how much faith did it take to climb? None. It took strength and a plan of attack, but not faith. And as long as I could climb and had the will to move, as long as I could reach that next outcropping, I was fine. But faced with the prospect of letting go? That took faith, faith to fall, and I didn't have much to give.

As long as we can keep conquering, going, achieving, or getting better, stronger, and higher we feel like everything is okay. But what happens when our strength runs out; when all our plans for climbing higher fail? What happens when we can no longer focus? What happens when control is taken from us or when we are forced to let go? That's when faith is required.

What most of us call faith is actually nothing more than human determination. It is confidence in our own ability, and that is nothing that resembles trust in God whatsoever. It's only when we are ready to let go that we are ready to believe.

173

June 20: Little Things

Malcolm Gladwell, author of the book *The Tipping Point*, makes this challenge: Take a piece of paper. Fold it in half. Do it again, and again, and again, until you have folded that piece of paper fifty times. When finished, how tall do you think the final folded piece of paper will be?

The size of a telephone book? As thick as a mattress? Not even close. Gladwell says the folded piece of paper would be as high as the distance from the earth to the sun – with only fifty folds (though no one has ever folded a piece of paper more than a dozen or so times).

It's called "geometric progression." Something that starts incredibly small takes very little time to become something extraordinarily huge. My father used to play a similar game with me when I was a boy. He would say to me, "What if I paid you to change four flat tires for me. Which would you rather have: $10,000 or a dollar for the first lug nut, but I'll double it every lug nut thereafter?"

I would always take the $10,000 and he would chuckle but never explain. I realized later that if I took the doubling dollar, at the end of the tire-changing session I would have much more than $10,000 – much more.

Do you believe that little things matter? Sure you do. And more so than hypothetical paper folds and lug nuts. The microprocessors in our computers, the antibodies in our bloodstreams, the placement of a decimal point or added zero on our bank statements, a single vote in a toss-up election.

Little things matter - especially the little things you do with the little life you have been given. You never know how it will all add up in the end.

June 21: The Confession Stand

My son used to love to go to the "Confession Stand." He doesn't want to make an appointment with the local priest, however. He wants a Slurpy, Coke, or an order of onion rings. Since he first learned to put words together, the "Concession Stand" at any sporting event is referred to as the "Confession Stand." Well "Amen" and pass the ketchup.

Growing up in the Baptist tradition, confession to a priest was not required. Baptists just couldn't bear the thought. That and the fact I came of age out in the country where everyone had a clothes line rather than an electric dryer for their clothes. When your bloomers and holey socks (not holy socks) are swinging in the breeze for God and everybody to see, there's not much left to hide. I think that is the point.

"Confess your sins one to another," the Apostle James said, "that you may be healed." These are hard words to practice when we have so privatized and individualized our faith that we prefer to hide our troubles, struggles, and failures from others. We keep our dirty laundry stuffed in a dark, putrid closet.

Yet, when we do not share our lives one with another – even the ugly parts – we miss out on the healing power the community of Christ can offer. We all need someone to whom we can bare our souls, someone who will help us carry the load and point us toward grace - grace for everyone.

For those who bear their souls, they find relief and liberation, and for those who hear and respond in love, they participate in the restoration of another. Then both can "cast their cares on Him who cares" for us all. So give me your hand. We will go to the Confession Stand together.

June 22: The Messiah

Antonio Stradivari was the master instrument maker of the last five hundred years. His name is most closely associated with his violins, violins that are unsurpassed in beauty and legendary sound. Classical musicians say that playing a Stradivarius is like driving a high-performance automobile.

Stradivari made several thousand of these sport car violins over his career and several hundred of these survive. But if you want to get your hands on one of them, it will cost you several fortunes.

The top five world record prices paid for any musical instrument are for Stradivarius violins. For example, in 2006, Christie's auctioned a Stradivarius called "The Hammer" for a record $3.5 million. But even that cannot touch the worth of Stradivari's most priceless violin: "The Messiah."

So precious is the instrument, the owners bestowed it to a British museum where it remains today. As a condition of the bequest, however, the museum can never allow the instrument to be played. "The Messiah" may be the world's most perfect and expensive instrument; yet, it sits inside a glass box, untouched by musicians and unheard by lovers of music.

Those who follow Jesus have a similar challenge and opportunity. The one we accept as our Messiah was born into the world to produce beautiful music. Nevertheless, this invaluable gift of God can be locked away in observational casing, but possessing and professing faith in Christ is no good unless we share Jesus with the world.

A final note about Stradivarius' "Messiah:" If someone could get his hands on this little beauty to play, it would likely sound terrible. Violins, like most stringed instruments, have to be played in order to retain their sound. The easiest way to destroy an instrument – or faith – is not by using it, but by locking it away.

June 23: Cracked Pots

There is an Eastern Indian tale about a waterbearer with two water pots. Each pot hung on the end of a long pole which the waterbearer carried across his shoulders. One of the pots was perfect and always delivered a full pot of water at the end of the long walk from the river to home.

The other pot had a crack in it. It leaked terribly and arrived at home with only half its load. The perfect pot was proud of his accomplishments, but the cracked pot was constantly ashamed of himself.

Finally, no longer able to endure his disgrace, the cracked pot spoke to his owner: "I am ashamed of myself and I must apologize. I have been able to deliver only half my load because this crack in my side causes water to leak out all the way back to your house. You can't get full value from your efforts."

The waterbearer smiled. "As we return home today," he said, "I want you to notice the beautiful flowers along the path." And sure enough, as they traveled away from the river, the cracked pot noticed the colorful flowers on his side of the path.

The waterbearer said, "I planted flower seeds on your side of the path, and every day while we walk from the riverside, you water them. Without you being just the way you are, the world would be less beautiful."

We are all, in our own way, cracked pots. But if we will be good stewards of our troubles, our limitations, and our imperfections, God will use these to change us and to grace his world. We are the only instruments God has to reveal his glory. And in our brokenness and weakness, the beauty of God will rain down over the entire world.

June 24: Just Decide

A farmer hired a worker and told him his first task would be to paint the barn. It should have taken about three days to finish, but the hired man was finished in one day.

The farmer then instructed his hired hand to cut wood, telling him it would require about four days. The hired man completed the task quickly and was finished in two days, again to the farmer's amazement.

The next task was to sort potatoes. The farmer instructed the hired man to arrange the potatoes into three piles: 1) Seed potatoes, 2) Food for the hogs, and 3) Potatoes for the market. Judging by the speed at which the worker had completed the other assignments, it would be an easy task. But at the end of the day, the potatoes were still in one large pile. "

What's the matter? Why aren't you finished?" the farmer asked. And the hired man replied: "I'm sorry. I can work hard, but I can't make decisions!"

Do you have a hard time deciding? Here is some advice then: Quit deliberating and start acting. We get paralyzed at the crossroads of decision because we are afraid of the consequences, or we fear disappointing someone who is counting on us, or we think God will punish us if we make a bad move. But the snag for most of us is not the making of a decision. It is finding the courage to do what we know we should do.

We may not always feel as confident as we would like when we "make our move." We may struggle with doubts and fears and second guesses. Still, faith is more about the choices we make, not the emotions we feel. So get started. Don't mess things up by thinking about it too long.

June 25: In The Light

Leo Tolstoy compared religious rules to the light given off by a lamp post. It dispels the darkness, so long as one stands in the light. But the lamp post has limitations, Tolstoy said. One had to stay put to stay out of the dark.

But following Jesus, Tolstoy said, was like a light or lantern fixed to a pole. A person could carry that pole out in front of him and travel anywhere he liked. Tolstoy never held a flashlight, but we have and can understand the analogy that way. To remain a rule-keeper, is to remain under a street lamp. To follow Christ, is to take a flashlight in hand, and go somewhere – to explore, to pierce the dark, to have a faith that is dynamic, not static.

Many people are locked into keeping the rules. They stand in their little circle of light, unmovable, barking at the street traffic and cursing the darkness. They might as soon be chained to a post. They are imprisoned, not growing or going anywhere.

Religious rules, or to use biblical language, "The Law," has been eclipsed by Jesus. Yes, the rules were all we had, once upon a time, but now we have something better – we have Jesus himself – showing us the way. And while the law was instructive and useful, ultimately, it could only constrict and confine. In the words of the Apostle Paul, "The letter (the rules) kills;" it can't give life.

Christianity is not a heavy obligation to stagnant, inanimate rules. Rather, Christianity is the free enjoyment of a relationship with a living person. This is Good News: God, who is now present in Christ, calls people of faith to follow Jesus, not to follow the rules. This is the liberation so many have been longing for.

June 26: Regrets

Charles was a hard man, just plain mean; and he was on his deathbed. The hospital staff, recognizing his attitude and condition, called for a pastor to pay him a visit. Lucky me.

But it didn't take long for our conversation to turn to the end of life. Gigantic tears formed in Charles' eyes. The hardened façade crumbled, and he said, "I need to tell you something."

Charles took me back to the French countryside. It was the weeks following the D-Day invasion. The now old hospital patient recalled being a young GI forced into guarding a captured Hitler youth. Unexpectedly, the boy produced a knife from his boot and attacked Charles. In the struggle that ensued Charles killed the young man. Charles concluded his story by saying, "I have prayed for that boy's soul every day of my life."

His body shook with a grief that was decades old, but a grief as fresh as the telling of the story. After this confession Charles improved dramatically, climbed off his deathbed and went home. I had nothing to do with his turnaround. It was the result of him unloading his regrets.

We all have regrets. We can resist and fight against these, allowing the past to drive us to self-abuse and destruction, one day waking up hardened, calloused and nasty, having failed at living – not because mistakes were made or because we have regrets – but because of what those regrets were allowed to do to us.

Or, we can take those same circumstances and learn from them. Let them draw us to a generous God. Experience his grace, learn to grant that grace to others, and find that the time of sorrow is not time wasted. Sorrow that leads us to God, leads us to our own salvation.

June 27: Left Hanging

Henri Nouwen compared the leap of faith we must make to follow Christ to the courage of a trapeze artist. This is something Henri knew about first hand. As a young man he was a member of the "Flying Rodleighs," a high-wire circus act.

He said, like a high-flying trapeze artist, we must let go of the security we have had, to take hold of what is coming to us. And like a trapeze artist, we cannot do both at the same time.

In the moment that a trapeze artist moves from one trapeze bar to the next, she must leave the relative security of holding on to something solid, something that has her confidence, and keeps her from falling. Then she must stretch out for the bar that is coming to her. In those milliseconds, which probably seem like an eternity, she is hanging there in midair, with nothing. She cannot go back to the security she has known. Nor can he speed the next trapeze bar to her. It is an act of faith.

The life of following and knowing Christ is lived in those moments between the trapeze bars. We cannot go back to our former lives, the way we used to believe, think, and live. We let those things go in order to follow Christ.

But have we yet taken hold of Christ? No, we have not. As the Apostle Paul said, "I do not consider myself yet to have taken hold of it. But one thing I do: Forgetting what is behind, I press on."

Faith is not the game of playing it safe. Faith is living without a net. Not because we love the adrenaline rush, but because we can't go with Christ and stay where we are at the same time.

June 28: Stumbling Toward Surrender

Jacob lived up to his name. "Jacob" means "heel grabber," or "one who causes others to stumble." Today we might use words like swindler, trickster, or con-artist. Jacob was the kind of guy who always found a way, through an abundance of guts or a lack of conscience, to get what he wanted.

But one night this shyster met his match: God came out of the night to confront Jacob, and all night long the two battled, with neither one prevailing. Finally, God dislocated Jacob's hip with the command: "Let me go."

Jacob had no tricks left in his bag; no strength to seize what he wanted; no deception remaining to take what didn't belong to him. And yet, he had something left: He collapsed to the ground, hanging on to the ankles of God, and asked for what he couldn't get on his own: A divine blessing.

It is preposterous. But Jacob's wish is not the most outrageous part of the story. That part of the tale belongs to God, because God, inconceivably, grants the request. Jacob doesn't get what he deserves, he gets grace instead. He gets the one thing he has been after his whole life: God's blessing. But it came only through exhausted surrender.

God says to Jacob, "You have wrestled with God and prevailed. Your name is now Israel." And to this day, every time we call the nation of Israel's name, we recall a man sleepy, stumbling, and limping across the river into the Promised Land.

To wrestle with God is to face the truth we have refused to admit about ourselves: Our self-reliance will never get us the blessing we want. So maybe it is better to be wounded by God than to retain the false trust in our own abilities.

June 29: Pew Potatoes

Christians are over-eaters. Not necessarily at meal time, though you will find a few rotund Bible-thumpers in front of you at the Sunday buffet. We overindulge when it comes to our "spiritual food."

"Give me good music. Give me good preaching. Pass the bread and pour the wine. Fill up my belly." And before you know it we are so plump and drunk we can't get off the pew to help our neighbor.

We have become spiritually obese: Pew potatoes that sit, feast, and nap, but refuse to get up and "work it off" in the fields of God's farm. So we are fat, slow, and unfit.

There are more than 300,000 churches in the United States, and Americans give $93 billion dollars a year to houses of worship, while buying $5 billion of Christian products to aid in personal spiritual growth. We have more than we need – spiritually and physically.

So to lament that you can't get spiritually "fed" is like complaining of starvation while standing in line at the all-you-can-eat Chinese buffet. We're not hungry. We aren't getting rid of what we have been given.

The challenge for us is to do something with what we have been given; to take the hundreds of sermons, the countless books and Bible studies, the millions of words that have crossed our ears, and put them to action in our hearts, hands, and feet.

We must take the multitude baskets of broken bread and jars of flowing wine spread out on the table before us each week, and share it with those who are hungry and thirsty.

Our challenge is to push away from the table, shake off the sluggishness of too many carbs and too much wine, and get back to work in God's world.

June 30: Getting Home

Years ago I flew into Atlanta, Georgia on an especially stormy night. The cloud cover was so dense, I could not see a single light below, not a single landmark.

As we circled, lurched, jerked, and dropped, I dug my fingernails deep into the arm rests. Then, without warning, I felt the hardened thud of striking the runway. Safe and sound we coasted to the terminal. Incredibly, the pilot had landed the plane, not only in the dead of night, but in zero visibility.

As I disembarked from the plane the pilot was standing at the door wishing us a fine evening. I stopped, and pointing out the window asked him, "How did you land this plane in that?" He answered, "It was no sweat. I just trust the instruments."

If this pilot had tried to feel his way toward the runway, we would have never made it home. To fail to trust the instruments – pointing us along on the journey – would have been a disaster.

Most times we can't see what waits for us on our way home. The clouds are too thick; the view too obscured. We can't even see where our next footstep will land. But in the absence of certainty, we reach forward in faith.

God has placed the occasional marker as he speaks to us through his instruments – the Scriptures, in prayer, through the wisdom of those around us – and we trust those instruments to point us in the right direction.

The pilot who answered me so confidently as I left the plane that evening was skilled at hiding his apprehension. But he could not hide the circles of sweat that bled through the underarms of his coat. Still, sweating bullets or not, his trust in the instruments had gotten us home. It always will.

JULY

July 1: Step By Step

A friend complained to me about his weight gain after going to the doctor. "Something must be wrong with their scales," he protested. "Last time I went to the doctor I was nowhere near that heavy!" So I asked the obvious question: "When was the last time you went to the doctor?"

After a few calculations he confessed it had been about ten years. So we made a few more calculations and discovered that his "rapid" weight gain was only two pounds a year - but he had gained those pounds every year for a decade.

The change in his body – like most change – wasn't immediate. He didn't go to sleep one night, with the body of an athlete, and wake up the next morning resembling something like a nicely marbled piece of veal. The change occurred incrementally, step by tiny step.

You don't fall out of shape spiritually in a day; or week; maybe not even a year. It happens over time. One day you feel strong, able, and fit. Then, after what seems like only a short time, you find yourself winded and tired, overweight and slow. But if you observe closely, you likely got that way over years.

What to do? Well, just as declining takes some time, so does getting back into shape. You'll have to work those spiritual muscles; return to healthy, daily disciplines; and relearn to pray and meditate. You won't feel spiritually strong overnight and you'll have some days when you wonder if getting fit again is really worth it.

But it is - worth it, that is. Because everyone feels better when they are lighter, stronger, more focused, and healthier. You'll get there if you stick with it. The change in your spirit - like most change - won't be immediate, but step by tiny step.

July 2: Six Months

This is it: The year is half over. Six months past and six months to go. How are you doing? Are you making changes? Keeping your New Year's resolutions? Are you becoming a different person? Or are you right where the year began?

The danger most of us face is paralysis; not of the body, but of the soul. We get stuck, unable to move. Still stuck in a job we loathe. Still planning to take that big chance, or make that big move.

Still at odds with the long-estranged loved one with whom we hope to one day reconcile. Still tripping over the same addiction, still trapped in that same poisonous relationship, still entrenched in the same soul-sucking routine. Time is far too short to live like this, and deep in our hearts, we know it.

The resplendent Erma Bombeck, who cannot be improved upon, provides a summary on this point. She wrote, "I have learned that silver tarnishes when it isn't used, perfume turns to alcohol, candles melt in the attic over the summer, and ideas that are saved for a dry week often become dated.

"When I am asked to give an accounting of my life to a higher court, I think it will go like this: 'So, empty your pockets. What have you got left of your life? Any dreams that were unfulfilled? Any unused talent that we gave you when you were born that you still have left? Any unsaid compliments or bits of love that you haven't spread around?'

"And, I will answer, 'I have nothing left to return. I spent everything you gave me. I'm as naked as the day I was born.'"

Six months past and six months to go. You still have time to make some changes. Get busy.

July 3: Set Free

On July 3, 1863 the largest battle of the American Civil War came to a merciful end outside the village of Gettysburg, Pennsylvania. Some of the fiercest combat on the last day of the battle involved what historians call "Pickett's Charge."

Led by George Pickett, 14,000 Confederates attempted to take Cemetery Ridge held by Union troops. The battle lasted less than an hour and not half of the Confederate troops survived, a bloody end to the deadliest battle in the Civil War's history.

Fifty years later, on July 3, 1913, surviving veterans of that day returned to Gettysburg for a reunion, and an impromptu reenactment. The Union veterans took their position on Cemetery Ridge, and the Confederate veterans marched across the open field as they had done fifty years earlier.

As the old Union soldiers moved from the ridge to rush down at the old men marching across the field, they raised their voices. But it wasn't a battle cry. It was a lament. The soldiers from both sides threw their arms around each other and wept. The old animosity and bitterness was gone.

"While we were still sinners," the Bible says, "Christ died for us." Once we were God's enemies but in Christ God took the necessary, loving steps to reconcile us to himself. So it is that when we love those who are our enemies, we are reflecting the nature of God.

Forgiveness of our enemies is not natural, because humans are innately violent. But when we are changed by Jesus, we are set free from the slavery of our human nature. To follow Christ means we have found a new way to live, set free to love those we once hated; for when we are set free - free at last - that is the greatest victory of all.

July 4: A Garden In The Wilderness

Roger Williams, theologian, founder of Rhode Island, America's first Baptist, and champion of religious and civil liberty a hundred years before the United States Constitution was penned, said communities of faith were like vulnerable, flowering gardens. Governments, on the other hand, were what he called "the wilderness."

Williams believed that those churches and faith groups that chose to mingle their religion with political power were permitting the wilderness to intrude upon their gardens. As such, they would be manipulated by politicians, policies, and the government, thus compromising on issues of love, justice, and mercy.

Or those same churches would become the manipulators themselves, using political power to force their beliefs on others. Either way, when church and state drank from the same cup, it would be the church that would be poisoned.

Roger Williams' counsel to the Christian church in his day is lasting: Learn to live in the world, but don't be a part of it. Or he might say, "You can plant a garden in a wilderness without having the wilderness in the garden."

As Christians, we have the right, privilege, and freedom to live out, practice, and share our faith in this country we love. But we do not have the right to force our faith on others or demand that society at large endorse our particular religious view.

When we as Christians do make these kinds of demands, we violate the spirit of Christ. We lay down the instrument of love for the devices of manipulation, coercion, and force. We let the weeds of the wilderness overtake the garden of faith.

I hope we can continue to tolerate a variety of fruits and nuts in our religious garden; even those we have little taste for. It's the only way we can maintain a garden at all.

July 5: Investing In Hope

In 1981, businessman Eugene Lang returned to the public elementary school he had attended five decades earlier in East Harlem. He was there to give the commencement speech for the graduating sixth grade class.

Speaking with the principal just before taking the podium, Lang learned that 75% of these kids would never finish high school. One, maybe, would go on to college. Lang was simultaneously heartbroken and motivated.

When time to make his address he cast his notes aside, notes about working hard and succeeding, and instead made a bold promise: "If you will graduate from high school," he said, "I will personally pay your college tuition."

The impact that Lang's promise had on the 61 children in the room that day was remarkable. Now (most for the first time) they had hope; real hope. And that hope became the fuel for their dreams and their futures. They worked hard, studied, and made improvements and plans they would have never made without such an offer being made to them.

Six years after that impulsive promise, more than 90% of that class earned their high school diploma and more than 60% went on to pursue higher education. In a class that might have seen one kid go to college (1.6% of the total), the improvement was nothing short of miraculous.

Lang made good on his offer. He picked up the tab on every student, and in time, many more students through his "I Have A Dream" Foundation.

Few of us can make so gutsy a promise as millionaire Eugene Lang, but I bet we can all do something to provide greater opportunity to someone who needs it. It's not charity (though charitable giving is a necessity too). It's an investment, the kind that leads to treasure in heaven, not on earth.

July 6: Toward The Light

In my grandmother's old house there was a stairwell that led from the basement to the first floor. Upon leaving the basement, the door would shut and lock automatically by means of a high tension closer, leaving you to climb the stairs in the dark. On the occasional times this happened to me, I immediately began pounding and clawing on the locked door behind me, terrified of the dark climb up the stairs.

But that door was locked, and no amount of banging or shrieking could reopen it. I had to find the courage to grope through the darkness, through that frightening unknown, to reach the unlocked door at the top of the stairs, always with a little light shining behind it.

Life, more often than not, is just like that stairwell. Everything is bouncing along splendidly until we reach some inevitable crisis, some roadblock, some door that locks behind us, leaving us in the dark. Disoriented, frightened, standing in a space we have never known, our first impulse is to go back.

Back to where life was predictable; back to that sense of safety that now alludes us; back to where we knew who we were and what we were doing. But that door is locked and the life we used to live is gone for good, and thank God, that life is gone for our own good, because we can never become the real people God is creating us to be by living in the past.

We must let the darkness do its good work, scrabbling through the transformational passageways, painful and dark though they be, and not fall back clawing and scrambling for our former lives. Those doors are locked, and can never be reopened. That's a good thing, because life is moving forward, toward the light.

July 7: Hospitality

Our friends moved from Chicago to the Deep South. One evening, as they were beginning to settle in, there was a knock at the door. Out on the stoop was a small-town Southern lady, gray-haired with apple pie in hand. She gave the usual "welcome to our town" speech and ended with an invitation for her new neighbors to join her for worship at the First Baptist Church the next Sunday.

"No ma'am," said my friend. "I'm an atheist." The poor woman was dumbstruck. To relieve the tension she turned to his wife: "What about you, dear?" Again, the answer was shattering: "No, I'm sorry. I'm Jewish." The charming saint from the First Baptist Church turned and left, taking her apple pie with her.

It used to be that everyone we met was a bit like "us." Not anymore. From religion and race, to politics and lifestyle, the diversity that now surrounds us is far greater than anything we could have imagined a generation ago. Thus, we exercise kindness toward those who are like us, and we keep our apple pies away from those we find unlike us. This is hardly "hospitality," Southern or otherwise.

In this day and age of "connection" and "social" media, we are actually more divided and disconnected than ever. A large reason for this is the lack of face to face community - especially with those we consider "different."

It is common in Eastern cultures to share tea with strangers as a means of welcome. It is an act of hospitable community building (like stopping by with a homemade dessert), because the more times "strangers" share tea together, the more like friends they become.

Tea and apple pies: There's something to sharing these with our neighbors that will be good for all of us.

July 8: Works Of Art

My wife loves a good garage sale. She also loves flea markets, thrift stores, junk shops, consignment exchanges, bazaars, and most any place she can find a bargain. She calls these adventures into the land of trading posts, "treasure hunts."

She's found a diamond in the rough here and there over the years, but for the most part I tell her that she has just accumulated scrap piles; piles around the house, in the garage, in the attic, and hiding in the backyard. But while she amasses her "treasures" in one heap, I move another heap out the door to Goodwill.

She lives by the mantra, "You never know when you might need something," and I by the opposite, "If you haven't used it in six months, you don't need it."

The truth of the matter is that she is on a reclamation mission. See, she makes art out of other people's junk. Broken glass, weathered boards, discarded jewelry; all the heaping piles are kept from the landfill and transformed into things of beauty. She's not looking for a diamond but what she can make shine like one.

This sounds a lot like the work God is up to in this world. He loves to take things - and people - who seem all but destined for the scrap heap and turn them into showcases of transformation.

No one puts junk in a display case or on a prominent wall for the world to see and appreciate. They put up art, beautiful paintings, and handcrafted sculptures. They show off what has taken hard work, skillful hands, and almost limitless patience to create.

God does the same. He's working on and with the debris of our lives to makes us things of beauty. And we will be, when he is finished with us.

July 9: Hope

Ancient philosophers used "hope" as a synonym for dashed expectations. It was nothing but starry-eyed, false anticipation that coaxed humanity "to its undoing," in the words of the Greek poets. Modern philosophy hasn't changed this view as Nietzsche thought of hope as something that simply prolonged suffering.

Even for those of us who are less philosophical, or maybe we are just more rosy than Nietzsche, we still struggle with this thing called hope, because it's hard to define.

"I hope my team makes the playoffs this year. I hope they have chicken on the buffet today. I hope my oncology report is negative. I hope to graduate in the spring." Surely hope doesn't mean the same thing every time we use it.

But for all of hope's ambiguity, it remains a worthy word, a lasting word; one of the three things that will last forever: "Now there remain faith, hope, and love, these three," Paul said. And with that, maybe he gave us a working definition. Hope is what lasts. More than human longing, more than personal aspiration, more than some head-in-the-cloud dream, it is the stuff of endurance.

Look at the clinical studies and practical examples of those who have survived the worst atrocities; prisoners of war, individuals subjected to prolonged abuse; others who have experienced various traumas. The survivors always have some intangible power to bend, but not break, under the pressure. It's called hope.

These individuals endured, persevered, and held on while suffering the "slings and arrows of outrageous fortune," taking "arms against their sea of troubles." But when the battle had ended and the waters had settled, they were found intact; hurt, but alive; battered, but not defeated. They had resiliency, which is the best synonym for hope that you can find.

July 10: By The Water

Psalm 1 describes a person rooted in the words and way of God: "They are strong, like a tree planted by a river. The tree produces fruit in season, and its leaves don't die. Everything they do will succeed."

It's not unlikely that Psalm 1 dates back to the time of the Jewish exodus out of Egypt. Egypt was, and remains, largely desert. But the country, for its entire history, has had one life-giving source of abundance: The Nile River.

Farmers have relied upon its annual flooding to deposit mineral rich silt on their fields, and they have dug canals leading away from the river so the streams of water will irrigate their crops, water their animals, and sustain their fruit trees. That is the image, a tree thriving in one of the most uninviting places one could conceive: The Sahara Desert.

It's more than three million square miles of waterless earth holding rocks, mountains, and sand dunes higher than sky scrapers. Temperatures can exceed 130 degrees in the day and drop to freezing at night. Gale force winds are common. The Sahara is the most caustic climate on earth, and still, there are trees growing and blooming in that endless desert, planted by the streams of water.

Is life easy for such trees? No, life appears impossible. Yet, the tough climate does not rob a well-nourished tree of its strength; it reveals its strength, for outer severity cannot exterminate the tree. It can only expose the tree's inner wellbeing.

So it is with people. When you see a person of character, stability, authenticity, and strength in an otherwise desolate landscape, you know that something life-giving is beneath the surface, for neither trees nor people grow green and strong in the desert without a supply of water.

July 11: All Or Nothing

William Law was an English priest and something of a mystic in the 1700s. He would have had an impressive career within the Church of England but his conscience got in the way.

Priests in the Anglican Church were required to take an oath of allegiance to the king. Law felt that this was a violation of his principles, as his ultimate loyalty belonged only to God. He tried to remain in the priesthood but that nagging oath kept coming up. Vocationally, he turned to teaching and writing instead. His writings, even after three centuries, are still in print.

The crux of all William Law has to say comes down to one word: Surrender. His writings, as pertinent as they were all those many centuries ago, are filled with phrases like, "the sweet resignation of the self," and "the sinking down into powerlessness." We have to give up our lives, Law inferred, to get in on the life God has for us.

He wrote, "God must do all, or all is nothing. But God cannot do all until all is expected from Him. And all is not expected from Him until by true and good despair we have humbly resigned everything to God."

At first blush this sounds so defeatist, something like "Christianity for Weaklings." Some will find it intolerable and object: "Give up? How can this be? Surrender is for cowardly milksops and quitters!" Such objections ignore the fact that there are some things that we cannot change, and what cannot be changed must be handed over.

Going further, such objections belittle the way of the cross. Read once again those familiar crucifixion accounts of Jesus, and there you will see that letting go requires more than a noble struggle, more than hanging on – infinitely more. It requires everything.

July 12: Room To Breathe

An unfortunate woman was found dead in the basement of her Connecticut home, found eventually, that is. It took rescuers several days to retrieve her body as the first floor of her house had collapsed on her under the weight of all the stuff she had accumulated over the years.

Her possessions, stacked to the ceiling with only a narrow, labyrinth-like pathway through it all, quite literally smothered her. Her death certificate said so officially with the cause of death declared as "Accidental Traumatic Asphyxia." This is a dramatic example, of course, but accumulating those things that fall outside the realm of the necessary, will take your life just as certainly.

Jesus said it like this: "Don't store up treasures here on earth, but store your treasures in heaven. Seek the Kingdom of God above all else." These words are directed at every packrat, collector, hoarder, attic squirrel, and garage-gatherer among us. Hang on to too much stuff, and it will take your life from you.

The most deeply spiritual thing that some of us could do is have a garage sale; or sell a property, or dump a portfolio, or write a big check to a homeless shelter. Because our spiritual lethargy has nothing to do with a poor prayer life, the lack of reading the Scriptures, or any failure with other disciplines: We are carrying too much baggage, trying to manage too much stuff. We have too many possessions, too many obligations, and it's a recipe for misery.

When we simplify, we are doing more than getting rid of the weight of physical possessions. We are making space to breathe, to thrive, to live. By giving up some of the things we carry or hoard, we aren't losing, we are gaining; gaining freedom to pursue life.

July 13: Before You Speak

"You must all be quick to listen and slow to speak." Those are the words of James in the New Testament. It reminds me of Demosthenes.

Demosthenes was a skilled orator from ancient Greece who made quite a name for himself. His ability to hold the attention of a crowd was legendary. But he was not always a skilled wordsmith. As a young man he had a terrible speech impediment. This became painfully evident when his inheritance was stolen and he had to argue his case in open court.

His speech was so bad, they gave him an ambiguous nickname in the Greek, meaning either "stutterer" or "sphincter" (While neither is flattering, I prefer the former over the latter). He was laughed out of the courtroom by the judge and everyone in attendance.

But Demosthenes was determined. He secluded himself in a cave and began studying the methods of the great orators of the past. He stuffed rocks in his jowls, a crude form of speech therapy, forcing himself to slow down when he talked. Then he shaved off one side of his facial hair so that he would be too embarrassed to go into public.

That way, he had to remain in isolation practicing until his hair grew back, and would face no one until he was properly prepared for the task. This would be a good practice for most of us.

Shave off half our hair? Live in a cave? Stuff rocks into our mouths? Well, yes, if doing these things makes us slow down; if these cause us to listen; if such drastic measures force us to choose our words wisely and carefully.

We might not make a name for ourselves by following Demosthenes' radical example, but we might learn to think - and wait - before we speak.

July 14: Rudderless Boats

There is a Zen story about a man who was boating on a river, the morning fog hanging just above the water. Through the mist he saw another boat. He noticed that the other boater was holding a steady course - coming straight at him - and not deviating.

The man called out a warning, making his location known. Still, the other boat came at him, faster and faster, not changing course. The man began to yell, waving his arms, and instead of gently steering out of the other boat's way, soon the man was standing in his boat, cursing and shaking his fist.

Finally, the other boat smashed into him, threatening to sink both vessels. The man was beyond furious. He leapt into the other boat ready to fight, but the other boat was empty. It was a pilotless ship. The man's anger evaporated when he realized there no one to be angry with; there was no one to blame.

This is the story of our lives, the story of making peace with many of the things and people that frustrate us. There are a lot of wayward boats out there. Most of them we can simply sidestep, sliding gently out of their hurried way.

Others crash into us. We can begin screaming, blaming, cursing and shaking our fists at them for what they have done. But we're waging wars with rudderless vessels, as most of the people who hurt us are people pushed along by the currents of their own pain and suffering. They aren't "in charge" of their feelings or actions. We just got in their way.

It's much easier - and safer - to simply get out of the way of runaway people. And when we can't, the better part of wisdom is to not argue with an empty boat.

July 15: Working On A Building

All across Europe you can find some of the most beautiful architecture on the planet; Christian cathedrals built during the Middle Ages. They are stunning, beautiful, awe-inspiring buildings, remarkable in engineering and aesthetics. However, they are only buildings. The church is a people, not a structure of wood or stone.

"You are the building stones of God's sanctuary," Peter told the early church. Not a fancy building with a spire, steeple, or stained glass. And Paul was just as forceful: "You are the temple of God, and God himself is present in you!"

If you go way back to the prophet Isaiah you find the same sentiment: "The Almighty doesn't live in houses made by human hands! Heaven is his throne; the earth is his footstool - what are you going to build to contain him?" Nothing - no matter how majestic the cathedral, no matter how elegant the church - he won't fit. He has chosen to make his dwelling place, his sacred space - within you.

Songwriter Wes King wrote: "You live on the highest mountain; you swim in the deepest sea. You dwell in the grandest canyon; yet you make your home inside of me.

"You call to the leaves in springtime. You speak to the kings of men; you breathe life, life into a baby. Yet you make your home inside of me. You walk through the starry heavens; you run to the soul that seeks. You climb the hill of sorrow. Yet you make your home inside of me."

So if you are going to put time, energy, and money into building something, put it into people. That's where God is investing. Resist the temptation to make faith about the monuments we might build. The building we are working on is the human soul, not a physical building.

July 16: Unanswered Prayers

Soren Kierkegaard told a story about a schoolboy who refused to learn. The teacher tried her best to engage him and get him to apply himself, but he simply would not. Finally she asked the boy, "What is it you want to do?"

He answered: "I want to sit in the back of the room, draw pictures, and take a nap." Exhausted, the teacher granted his request. The boy got what he wanted, Kierkegaard said, because the teacher had given up on him. He adds, "Beware when God answers some of your prayers." It could be that he has "given up" and allowed you to have your own way.

Tony Campolo was fond of comparing Kierkegaard's parable to an incident in his own life. When Campolo was eight years old, he went to a Saturday afternoon matinee and saw a cowboy movie about Hopalong Cassidy. From that seminal moment, all young Tony wanted to be was a cowboy. He became obsessed with it.

He goes on to say, "Wouldn't it have been weird if, when I was seventeen and asked my father about going to college, he had exclaimed, 'College! What are you talking about? When you were eight years old you said you wanted to be a cowboy!

"I bought you a thousand acres in Texas with a horse and a hundred head of cattle. It's all waiting for you because that is what you said you wanted!'" Campolo concludes: "I'm glad my father didn't give me what I wanted." And he reiterates Kierkegaard's warning: "Beware when God answers some prayers."

God may refuse to give us what we ask for because he actually loves us and wants us to learn, grow, and experience change. By saying, "No," it might be God's way of preparing us for something better.

July 17: Off The Chain

Jesus isn't interested in making us keep the rules. He came to neither abolish nor add to all religious legal codes. He came to set us free from their necessity, changing our hearts. By providing us with the inner power to "do right, love mercy, and walk humbly with God," outside motivations are no longer required.

Now, to think of spirituality without rules is a radical departure for many of us because we have based our relationship with God on rule-keeping, measuring up, and following the jot and tittle of every bit of religious moralizing.

But as soon as we get into a situation for which there are no exact rules, we have no inner compass to direct us. So we fail resulting in feelings of guilt, fear, and shame; or we keep adding to the thickness of the rule book with more regulations. Christ came to set us free from all of this, the bonds of legalism and the chains of disgrace.

Jesus didn't arrive – and thanks be to God for this – with more and better rules, a heavier and stronger chain. He arrived with a transformative, liberating way to live that moves us to right thinking, right feeling, and right actions.

Clarence Jordan said "Keeping the religious rules is like chaining a vicious dog to a tree. With the dog chained the owner could then report, 'You know, my dog has never bitten anyone. He must be a good dog.' Wrong! The goodness of the dog is based solely upon the strength of the chain."

Jesus' intention is to change the very nature of the human species, not to manufacture a more robust chain. By transforming the human heart, Christ shows that chains not only fail to change us, but that those chains are no longer necessary.

July 18: All Who Will Come

Will Campbell was a self-proclaimed "bootleg preacher" from Mississippi with a Baptist ordination, a foul mouth, and a love for Jesus, Bourbon, and country music. He was best known for his tireless work toward racial equality and his no-compromise, no pulled-punches attitude when it came to reconciliation.

"God is ready to forgive and restore all who will come," he preached for decades. When asked how he would summarize his theology and his work, in Campbell's iconoclastic style he answered, "We are all bastards; but God loves us anyway."

This belief was put to the test during the racial violence and upheaval of the 1960s. One of Will's colleagues, a Civil Rights worker named Jonathan Daniels, was shot and killed by an Alabama sheriff. The sheriff was acquitted.

Will retreated to a friend's home to grieve and rage. There, the friend put a pointed question to Campbell: "Which one of those two bastards do you think God loves the most - Jonathan or that sheriff?" It was a shattering confrontation, and Campbell's own salvation. He said:

"Suddenly, everything became clear. My twenty years of ministry had become, without my realizing it, a negation of Jesus, a denial of the faith I professed. That sheriff was indeed as loved by God as Jonathan. And if loved, forgiven; and if forgiven, reconciled. Damned if that revelation didn't make a Christian out of me. And I'm still not sure I can stand it."

This is the category-exploding, boundary-breaking, world-upturning gospel: God's grace trumps everything. God's love welcomes all who will come. God's forgiveness is no "respecter of persons," even those persons for whom we ourselves have little mercy. Yes, this is sometimes more than we can stand, but it is the no-compromise, no pulled-punches message of reconciliation.

July 19: Like Father, Like Father

When I was a kid my father was brilliant. He seemed to understand or know everything. He could do math in his head; could read the hardest words; fix anything broken, and solve any problem. He was a virtual Einstein.

But as I got older I discovered my father was growing remarkably stupid. In just a few short years, somehow, he became a backward, bumbling simpleton with not the slightest indication of how the world works. He offered inane advice on money, education, and the opposite sex. He set ridiculous boundaries in regard to my time, work, school, and friends. A few times he even dared to critique or forbid my well-made decisions. What an idiot.

Then, when I became an adult, my father experienced a dramatic recovery. His counsel improved drastically – almost overnight. His words were far sounder than I could ever remember. His intellectual turnaround was miraculous, and since then, I have been glad to see him doing so well again.

What bothers me now is the fact that I am my father's son. I get more like him every day: The cadence of my voice, my mannerisms, the gray in my beard, my dietary habits, my elevated cholesterol. Even my own mid-life plunge into idiocy: My teenage sons treat me as if I already have dementia. "Bless his heart," their eyes say, "he doesn't have a clue."

But I'll get better, in a decade or so. My mental capacities will improve as my own father's did. Maybe then I won't be such a bonehead, and my children will find me worth listening to again. It's really too bad that we fathers take these short trips into stupidity when our children are at such vulnerable junctions in their lives. They sure could use a little help.

July 20: Throw A Line

Why do you pray? Because you were taught it was a good discipline to maintain? Because you always have, for as far back as you can remember? To quiet your mind? To get God to "do something" for you or those you love?

The reasons are manifold, but really, what good is prayer if it isn't changing those of us who pray? Because if prayer only feeds our narcissism and the human tendency to self-aggrandize our egos (give me, me, me what I, I, I need), then I seriously doubt that God is doing very much listening. Why would he?

If all we want is a change of circumstances, be it in regards to our health, finances, job, church, spouse or a hundred other things, we miss the point that God seems more interested in changing us, rather than changing our surroundings. To give us everything we desire converts God into a divine vending machine. And honestly, I've never seen it turn out well for those who get everything they want out of a vending machine.

I love the image painted by the great Methodist missionary E. Stanley Jones (who spent the bulk of his life working in India). He said, "Suppose you go fishing early one morning, and launch your little boat into the water. After a while, you are finished, and you wish to return home. What do you do?"

He answers, "You throw a line to shore and begin to pull. Are you pulling the entire landmass to yourself, or are you being pulled to the shore?"

The answer to his question is as enlightening as it is obvious. Prayer is not the means by which we pull God to us and in our direction. It is the means by which we are drawn to God.

July 21: Look To Jesus

I counseled with a woman whose understanding of God was nothing short of horrific. For her God was always lurking as an unpredictable bogeyman; an enraged, vicious, and cruel sadist. It was no surprise that she lived in abject terror.

Her conclusions about God, however, were not her fault. They were imposed on her, as this single story makes evident: She was twelve years old and her father had come home drunk, as usual. He pulled a revolver from his chair-side table and called her over to his lap.

He cuddled her in his arms for a moment and then placed the cold steel of the revolver against the back of her head. "Did you know I could blow your brains out right now?" he asked her in a menacing whisper.

He quickly put the gun aside and held her close again, only to return to the gun and repeat the question again and again over the space of the evening. One moment he was tender and loving, and the next he had a gun barrel pushed against her skull with the hammer cocked.

This is a horrible story. More so, it is a horrible experience for anyone to live through, and it has caused her all types of emotional disturbances over her lifetime, not the least of which is her thinking about God. For her, God is just like her drunken father.

How can her thinking, grounded in such grievous experiences, ever change? I'm not exactly sure, but I know the general direction to point her - and others with such heinous theological images: Look to Jesus. If Jesus is, as the Scriptures say, "the exact representation of God," then God can be nothing but loving, welcoming, compassionate, and graceful; especially to a child welcomed safely into his arms.

July 22: Noisy

Maybe God used to move within your heart, he once whispered in your ear - or maybe you have never had such an experience at all. God might speak to others, or you used to know what it was like for God to speak to you, but now you've grown hard of hearing.

The troubling thing is, when someone's hearing begins to erode, his or her life only gets louder, further magnifying the problem. The TV volume is cranked up to the unendurable decibels of a jet fighter. Warning bells and alarms are ignored, so they keep blaring. Communication becomes difficult, a game of escalating voices. Hearing anything becomes impossible.

While we wish God to shatter his perceived silence with thunderclaps, earthquakes, and firestorms, why should he speak to us over the noise of our lives? Why would he add to the commotion? His voice will only get lost - and it does - in the dissonance that surrounds us.

We have to get quiet to hear his "still, small voice." We have to "put on our listening caps," as our elementary school teachers told us, to hear what God has to say. So, you might not be hard of hearing at all. It could be the pandemonium within and without; the sound and fury that has been absorbed into your heart, mind, and very soul.

We have to turn down the volume around us, not to hear ourselves think, but to hear anything – even the Maker of the Universe – when he gently speaks our name.

David Beavers says it impeccably: "Spend the day alone, without a phone, without a book, or a computer. There, listen to and observe the insane, obsessive, cyclical and compulsive chatter that drives you - inside and out. It is nothing more than noise, and noise is the problem."

July 23: To The End

In Jesus' story called "The Parable of the Prodigal Son," much has been said and written about what the father does to welcome his wayward child home. The father leapt from the porch, ran to the boy, embraced him, dressed him in fine clothes, put a ring on his hand, new shoes on his feet, and threw a monstrous party.

What gets less attention is what the father didn't do, and there is as valuable a lesson in his inaction as his action. Yes, when it was time, the gracious father was abuzz with activity, but for the longest time, he just sat on the porch.

Reset the scene: The man took his fortune, ran to a far country, and promptly exhausted his enormous wealth. He ended up living in a pig pen. Meanwhile, his father remained at home - waiting possibly for years - and never chased after the boy, though he must have known the disaster that had overcome his son.

The father was wise enough to know that he couldn't make the boy change. The prodigal had to "come to the end of himself," and even a magnanimous, gracious father with all the help his son would ever require, could not do that for him. Attempting to intervene before the young man was finished with the pig pen, would have only resulted in failure for everyone involved.

I suspect we all have people in our lives that we want to "help." Addicts. Codependents. Emotional junkies. Friends or family who go running over Fool's Hill every chance they get. It's hard to practice restraint with those we love, but there is no other choice, because we can't change, rescue, or make them see the error of their ways. They will have to come to the end of themselves, for themselves.

July 24: In The Actual

Family life isn't easy, even though we preacher-types don't always acknowledge this fact. We give the impression that if your family is not constructed of a spiritual bring-home-the-bacon father, a faithful, loving stay-at-home mother, and two and a half obedient, compliant children, then your family isn't "biblical" and your work is defective in some way.

This is absolutely preposterous. If ineptness at home were a disqualifier, no family would ever have a future, for every family is dysfunctional in one way or another; it's simply a matter of degree.

This proves true especially with the "biblical" families found in the Scriptures. You will be hard pressed to find a family in the Bible – not even Jesus' own family that once tried to hide him in a padded room – that is not seriously flawed.

"Biblical" families, with all their murder, adultery, polygamy, sexism, violence, and envy were far less healthy than most of our families, and I think that's the point. If God can use them, if God's goodness isn't thwarted by them, then he ought to be able to use, bless, and preserve our families too.

So if you are in your third marriage, well, make this third one the charm. If one of your children won't speak to you, talk to the ones who will. If your in-laws hate you, treat them with respect and just get through each holiday. If you are attempting familial reconciliation and your efforts seem stymied, stay at it.

When it comes to family, there is the way we "wish" things were, the way things "ought" to be, the way things "should" be, and then there is the way things really "are." God and grace come to us there, not in the hypothetical, but in the actual.

July 25: Fragile

The person with a big ego is not confident, bold, and daring. Such a person is fragile. His drive and focus is not the result of his abilities, but his feelings of inferiority. The one who "tries hard," finds it hard to measure up.

Helen Shucman said the ego-driven person is "affected by everything" with no sense of identity or grounding, no internal peace, no satisfaction. He is shaky, insecure, and afraid. Consequently, he goes hustling for love and validation, trying to to shake down approval from every person and situation he encounters; here and there, trying this and trying that; reaching high and reaching low, straining for everything.

The good news is a person can get off this never-ending hamster wheel. We all can. We can quit doing and saying things we don't mean, clutching to approval we don't need, wasting time and energy we don't have. We can be free from the merciless crowd, free from our pride and insecurities, free to become people who no longer need the flattery of others, flattery which lasts about five minutes, and then the exhausting, self-caging exercise must begin again.

How do we get free? Simple acceptance. Of yourself. Your world. And your place in it. It is enough. You are enough. So settle down. You can't win every game. You can't make every person love you. You can't react to every voice that calls to you. You can't prove to every person you meet how lovable, capable, smart, sexy, accomplished, and worthy you are.

Try to do all of this, and you will be an ego-driven, self-centered maniac; or you will be as fragile as glass, a needy little imp that never experiences a single moment of rest. Either way, you will never be free.

July 26: Greener Grass

Gretchen Rubin says there are two kinds of people in the word, or at least two ways to make decisions. There is the "satisficer" (yes, apparently a real word) and there is the "maximizer."

"Satisficers" are those who make a decision once their basic criteria are met. This doesn't mean they settle for mediocrity; their criteria can be exceedingly high, but as soon as they find what they are looking for, the search ends and they get busy being happy.

"Maximizers," on the other hand, want to make the optimal decision. They go looking for a recipe, a new car, an apartment or even a spouse that is perfect. Even if they find something (or someone) that is exceptional, they can't make a decision or commit. And even if they do, they languish about in regret, always thinking about what "might have been" or the grass that is greener on the other side of the fence.

Studies suggest that "satisficers" tend to be happier than "maximizers." This is because "maximizers" spend a lot more time and energy, not only coming to a decision, but because they fret and stew long after the decision is made, wondering if they made the best choice.

Here is a word of wisdom: Life will never - never - be exactly as you wish it to be, no matter how much time you take making that perfect decision. Decisions require wisdom - and God will give exactly that if you ask for it - but decisions do not require perfection. That's what grace is for, and God will give you plenty of that too.

Besides, that greener grass on the other side of the fence? It doesn't exist. The only place the grass is greener is above the septic tank, and trust me: You won't be satisfied living there.

July 27: Never Unloved

Once in a religiously charged discussion with another, I was asked rather accusingly, "Don't you love God?" My answer was simply, "I don't know," because sometimes I don't know how true my love for God is. It waxes and wanes according to my circumstances, mood, and the levels of caffeine and serotonin in my bloodstream.

So no, I don't know how strong my love for God is because it is a frail, human love subject to my very real limitations. But I do know that God loves me. I know that God loves you, and that makes all the difference.

Such love has a name. In the Hebrew language it is called, "Chesed," and is usually associated with God's parental love for his children. It is a word for which there is no easy English equivalent. Some call it grace, some mercy, or kindness, but these attempts fail. "Chesed" is all of these things and more, the central Hebrew virtue to which all acts of charity and goodness are attached.

Dr. Ralph Davis writes: "Chesed is where love, strength, and steadfastness interact with each other, not merely kindness, but dependable kindness; not merely affection, but affection that has committed itself." And I will add that such a commitment is always there - whether it is deserved, earned, justifiable or otherwise.

One rabbi, explaining so plainly, says, "When a person works for an employer, and then he gets paid, that pay is really a recycling of his own deeds. It isn't love. It isn't kindness. It is earned. But an act of 'Chesed' cannot be recycled. It is something given or granted without cause."

"Don't you love God?" is the wrong question. Because we have all been unloving, undeserving, unkind, and unhappy toward God. But thank God, we have never been unloved.

July 28: Cleaner Windows

A young couple moved into a new home in a new neighborhood. The next morning while they were eating breakfast, boxes still strewn across the house, the man watched his neighbor hanging the wash outside.

"That laundry is not very clean," he said. "She does not know how to wash correctly. Perhaps she needs better laundry soap." This went on day after day: Eating breakfast, complaining about the neighbor's dirty laundry, and unpacking boxes.

A month or so passed, and the man was surprised one morning to discover the neighbors' brilliant clean laundry on the line! He said to his wife, "Look, she has learned how to wash correctly. I wonder who taught her how."

The wife said softly, "Nobody. I got up early this morning and washed our windows."

Think about how many times a day you make judgements or come to conclusions about others. Such conclusions are usually based only on outward appearances, based on what we see. A person on the news. The barista from whom you buy your coffee. Strangers seated on the pew across the aisle at church. A neighbor to whom you've never spoken.

You know essentially nothing about these people but you make up your mind about who they are, what they do, and their many shortcomings. To such attitudes Jesus said, "Why worry about a speck in your friend's eye when you have a log in your own? How can you think of saying to your friend, 'Let me help you get rid of that speck in your eye,' when you can't see past the log in your own eye?"

Cleaning our own dirty windows and straightening out the cluttered boxes in our own houses before turning our attention to anyone else is a far healthier use of our time and energy.

July 29: Behind Every Beautiful Thing

On this day in 1890 the extraordinary but tormented artist Vincent Van Gogh took his own life. Van Gogh produced hundreds of paintings, some of which are the most valued in the world.

Van Gogh never set out to be an artist. He wanted to be a pastor. "God has sent me to preach the Gospel," Vincent wrote as a young man. But he failed the seminary entrance exam and flunked out of missionary school. When he became a pastor he was fired within months. This painful rejection turned him to the easel.

In one of his iconic paintings, "The Church at Auvers," Van Gogh's pain from being rejected by the church bleeds off the page like his hues of blue and starry nights. A road leads to a massive house of worship. Yet the path, upon arriving at the church, is suddenly diverted, because this church has no doors. After being rejected by the church, Van Gogh concluded that there was no way for him to get in.

Feeling like his calling had been redirected, Van Gogh picked up his brush as an artist in God's service. The one who felt rejected by the church said, "The great artists, the serious masters, tell us in their masterpieces what leads to God. One writes it in a book; another in a picture."

It was Vincent Van Gogh's pictures - his glorious interpretations - that he used to lead people to God. And he did so with his rough edges and broken pieces; his fragmented mind and his constant illnesses; with his short, remarkable life; bringing the world priceless joy out of tremendous pain.

But that's always how it works."Behind every beautiful thing is some kind of pain," to quote Bob Dylan, and God uses pain to bless and beautify the world.

July 30: Change Your Mind

An old friend of mine is an addiction therapist, coming to his line of work honestly, as an alcoholic. The addiction ran roughshod through his marriage, family, and career until finally his life collapsed. But he got sober, obtained a professional counseling credential, and went to work helping other addicts reach sobriety.

Today he is a sort of evangelist for recovery and often says, thumping his Big Blue A.A. Book, "Nobody's gonna change 'cause they feel like it. A man's got to change his thinking." Bad thinking equals bad living.

We in the faith community are extremely skilled at assessing what people are doing wrong. After all, we want people to live whole, healthy lives and that's a good thing. But we can't begin with someone's behavior (Have you ever told a drunk to just "quit drinking?" How did it work?). We must begin internally.

"As a person thinks in his heart," the Proverbs say, "so is that person," because what one thinks affects the way one feels, and how one feels leads directly to one's healthy or unhealthy behaviors. But most of the time we mistakenly focus on modifying behavior rather than changing the deep motivations that lead to actions.

Training the mind and heart to be different, that is to "fix our thoughts on what is true, honorable, right, pure, lovely, and admirable" or to "take captive our rebellious thoughts" takes vigilance, but it leads to transformation.

How long will this take? About two months, according to experts. If you are especially malleable, your thinking pattern might change in a few weeks. If you are more stubborn, maybe six months. The point is, changing your way of thinking doesn't happen overnight - but it doesn't take forever either. Learn to change your mind, then you can change anything.

July 31: Peepholes

Have you ever gone "peephole" driving? I bet you have. On a cold morning, snow or frost has covered your windshield with ice. You are in a hurry, so with a quick shot of wiper fluid and a blast of defrost, you clear a tiny sliver and start down the road.

You are hunched over the top of the steering wheel, in the dark, looking out a slit. You get about a half-mile from home before you realize how incredibly stupid you really are. You can hardly see a thing. But what you do see, fearfully enough, is a bunch of other drivers doing the same thing as you!

This as an apt metaphor for how we live our lives. Our worries and troubles descend upon us like a near impervious shroud, blinding us, making us afraid, making it so we can't see where we are going. Of course, most people we meet are in the same condition: Squinting through peepholes, getting nowhere fast.

This is a reason I love one of Paul's great prayers. But more than admiring it, I want to experience and live it: "I pray that the eyes of your heart may be enlightened in order that you may know the hope to which he has called you."

If we focus only on our personal tribulations, the unrest of the world, the pure meanness and nastiness that seems to drive some people; then before long we will be as blind as proverbial bats, unable to see any safe path in the world. We will become nothing but fearful, cynical, pessimistic old sourpusses that have given up on everything and everybody.

Hope doesn't work like that. Hope gives us hearts to believe and eyes to see. Hope opens the path to a better - and brighter - future.

AUGUST

August 1: It All Fits Together

At the memorial service of a dear, college friend, I said: "All of creation - cancerous bodies, broken hearted-families, widowed husbands, those of us with more questions than answers - we all long for God's new creation and redemption to come.

"We must remember, this is not all there is. This is not even a fraction of all that is. We live on the tip of an iceberg with the vastness of all God is and has planned for our futures lying somewhere beneath the surface. God will achieve merciful justice."

But I admit, I don't know how the details of God's ultimate justice will work its way out. Words from Walter Brueggemann helped me, however, in my confusion. Brueggemann had a friend, he said, who wanted to learn to become a carpenter.

The friend found an experienced, patient, carpenter who would teach him the trade and they went to work, but the work just didn't work. Brueggemann's friend couldn't make his hands do what needed to be done. His efforts were a disaster.

After a great deal of frustration the carpentry teacher said, "Look, I can't teach you how to be a carpenter, but I can teach you how things are put together." For Brueggemann's friend, this was the answer for which he was looking. Now, he could look at furniture or construction with a new respect, if not reverence, for while he couldn't do the work himself, he had an appreciation for how it all fit together.

I don't know how God's final justice and kingdom will come. And I certainly can't do anything to bring that justice to bear, myself. But in Christ I'm beginning to see how it all fits together. And that brings me a new appreciation – a new peace – that I would not have otherwise.

August 2: On The Road

Christianity is a fluid faith for a pilgrim people. It is a spirituality of movement. But look at how we have structured it, and it is easy to see why we most often view Christianity as an incorrigible, fixated fortress rather than a dynamic journey.

Our doctrines, constructed and accumulated over thousands of years, stack up like immovable stones. The buildings that contain our worship services are almost always built of rock, granite, or the hardiest material we can find.

Or try being an idealistic reformer who seeks to change a church's policy or its strategy to meet the world where it now is. If you're not taken out behind the vestry and quietly crucified, you'll find that change in the church usually moves with all the terrifying speed of a melting glacier.

This betrays our roots and the trajectory set for our faith from its beginning. Before his death, Jesus described himself and faith in him like this: "I am the true and living way." This had such a profound effect on the first followers of Jesus that the earliest self-description of Christianity was "The Way." It was the Path. The Road. It was the constantly evolving, opening arc that took this "band of gypsies down the highway."

It doesn't appear that Jesus came to establish an inflexible, competitive religion that would be pitted against other belief systems. No, he came to show us how to live the life of redeeming love, love for God and for others.

There's nothing about love that should be turned into coldblooded institutionalism; be used to exclude, marginalize, or separate. This Way can only take us further down the road and deeper into the heart of God. And while love is often "a road less traveled," it is the worthiest of journeys.

August 3: Former Things

When I first taught my son to drive he had the nasty habit of looking over his shoulder to see what was behind him. He would do this even while driving at a fairly decent speed, resulting in several near crashes (along with a great deal of screaming from his instructor and added gray hairs to my head).

That habit, now thankfully broken, was indicative of the human condition. We are always peering over our shoulders at what is behind us; always trying to re-envision a better past. So it should be no wonder why we can't keep our lives on track, why we keep crashing into the metaphorical ditch: What else could happen when we maneuver through life while looking backwards?

But for most of us, there's a lot of junk to look at back there. The tragic death of a child. Unjustified suffering or inexplicable hardship. Betrayal by a spouse or partner. A personal sickness or disease. Self-inflicted wounds of stupidity and poor choices: All of these call us to look at and live in the past.

Yet, we are all moving forward. That is where life is lived. That is where God is leading, and the road he is creating. As said with the prose of the prophet Isaiah: "Forget the former things; do not dwell on the past. See, I am doing a new thing. I am making a way in the wilderness."

Simply, there comes a day when we must fix our eyes on the road before us; a day to quit working so hard on what is long gone; a day to blackout the rear windows of life and see the God-given road that leads into future. Looking over your shoulder is a habit that can be broken. Break it today.

August 4: A Wonderful World

Today marks the birthday of a man called, "the beginning and end of music in America." Born in the sweltering heat of a New Orleans' summer, the grandson of former slaves, and suffering abject poverty, that man was Louis Armstrong.

Louis' most iconic song, "What a Wonderful World," was released in 1967. The southern states were fighting desegregation, and the U.S. Army was fighting in Southeast Asia. The Apollo 1 spacecraft was burning on the launchpad, and the Cold War was burning in Eastern Europe. The Israelis were at war with their Arab neighbors, and police departments were at war with African-Americans in the country's major cities.

How could Louis Armstrong sing this song about rainbows and unicorns when the world looked like it was going to hell in a hand basket (as it still does today)? Armstrong answered, "It seems to me it ain't the world that's so bad, but what we're doing to it. All I'm saying is: See what a wonderful world it would be, if only we'd give it a chance."

That conclusion hints of Scripture. God created this wonderful world and called it "good." What went wrong? We did. Humanity was to serve as the steward and curator of God's world. It was – and will always remain – humanity's role to be creation's protector; to maintain the goodness of God's world. We have largely shirked that responsibility.

Yet, this world means something to God, because God wants it to be wonderfully "good." Thus, We throw ourselves into the fray of this fractured world – healing the sick, making peace among enemies, feeding the hungry, working for justice, protecting and sustaining resources, creating harmony – because we believe "it ain't the world that's bad, but what we're doing to it." Let's give the Wonderful World a chance.

August 5: Bad Dogs

I have yet to see this disproved: Those most obsessed with being right always end up being hardhearted. Whether it comes naturally, a default setting in some people, or is the result of their environment, there are people who not only must be right about all that they believe, they must show how others are wrong.

A friend of mine calls this the "bad dog syndrome." Those with an overinflated sense of correctness point their fingers at those who don't measure up and cry, "Bad dog! Bad dog!" All that is lacking is a quick swat of the rolled up newspaper to the nose. For these scolding perfections, the drive to be error-free prevents them from genuinely loving people.

Granted, there's a lot to scold in people; surrounded by a culture that is arrogant and defiant; that flies in the face of justice and right; a culture that is charged with evil and corruption, it's a real test to remain loving followers of Jesus.

It's much easier to get cynical, grumpy, and angry. It's easier to point fingers at the evil-doers; easier to identify and ostracize the heretics; easier to take our rightness and our righteousness and wear it like a badge; easier to stand on our "principles" and even suffer for them, than it is to be gracious toward others. It's easier to kick the "bad dog" than to love the mutts and mongrels.

The truest truth we can hold to is love, for God is love. It's not that God ignores injustice or wrong-doing (or wrong-believing). He simply wants to love and redeem more than he wants to scold "bad dogs." So, you can try to prove how right you are or you can love. It's hard to do both at the same time.

August 6: Marbles

Next time you hear the phrase, "Losing my marbles," you might think of this:

"Let me give you a lesson on getting your priorities straight. I sat down one day and did the math. The average person lives about 75 years. I know, some live more and some live less, but on average, folks live about seventy-five years.

"I multiplied 75 times 52 and I came up with 3900, which is the number of Saturdays that the average person has in their entire lifetime. Now, stick with me, I'm getting to the important part.

"It took me until I was 55 years old to think about all this in any detail, and by that time I had lived through over 2,800 Saturdays! So I got to thinking that if I lived to be 75, I only had about a thousand of them left to enjoy. That's when I went to a toy store and bought every single marble they had (I ended up having to visit three toy stores to round up the correct number of marbles).

"I took them home and put them inside a large, clear plastic jug right here on my desk. Every Saturday since then, I have taken one marble out and thrown it away. I found that by watching the marbles diminish, I focused more on the really important things in life.

You see, there's nothing like watching your time here on this earth run out to help get your priorities straight; and this morning, I took the very last marble out of the container. I figure that if I make it until next Saturday then I have been given a little extra time. And the one thing we can all use is a little more time, if we will do something with it."

August 7: Buckle Up

It is widely known that Muhammad Ali was not only "the Greatest," in the boxing ring, but he was a great flyer. He loved to travel by airplane, and was never afraid (I love to travel as well, but I don't enjoy flying. It usually takes a combination of prayer, Bourbon shooters, and an Ativan to get me off the ground, but I digress).

Ali, the former Cassius Clay, claimed, in all his humility, that no plane could ever crash while he was on board. God would protect him. Reports are told that he would get on a plane and tell all the other passengers not to be afraid, as they were safe so long as he was on board.

There are conflicting accounts, but it seems that Ali was on a cross-country flight to Los Angeles when the plane encountered heavy turbulence. The pilot turned on the "fasten seat belts" sign and everyone promptly buckled up - everyone except Muhammad Ali. He was not afraid.

One of the flight attendants came by and said forcefully, "Sir, for your safety, please buckle your seatbelt." Ali responded, with all his bravado, "Superman don't need no seat belt!"

Without breaking stride the attendant responded just as confidently, "Superman don't need no airplane, neither!" Ali buckled up.

None of us are as strong as we think we are. Fearfully and wonderfully made? Yes. Capable of incredible achievements? Yes. The crowning glory of God's creation? Yes. Able to leap tall buildings with a single bound? Not even close.

There's no shame in admitting what we are: Frail, susceptible to fear, made of dust. God made us this way; made to fly high, yes, but always dependent upon him and his grace. God may have given us wings, so to speak, but no red capes.

August 8: Reconciliation

In the summer of 1993, white rule was ending in South Africa. As the first free elections were about to take place, the country descended into violence. White fundamentalists attempted to hold to power, and disenfranchised young blacks rioted in the streets.

A mob of these angry young men spotted Amy Biehl, succeeded in stopping her car, and she was stoned and stabbed to death. Biehl was not their enemy, however. She had been in Cape Town for a year, a Stanford graduate and Fulbright scholar studying and working to end apartheid. She had a plane ticket in her car to fly home to California the next day.

Four members of the mob were charged and convicted of murder. The prosecution asked for the death penalty, but the judge sentenced them to eighteen years in prison, saying he thought that they had a chance to become useful citizens. Four years later, these four men applied for a pardon before the nation's Truth and Reconciliation Commission.

At the hearing, the men admitted their role in Amy's killing and said that they believed they had to kill whites to force the government to relinquish power. They each received a pardon and were set free.

More remarkably, they received a pardon from Amy's parents and family. Two of the men who killed Amy Biehl, in fact, now work for the charity that Biehl's parents founded after she was killed.

The only way to stop the continual and rampant hate in this world is to make peace. The only way to make peace is to forgive. The only way to forgive is through the unrelenting love and forgiveness of God. We are the images of God's love, a love that will bring reconciliation to the world, a reconciliation that is heaven come to earth.

August 9: An Autobiography

Portia Nelson was a pianist, vocalist, songwriter, actress, cancer survivor, and painter - roughly in that order. She was also a composer, savvy business person, and photographer. Best known for her Hollywood and Broadway rolls, she has been under-appreciated as an author. In 1977 she wrote a book entitled, *There's A Hole In My Sidewalk: The Romance Of Self-Discovery*. It is a gem of a little book, and it contains an original poem I find extraordinary (Nelson was also a poet, it seems). Her poem is entitled, "An Autobiography in Five Short Chapters."

I. I walk down the street. There is a deep hole in the sidewalk.
 I fall in. I am lost; I am helpless.
 It isn't my fault. It takes forever to find a way out.
II. I walk down the same street. There is a deep hole in the sidewalk.
 I pretend I don't see it; I fall in again.
 I can't believe I am in this same place.
 But it isn't my fault. It still takes a long time to get out.
III. I walk down the same street. There is a deep hole in the sidewalk.
 I see it is there but I still fall in; it's a habit.
 But my eyes are open and I know where I am.
 It is my fault. I get out immediately.
IV. I walk down the same street. There is a deep hole in the sidewalk.
 I walk around it.
V. I walk down another street.

This autobiography isn't Portia's alone. It's the story of most people in the world. The quicker we can recognize the things that trap, ensnare, and snag us, the quicker we can take responsibility for "falling" into them. It's only then that we can get to happier chapters in our own stories.

August 10: Surprise

The late Bruce Larson loved to tell the true story of friends who had planned the great American vacation. They were going to drive from their home in Alabama to California and back again.

The trip was planned in exact detail: The cities they would visit, the roads they would take, and the sights they would see. Just days before the trip, however, the husband/father was prevented from going because of work. The family was heartbroken, but he insisted that the family do without him. And they did.

The man finished his assignment in a couple of days and then unexpectedly flew to Denver. There he hired a driver to take him to the Continental Divide. Knowing the exact plan his family was following, this spot was where his wife and kids would pass later in the day (Note: Larson's story predated cell phones).

The man stood there on the road for hours waiting and praying his wife had stuck with the itinerary, and hoping to see the family station wagon coming down the road. Indeed, when it rounded the curve, Larson's friend stuck out his thumb to hitch a ride from his family who thought he was thousands of miles away. His wife almost ran the car off the road in complete shock.

When Larson asked his friend, "Why did you go to all that trouble?" he answered: "Bruce, it's like this. One day I'm going to be dead, and when that happens I want my wife and kids to say, 'Dad sure was a lot of fun wasn't he!'"

Life is full of surprises, some good and some not so much. Live your life as a surprise, a shocking, joyful bolt of amazement. You will enjoy your days so much more, and so will those around you.

August 11: The Tiger

From Frederick Buechner:

"Ramakrishna told a fable about a motherless tiger cub who was adopted by goats and brought up by them to speak their language, emulate their ways, eat their food, and in general to believe that he was a goat himself.

"Then one day a tiger came along, and when all the goats scattered in fear, the young tiger was left alone to confront him, afraid and yet somehow not afraid. The tiger asked him what he meant by his unseemly masquerade, but all that the young one could do in response was to bleat nervously and continue nibbling at the grass.

"So the tiger carried him to a pool to look at their two reflections side by side and draw his own conclusions. The truth gradually became clear. Lashing his tail and digging his claws into the ground, the young beast finally raised his head and the jungle trembled at the sound of his roar.

"Human beings as they usually exist in this world are not what they were created to be. The goat is not really a goat at all - he is really a tiger - except that he does not know this. Or, to use another language, we were created in the image of God, but something has gone awry.

"We were created to serve God and each other in love, but each of us chooses instead to serve himself as God, and this means wrenching ourselves out of the kind of relationship with God and men that we were made for.

"Yet, there is still enough of the tiger in us to make us discontented with our goathood. We eat grass, but it never really fills us. We bleat well enough, but deep down there is the suspicion that we were really made for roaring."

August 12: Woodpeckers On The Wall

On August 12, 1961, leaders of the German Democratic Republic signed an order to close the border between East and West Berlin and to erect a massive Wall dividing the city. Roads that ran into West Berlin were destroyed. Barbed wire and land mines were put into place. Concrete and steel were piled into place along the 27 miles of city border.

But this Wall, like all things evil, did not last. On an autumn night in 1989, East Berliners defiantly cascaded over, around, and through the iconic Wall that had separated families, friends, and a country for a generation. They were met on the other side by their brothers and sisters, who received them with open arms.

In the weeks that followed that revolutionary night, people from all over the world came to Berlin with hammers in hand to knock a piece of the Wall down. Some came for souvenirs. Some came to participate in a historical moment. Some came simply out of curiosity, to get in on the action. All came to do their part in tearing down one of the ugliest symbols of restriction, tyranny, and injustice ever created.

The nickname given to these unnamed, unknown people who tore down the Berlin Wall piece by piece and blow by hammer blow was the Mauerspechte: The "woodpeckers on the wall."

This is how all evil is overcome. Not in one fell swoop, but by the accumulation of small thumps. Bit by bit, year by year, with blood and tears, we keep pounding on the walls of exploitation, corruption, violence, and oppression.

God knows this world could stand a few more "woodpeckers on the wall" today; those, with hammers in hand, who will persistently and defiantly chip away at what stands in the way of peace, justice, and restoration.

August 13: Sticks And Stones

From all reports, Juergen Peters was a bright, sweet, young man. But Peters was often troubled, depressed, and empty. After a dispute at work one day he turned unusually dark. He walked off his job and climbed to the top of a water tower with every intention of jumping to his death.

At some point Juergen, thankfully, was convinced by a negotiator to change course. He carefully began climbing down the narrow iron ladder to the ground. Some in the crowd that had gathered felt deprived of a sensational conclusion. Someone yelled out, "Jump, you coward, jump!"

As Peters descended the tower more and more spectators began to jeer and deride him. He hesitated, looked down at the crowd, and then climbed back up. When he reached the top again, he moved out on the ledge and flung himself off.

If Juergen Peters had made it safely to the ground that day, I don't know if he would have received the mental health intervention he so badly needed. But I do know this: The cause of death may have read "suicide," but those in the crowd could have been detained as accomplices to the crime.

This is a tragic, dramatic story, but a necessary one, for we are destroying one another with our words as hateful, spiteful rhetoric spills out in all corners of society. The children's rhyme goes: "Sticks and stones may break my bones, but words will never hurt me," but that's a boldface lie.

Words hurt. Words can lodge so deep in the memory that decades of living cannot erase the pain. Words can crush, destroy, and yes, even kill. But they are not just killing others. We are burning our whole world to the ground. May God give us the grace to keep our mouths shut.

August 14: Faith In The Right Place

The "Flying Wallendas" were an old circus family from Germany. They came to the United States in the 1920s, and their safety net got lost somewhere as they crossed the Atlantic. Thus, they performed without it. For this feat the Wallendas received an uproarious 15-minute standing ovation from the crowd. They never used a safety net again.

The patriarch of the family was Karl Wallenda. He performed until he was in his mid-70s, but died after falling from the wire in 1978. He had been supremely confident over the years, never thinking he would fall.

To that point, it is said that he once asked the crowd at a performances if they thought he could cross a wire strung between two buildings. The crown cheered and affirmed their belief; they hadn't paid their money for nothing.

The promoter of the event was particularly enthusiastic, whipping the crowd into a frenzy. Wallenda then invited the promoter, and anyone else who was willing, to ride on his shoulders while he crossed the wire. There were no takers. No one was willing to put their enthusiasm to the test.

Honestly, I wouldn't have accepted the invitation either, and not because I don't have faith. I just don't have faith that someone can carry me on their shoulders across a high wire, ten stories in the air.

In regards to faith, it's not that we don't have enough of it (Jesus said a mustard seed's worth was more than enough to move mountains). The challenge is to place our faith in the right person.

The amount of faith you have is inconsequential. But the object of your faith is absolutely critical. It's not how much faith you have that matters. It's in whom that faith has been placed that makes the difference.

August 15: The Bright Side

On most days "people of faith" are trusting and unquestioning. But on other days, we are as cynical, jaded, and suspicious as a room full of Doubting Thomases. We are struck with doubt, our hearts are filled with questions, and we rage against heaven demanding answers that never seem to come.

But there is a bright side to doubt. It's a signal flare for a little extra help. For example, the lone survivor of a shipwreck washed up on a deserted island. Every day he prayed to God to send someone to rescue him, and every day he scanned the horizon for help, but none came.

Exhausted, he eventually began to make a life on the island. He built a hut out of driftwood and palm branches to protect himself from the elements and to store his few possessions. Then one day, after scavenging for food, he arrived home to find his little hut in flames, the smoke rolling up to the sky.

As if shipwreck and loneliness were not enough, now his only home and few belongings were gone. He cried out: "God, why did you let this happen to me!" Early the next day, after a shelterless night, he was awakened by the sound of a ship approaching the island. It had come to rescue him! Tears of joy streamed down the man's face.

"How did you know I was here?" he asked his rescuers. Incredulously, they looked at him and answered: "Of course we saw your smoke signal asking for help."

Doubt, rather than driving God away, may in fact, bring him to us. When we feel as if faith is burning to the ground, it just might be the necessary signal for God to somehow, someway, appear to us, in a way we never dreamed possible.

August 16: The Elvis In Me

It was August 16, 1977. We were sitting at the corner of College and Line Streets; my mother driving, my sister in the backseat, and me riding shotgun. It was at that precise moment and time that the crackling radio announced that Elvis Presley was dead.

Raised as I was in a Christian fundamentalist household, that "filthy rock music" was not allowed in the house. No Stones. No Dylan. No Hendrix. The only artist that got a pass was Elvis. In my mind's eye, not only do I remember the day of his death, I see all his records stacked on my family's bookshelf, right next to the King James Bible.

In his lifetime Elvis received three Grammys. None of these were for his rock or popular music. All were for his gospel recordings, and he loved that genre the most. In the end, the man was a contradiction - just like his records were - sitting next to our family Bible.

He was the King of Rock and Roll, yet his highest career achievement was in gospel. He had 150 albums reach gold or platinum status, but the songs he played the most were the hymns he learned in church.

He was the icon of the sexual revolution, had some 10,000 doses of pain killers and amphetamines prescribed to him in his last year of life, but still called the Bible his favorite book. He died with a dozen substances in his bloodstream, but with a book about Jesus clutched to his chest. He was a conflicted person. Aren't we all.

We each have a bit of Elvis within us as our better angels and howling devils compete for dominance. It's no secret which direction the battle will go. That part of us that we nourish will always carry the day.

August 17: The Rabbit

Why do people become Christians? There are more than a few reasons, but one thing is certain, those who follow Jesus for a lifetime are those who have seen and experienced him for themselves.

They do not live off the back of their minister's faith or through the experiences of others. They don't rely upon what their friends, mentors, or books say. Rather, they have come face to face, somehow, with the risen Lord.

A young man went to see his grandfather, an old man who had been a follower of Jesus his entire life. When the young man arrived they embraced and after a while the grandson asked his grandfather, "Pop, why is it that some people who follow Jesus give up? And then there are people like you, who stay at it their entire life?"

The old man said, "Let me tell you a story. One morning I was sitting here and all of a sudden, a big old white rabbit jumped into the yard. My dog took off after that rabbit. Soon a few more dogs joined him.

"Gradually, the other dogs dropped out and went home, discouraged and worn out. Only my dog stayed with the chase till the end of the day. That is the answer to your question." The young man thought a while, but didn't get it.

The old man said, "Son, why did the other dogs give up on chasing the rabbit? Ain't it easy to see? The other dogs had not seen the rabbit. They only heard the barking. But once you see the rabbit, you never give up the chase. I have seen the rabbit for myself and that is what keeps me at it."

As you are on your way, look for the "rabbit" and experience Jesus for yourself.

August 18: The Pursuit

I find it ironic that the word used to describe our uniquely consumeristic way of life is "Consumption." It is a word that described tuberculosis, a disease that ate away a person's ability to breathe, that devoured one's wellbeing.

Maybe that definition should stand today, describing the culture we have created. Consumption is depleting us and we are suffocating. How then, can we be happy?

Whenever I have taken a group of Americans to a developing country, one of the first observations that the Americans make is how happy the people are. Largely, this is true, but a missionary in Honduras told me once, "When children reach a certain age here, they begin to see what they can have and they see what they don't have. It creates in them a greed and desperation that they did not previously have."

He wasn't glorifying poverty, as if ignorance would be bliss. He was simply pointing out that the desire awakened within them resulted in so much unhappiness - and he was quick to point out that through today's extensive media - it was the wealth of North America and Europe that dangled out there in front of these kids and young adults like a carrot on a stick; a carrot they will never be able to reach.

We suffer the same disease, though our poverty is greater than most of the world's riches; we keep striving and scheming. We are truly blessed that in our society we have the means, education, and general wherewithal to engage in what we call, "life, liberty, and the pursuit of happiness."

Yet, we are too dense to see that the pursuit itself robs us of the intended goals. The longer and harder we pursue, the less life, liberty, and happiness we seem to be able to possess.

August 19: Root Causes

There was a small village on the edge of a river. One day a villager noticed a baby floating down the river! She heard crying in the distance and looked downstream to see that several babies had already floated by.

Other villagers began to notice that even more were coming from upstream! They didn't know how long it had been going on - maybe years - as they had been busy with their work and their lives. But now that they saw the problem, they had to do something.

Watchtowers were built on both sides of the river and rescue teams maintained 24-hour surveillance with zip-lines and baskets. But the number of babies floating down the river only seemed to increase. So the villagers built orphanages and took the babies in, and life in the village found a new normal as enormous resources were used to save the babies.

Then a villager finally asked the obvious: "Where are all these babies coming from?" No one knew. He said, "We have to go upstream and stop whoever or whatever is causing this." But not everyone agreed.

"We have lives here," some said. "If you go upstream, there won't be enough people to pull the children from the water," said others. "There must be something terrifying up there that would cause all this," still more protested.

But a few villagers decided to make the dangerous journey up river. They didn't know what they would find, and they didn't know if they would be able to do anything, but they had to go. Yes, some had to help at home, but some had to get to the source of the problem.

Let us never be content with only treating symptoms of our community's troubles. Let's go further. Let's go to the root causes.

August 20: Unsettling The Settled

"God said it, I believe it, and that settles it." This slogan is one of today's common bumper sticker defenses of the Bible. This view characterizes the Bible as a divinely dictated book of statutes whose truth is crystal clear to anyone who has sense enough to simply read. Of course they fail to clarify that what they call the "truth" is their view of the truth, shaped by their unique set of circumstances, experiences, and presuppositions.

Thus, "believing the Bible" can create hard-hearted, judgmental, graceless religionists who patrol society with weapons of rigidity and arrogance. In such cases, both belief and the Bible have been misappropriated. Christians can become "settled" for sure, but are simultaneously nothing like their namesake, Jesus Christ.

But what if we begin to read the Bible descriptively rather than just prescriptively? That is, what if the Bible describes the human search for God – and God's interaction with humanity – rather than simply prescribing religious behavior? We could then read the Scriptures, not to confirm our righteousness and others' wrongness, but looking for how we can better know God.

And how does the Bible reveal God? By pointing us to its prime subject matter: The person of Jesus. The goal of the Scriptures is not to give us ideas about religion; not to help us form sharper or better doctrinal statements; or to build theological armaments against those who believe differently than we do, or to answer all of our questions. It is to bring us face to face with Christ, and to become like him.

I'm not advocating setting the Bible aside, but to actually embrace it, and see to whom it points. This may be an unsettling way to approach the Scriptures, but being "settled" isn't the point; knowing and becoming like Jesus is.

August 21: Refrigerator Rights

Therapist Will Miller says that your refrigerator says a lot about your relationships. Here's how: There is a knock at the door. It is a salesperson. You invite her in. She begins to present her materials, but pauses to go to your refrigerator and begin making herself a sandwich. She rattles through the drawers for lettuce and cheese, turkey, and mayo.

She goes to the pantry and gets out the bread, a plate and a knife. She returns to the fridge and grabs herself a beer or pours a soda. Then she carries her meal into the living room, picks up the remote, changes the channel to what she wants to watch, props her feet on the coffee table and makes herself at home. You would probably be annoyed.

Now, suppose there is a knock at the door. This time it is your best friend. She comes in, and after a few minutes, goes over to your refrigerator, opens it up and begins making a sandwich.

She rattles through the drawers for lettuce, cheese, turkey, and mayo. She goes to the pantry and gets out the bread, a plate and a knife. She returns to the fridge and grabs a beer or pours a soda. In this case you are not offended at all. Why? Because your friend has "Refrigerator Rights." She is welcome.

Being Christians, to a large extent, is about earning and maintaining "Refrigerator Rights" with others. It is about reaching a place of deep connection with those who are on the same journey with us.

This is far more than the generic "fellowship" we often settle for - a doughnut and sip a cup of coffee together. This is "Refrigerator Rights; a place where we are welcomed into the lives of others, and they are welcomed into ours.

August 22: The Cowboy

One Sunday morning an old cowboy entered a church just before services were to begin. The old man wore tattered jeans, a denim shirt, and boots with very little shine left on them. In his hand he held a much beloved, much read, but worn Bible.

The church he entered was upscale in an exclusive part of town, and it was the largest and most beautiful building the old cowboy had ever seen.

The people seated in the pews were all dressed up in expensive clothes and jewelry, and they had expensive cars in the parking lot. When he sat down, others moved away from him and watched him with a cautious eye. They were appalled at his dress and disrespect.

The service began and there was incredible music and beautiful liturgy. The pastor preached his sermon forcefully with a dose of fire and brimstone. As the old cowboy was leaving the church the preacher approached him and asked the cowboy to do him a favor.

"Before you come back here again, have a talk with God and ask him what he thinks would be the appropriate attire for worship." The old cowboy assured the preacher he would do exactly that.

The next Sunday he returned wearing the same tattered jeans, same denim shirt, same dirty boots, and same worn Bible. Again, he was shunned and ignored. The preacher approached and said, "I thought I asked you to speak to God before you came back to our church."

"Well, I did," said the old cowboy. "If you spoke to God, what did he tell you the proper attire should be for worshiping here?" The cowboy answered, "Well sir, God told me that he didn't have a clue what I should wear. He said he's never been in this church before."

August 23: Do Something

Larry Walters, a truck driver from Long Beach, California, visited his local army surplus store and purchased for himself 42 huge weather balloons. He filled the balloons with helium and attached them to an aluminum lawn chair.

Then he grabbed a peanut butter and jelly sandwich, a few drinks, and a pellet gun (to pop the balloons when he was ready to land), took his seat and cut the ropes holding him to earth.

Immediately Walters soared three miles into the atmosphere, straying into the path of two commercial airliners. It was a short flight as Larry, near hypothermia, began shooting the balloons with his pellet gun.

The authorities were there on the ground to meet him, but they didn't know exactly what to charge him with. Ultimately, he stood trial for "operating an aircraft without an airworthiness certificate," and operating an aircraft "without maintaining communication with an airport control tower."

Now the obvious question: Why would someone do such a thing? Well, besides saying it was the most fun he ever had, Walters explained: "I've had this dream for twenty years of going up into the clear blue sky. You can't just sit there. You've got to do something."

As we seek to follow Christ, it's not unusual to find ourselves in a Larry Walters' position. We have this almost instinctive draw to launch out into the clear blue, to reach for higher and better things, or to go deeper in our connection with God.

But what keeps our feet glued to the ground is the fear of cutting the moorings that hold us to the ground. We are more afraid of the unknown, than we are dissatisfied with what we know. Yet, there comes a time to "do something," because you won't get anywhere just by sitting still.

August 24: Know Thyself

In central Greece there was an ancient city named Delphi. It was the location of Apollo's Temple, where the Greeks and Romans made long pilgrimages to hear a word from the Oracle, a prophetess who was Apollo's spokesperson.

In the outer court of the temple was a phrase inscribed into stone (a phrase long associated with Socrates). The phrase, in English, was, "Know thyself." The Greeks understood that without a sense of personal identity, there was no real hope of growth, maturity, or getting on with life.

I think the Apostle Paul would agree with this, but his application would be radically different. He would say, "Yes, know thyself, but also know that you belong to Christ. Your identity has been swallowed up in him. Put differently, we "no longer live, but Christ lives in and through us."

The majority of our spiritual struggles, the greater part of the pain and regrets we carry around, the most stubborn roadblocks in our path to maturity are centered on the fact that we do not accept the truth about ourselves. The truth is this: When God looks at you, he sees Jesus. That is who you really are.

You are loved with an unquenchable love, a love as certain as the Father's love for Jesus. You are forgiven and made whole. The perfect life of Christ is now yours. He has made you as innocent as a new born baby.

Therefore, you are not what your parents may say about you; not what angry, judgmental religion says about you; not what the Devil whispers in your ear; not what your ex-spouse thinks of you, and especially not what you might think of yourself. You are who God says you are: Whole, forgiven, restored, free, and redeemed. That makes life worth living.

August 25: The Man Behind The Curtain

What do Kenosha, Wisconsin, and Cape Cod, Massachusetts, have in common? On this day in 1939, those towns hosted the first public release of "The Wizard of Oz."

I love the scene where Dorothy and her friends return to Oz's palace with the Witch's broomstick. In the midst of booming voices, thunderclaps, and lightning bolts, Toto scurries over to that mystical stall and pulls back the curtain.

"Pay no attention to that man behind the curtain," the Wizard warns. But the game is over. There is no great and powerful Oz. There is only Oscar Zoroaster Diggs from Nebraska.

We have been told that God is a terrifying "wizard," more forbidding than all the dangers of the world. We might as well throw ourselves out his palace window to escape his terrors than to remain in his presence.

This is all smoke, mirrors, and megaphones, for Jesus has done something that even the legendary Toto could not accomplish. He didn't pull the curtain back, he tore it asunder, showing us a God who isn't playing games or hiding his true identity.

In Christ, God decided he would no longer allow his reputation to be misrepresented. He would present himself as a mere mortal that he might enter our sufferings and undo the chaos of creation.

The coming of Jesus into the world was the coming of God into the world. And the cross of Jesus, in all of its foolish glory, did not change God – he has always been in love with humanity – it changed us.

With no heavy curtain obscuring our perspective, we see that God is more gracious, more wonderful, more welcoming, and more loving than we previously imagined; there is no reason to be afraid of him. He welcomes us home, and there's no place like it.

August 26: The Gospel According to Jesus

When Jesus began preaching his gospel in the Galilean hills, his message was clear and singular: "The Kingdom of God is at hand. It is here and now," he said. "It is today."

Jesus' intention, it seems, was not to rescue people from earth, per se, transporting them to a far-removed heaven. His intention was to put heaven inside of people. A gospel that ignores this fact – and this current world – because our status in the next world has been properly secured, is a distortion of Jesus' redeeming message.

Thus, the gospel according to Jesus, is not just about a harp-playing, cloud-riding, hymn-singing, glory-praising, pie-in-the-sky heaven. It is holistic, all-encompassing deliverance, now. I'm not denying the existence of the afterlife; but I do not believe that we have to die to personally experience the life God has for us.

Jesus' first disciples did not have the benefit of two-thousand years of Christian tradition and theology. All those disciples had were Jesus' words: "Follow me, for the Kingdom of God is at hand." They had no promises of a big heavenly payoff. No fluttering angels' wings, no crossing over the River Jordan to the Hallelujah Shore, no promises of golden streets or pearly gates, no "full assurance that you will go to heaven when you die." All they had was the invitation of Jesus to "Follow me." For them, that was enough.

I believe that how Jesus taught us to live and the life he has to give, is the greatest hope for the present. He offers redemption, in all its magnificent and diverse manifestations, as more than the blessed hope of heaven. He offers it as the blessed hope for today, because today – not tomorrow – is the day of salvation.

August 27: Christian Savages

The Barna Group, a long-tenured research organization that tracks "spiritual indicators" has declared Providence, Rhode Island as the most "unbiblical" city in America. This should come as no surprise, given Rhode Island's history. The state began as a haven for those who had been mistreated by strict biblicists - "Bible-Minded" people. Rhode Island's founder, Roger Williams, arrived in Massachusetts more than a century before the American Revolution.

Originally he was part of the Puritan effort to build that famed "City on a Hill," a divinely instituted nation where everyone would be "Bible-minded." But Williams relentlessly preached liberty of conscience and freedom from religious conformity.

Finding no home for his "radical" ideas, Williams eventually founded Rhode Island. And it was exactly that: An island, a sanctuary for all kinds of religious dissidents in the earliest years of the American colonies, surrounded by the stormy waters of zealous extremism. Jews. Quakers. Baptists. Catholics. Atheists.

They came in manifold and variegated expressions, and Roger Williams, this nation's first Founding Father of toleration and liberty, welcomed them all, in spite of being viciously hated by New England's religious establishment.

It was no wonder, then, when Massachusetts Governor, John Winthrop, asked Roger to recant of his beliefs, Roger responded, "I cannot; for I feel safer among the Christian savages, than I do among savage Christians."

Ironically, Roger Williams never lost his Christian faith, and to the end of his life, he was definitely a "Bible-minded" man. Maybe, if he were alive today, he would wish that more of his neighbors loved the Christian scriptures, but he would never force them to do so. He would say as he said: "Men's consciences ought never to be violated. For a religion that must be upheld by violence, is a religion that cannot be true."

August 28: Getting A Living

When Henry David Thoreau retreated to the woods of Walden he was wrestling with two questions, "How much is enough?" and more importantly, "What does it actually cost a person to obtain his or her possessions?"

His theory of personal economics came down to this: The cost of a thing is not the monetary price tag attached to it. It is the amount of one's life it takes to get it.

For example, if one wants a particular house, the sale price is not as important as the years it takes to pay for it. If one wants a car, a computer, a new iPhone, or designer label clothing; then the calculation involves more than the payments. Calculate how much time and life it will cost to acquire these things.

Quoting Thoreau he said, "If your trade is with the Celestial Empire" (his description for what Jesus called the Kingdom of God), "then very little is actually needed to live well and to be free.

"A modest home should be enough. Plain clothes will do. Instead of a hundred dishes, why not five; and reduce other things in proportion. Keep your accounts on your thumbnail. Simplify, simplify. And once you have secured the necessaries of life, then you can confront the true problems of life with freedom."

Thoreau brings us to the universal human ambition: We all just want to be free and happy. It's all a search for satisfaction. Is a "spirituality of satisfaction" too shallow? No, not if one is seeking genuine, soul-sustaining fulfillment.

But getting more won't get it done, because more and more of what is not good for you will only smother you. As Thoreau concluded, "There is no more fatal blunderer than he who consumes the greater part of life getting a living."

August 29: Be Careful

Coach John Wooden was the most successful men's basketball coach in NCAA history, winning an unprecedented 10 national championships at UCLA. More impressive than his coaching record, however, was his mentoring and leadership of the young men on his teams. He not only taught them how to play a game; he taught them how to live.

His teaching ranged from his "Pyramid of Success" - the attributes he felt people needed to succeed - to giving lessons for hours on how to put on socks (because little things matter and blisters sideline the best player). And he never allowed anyone's individual number to be retired because he believed so strongly in the concept of a team.

One of his most famous sayings goes like this: "Talent is God-given. Be humble. Fame is man-given. Be grateful. Conceit is self-given. Be careful." Then, he would tell this story to accompany his words:

Wooden and his UCLA Bruins won the first of their national championships in 1964. The game was played on Holy Saturday, the night before Easter, in Kansas City, Missouri. They celebrated late into the night, but on Easter morning, there was no way Wooden was going to miss church with his wife.

The couple was standing outside their hotel waiting on a cab to take them to church. Wooden says he was standing there thinking about the night before and the season that had just ended. He was so proud of his team and of himself. Then, out of nowhere, a pigeon flew over and pooped on top of his head, as if he were the only bombing target in Missouri.

He said, "I think the Good Lord was saying, 'Don't get carried away.'" The lesson stuck for the rest of his career. It's a good lesson for everyone.

August 30: Rohr And Remus

Richard Rohr says that spiritual transformation is most often achieved through great pain - emotional or physical. The pain strips away our defenses and forces us to "let go" of the things that keep us from growing. With Rohr, Uncle Remus teaches us the same lesson.

Remus was the fictional narrator of a collection of African-American folktales compiled by Joel Harris. Harris published them to showcase the unparalleled wit, intelligence, and resiliency of African slaves.

In Remus' perennial story, B'rer Fox constructs a doll made of tar and turpentine to capture B'rer Rabbit. Rabbit becomes so entangled in the trap he can't move. Fox begins to contemplate how to best do away with his enemy. Rabbit says, "Whatever you do, don't throw me in the briar patch!"

Fox does exactly that; grabbing the tar-covered Rabbit, he heaved him into the briar patch and waited for the whimpers of pain and death. After a few minutes Fox heard someone calling his name.

He turned around and there was Rabbit! He was sitting on a log combing his clean fur with a wood chip. The briars had pulled away all the stickiness that had ensnared him. "I was bred and born in the briar patch, B'rer Fox," said Rabbit. And he skipped away - Remus says - "as merry as a cricket."

Sometimes the only way to be rid of the things that have gripped you is to go into the briar patch. It's the great pain of the thorns and thistles; the chaos of being tumbled head over heels and landing with a thump; the shattering, ripping, and tearing, that leads to a less encumbered life.

To be as "merry as a cricket," you can't avoid pain. Your suffering, ultimately, will set you free from the things that have kept you trapped.

August 31: Never Failing

"Love is the irresistible desire to be irresistibly desired," said Robert Frost. Love is "when you can't fall asleep because reality is better than your dreams," quipped Dr. Seuss.

Love is an "incurable disease," wrote Thoreau, "for which there is no remedy but to love more." Plato, more pessimistic, said "love is a serious mental disease," and Shakespeare was the first to say, "love is blind." The Beatles said it was "all you need."

Emily Dickinson called it "pure immortality" and Tina Turner said it was a "second-hand emotion." Charlie Brown said love was being "able to share your popcorn," while Captain and Tennille sang that "love will keep us together," though the couple divorced after 39 years of marriage.

The Apostle Paul's definition has stood the test of time like no other. He wrote, in part: "Love is patient, kind, never possessive, and is not arrogant. Love does not take into account a wrong suffered. It bears all things, believes all things, hopes all things, and endures all things. Love never fails."

We can make Paul's definition even more real-world like this: "Love is the combination of patience, kindness, assurance, sacrifice, honesty, and perseverance.

How do you know if what you are feeling is "love?" If it is characterized by patience, kindness, assurance, sacrifice, honesty, and perseverance, then it very well could be.

So forget all these slushy, Hallmark card definitions: "Love is never having to say you are sorry" or "Love means we never have to argue." That's ridiculous. And "I love you because you are my hero." Well, get back to me when your superman or superwoman stumbles over a chunk of kryptonite.

Love is much more of a profound, unyielding commitment than a whirlwind of emotion. Emotions change, but love - real love - never fails.

SEPTEMBER

September 1: Back To School

The Buddha said, "When the student is ready, the teacher will appear." Well, ready or not, teachers are showing up in classrooms everywhere. It's time to crack open the books, slip the surly bonds of summer, and head back to school.

My counsel is to stay in school as long as you can – not to avoid employment – but to learn all you can. And more so, to learn to become a learner: For when you stop learning, you've stopped living.

We are always in school, or at least we should be, and those who feel they have matriculated to the point - in life or faith - where we think we know it all, or at least we know enough, we haven't graduated. We have quit.

We become fixated, immature masters of minutia, nothing more, and life grows incredibly small - looking like old men and women stuffed into preschoolers' chairs. Mystery is murdered, discoveries die, and gone is the joy and excitement of new, daily revelation.

How many treasures are forfeited by those who "know that they know that they know," but they have learned nothing new in decades? In the words of Russian giant Leo Tolstoy, "Even the strongest current of water cannot add a drop to a cup which is already full."

Maybe the always returning school year is an act of redemption, really, for we get another chance to learn our lessons; to take the same course, again and again if necessary, so we can get it right; to pick up the material that we have not yet mastered or refused to heed, and to go deeper.

In life's classroom the lessons must be learned for our own maturation and well-being, and the Teacher knows this. He is giving us every opportunity to succeed – if only we will.

September 2: This Is Going To Be Good

Communion. Some call it the Eucharist; the Lord's Supper; or the Sacrament of the Altar. The terms used by Christians are varied. But regardless of the theological technicalities involved, it's how we come to the table that is more important.

I was reminded of this when I attended an Episcopal service where a friend is the minister. It was a magnificent experience of sights, sounds, and beautifully orchestrated liturgy; so much unlike anything of my own Christian tradition, and infinitely more formal than my freewheeling approach.

It took me a while to catch on and to catch up. I sluggishly stood, always a few seconds behind the crowd, and wound up standing alone, dropping to the pew after everyone else took their seat. I fumbled with the order of worship, never able to find the readings or the songs on time. After the homily, and a number of other confusions, the invitation was offered to receive Holy Communion.

Finally something I understood! But I wondered: "Will I be welcomed?" because churches have tons of rules about who can and can't participate - even fellow believers. I gladly discovered that the invitation was for all. Even those who felt out of place had a place at the table.

As I knelt at the altar I was joined by a young family; dad, mom, and three small children. The youngest, four or five years old, stood right beside me at the rail, too short to kneel. I looked at him and smiled. He smiled in return, wiped his wet lips with the back of his tiny hand and coarsely whispered, in a voice that could have been heard at the back of the sanctuary, "This is going to be good!" And it was, because it's always good to be welcomed to the table.

September 3: Run The Race

Life is a race, a race best run with this biblical instruction taken to heart: "Strip off what slows you down and run the race God has set before you."

Just imagine a track meet where a gaggle of runners step onto the track and some are grotesquely overweight, looking more like sumo wrestlers than sprinters. Some are wearing stiff denim skirts and long, heavy canvas pants.

Others have on high heels or work boots. One is pushing a grocery cart full of junk food. Another has a backpack on her back. Some are carrying books; and some are dragging duffle bags. The starter pistol fires and the group lurches forward with no one staying in his or her lane. They crash, stumble, and fall over each other pushing and shoving.

One cuts through the infield trying to be the first to cross the finish line, though he's obviously cheating. Another runs straight to the concession stand for a chili dog and fried pickles. Another heads to the stands to visit with his family and friends who have come to see him "run" the race. A few stop just steps past the starting line to post their selfies on Facebook. It's a massive disaster.

That's how life is. Very few people ever get around to actually running. They are incompetent at living. Out of shape. Unfocused. Easily distracted. Always found in the shadow of the ice cream truck. And they wonder why life seems so hard - why they never seem to be getting anywhere - why faith is such a burden.

If you aren't in shape to run, throw off anything extra you are carrying, anything that will trip you up, and focus on running. You will run yourself "into shape," and find life lighter than it has ever been before.

September 4: Deep Water

Our spiritual journeys look something like what I saw one afternoon at a local water park. There was a kid, well past the toddler age, who caught my attention. He was almost as tall as I am, and was playing in the kiddy pool.

Sometimes he would venture into the ankle depths of the wave pool, but no further. He was either incredibly afraid of water, something I can appreciate, or he had the most overprotective mother on the planet, something I am familiar with too.

He had a life jacket on (US Coast Guard approved, no doubt). He had smuggled in a pair of goggles and a snorkel. There was a whistle around his neck. I watched him for a long time, and every time I passed the wave pool area he would be there, thrashing about in the shallows or sitting in the shade of a massive umbrella.

I wanted to go up to him (or the parents) and say, "You're in the kiddy pool! Come ride the rapids. Come shoot the tubes with us. Launch out into the deep water. You're dressed for it. Come on, let's have some fun!"

Jesus extends the same invitation to us: "Do you want to see something extraordinary? Do you want to experience a depth of faith and spirituality that you have never known before? Do you want to launch into the deep blue sea, leaving behind the mediocrity you have lived in for years?

"Then quit clinging to the side. Quit building sandcastles next to the shallows. Quit wallowing around in the kiddy pool, pining over what you wish could be. Let go."

You are already dressed for adventure. It might scare the stuffing out of you, but if you head for deeper water, you'll never want to go back.

September 5: Wait For Your Soul

The first Labor Day celebration was observed in New York City in 1882, meant to honor "the contributions workers have made to the strength, prosperity, and well-being of our country." Not many years later, it became evident that the American worker was such an exceptional and efficient creature, that work hours would soon be reduced to mere shadows of their former oppression.

Economists predicted that technological advancements would soon lead to a 15-hour work week. In the mid-1960s, congressional leaders boldly predicted a two-day work week by the year 2000. Yet, the predictions of "less work more rest," are a farce for today's laborers.

In the book of Genesis, on that final day of the first week, God rested. The word for rest means "to renew the spirit." Lettie Cowman, a devotional writer from a century ago, illustrates this with one of her stories from Africa.

She wrote about an Englishman who was exploring the deepest jungles, traveling like British royalty. He had so many possessions he had to hire an army of strong men from the local villages to portage his belongings through the jungle. On the first day of his grand safari he pushed the laborers at an exhausting pace. But on the second morning, the hired Africans refused to move.

Finally, one of the young men explained that they were not especially tired. Rather, they had gone too far and too fast on the first day, and had to "wait for their souls to catch up with their bodies."

Ms. Cowman concludes: "This whirling, rushing life which so many of us live does for us what that first march did for those poor tribesmen. But here is the difference: They knew what they needed to restore life's balance; too often we do not."

September 6: The Art Of Nothingness

I make a living using words – putting them on paper and ejecting them into the air. Being quiet is, by default, not my specialty. I wish it were different. I have always envied those who are quiet and meditative by nature.

That is my wish, but that is not my disposition. But, we ADD-types need some quiet here and there. We need to subdue our minds and soothe the chorus of voices inside our heads. But how? I can only return to a story involving Jesus and two sisters.

The two sisters were Mary and Martha who hosted Jesus in their home. Mary was a venerable St. Benedict, placid and peaceful, sitting at Jesus' feet in silence. Meanwhile, Martha was in the kitchen shaking and baking, jumping and jiving, busting her can while the more brooding types breathed the ether of serenity.

Martha's own ADD mind, being in overdrive as it always was, earned from Jesus an understanding, gentle rebuke. He effectively said (and I am paraphrasing here), "Martha, relax. It's okay to be busy, but don't overdo it. Do a few important things well; but let the rest of it go."

This is a prescription written by Jesus' own hand, for all us Martha-types who need a little less talk and a lot more contemplation: "Chill out. Take a walk. Linger over your coffee a few more minutes each morning."

Yes, we who are the hard-driving, multi-tasking, goal-orienting, noise-making, word-emitting Marthas of the world would do well to learn the art of nothingness. By creating times of quiet on our calendars and in our lives, we might not be transformed into spiritual mystics, but we might discover that God is easier to hear, for in the quiet places God will certainly speak.

September 7: The Blitz

"The Blitz," was a decimating bombing campaign launched by Nazi Germany against London beginning September 7, 1940. More than 30,000 bombs fell on the city over the next four months.

Hitler believed the "Blitz" would so terrorize Londoners that the country would collapse. The British government, including the bulldog Winston Churchill, predicted the same. They estimated that a sustained German bombing attack would kill 600,000, leave a million wounded, and would create such mass panic, that the city would be abandoned.

People would refuse to go to work. Industrial production would grind to a halt. The army would be useless against the Germans because it would be keeping order among the hysterical civilians. The government even set up psychiatric hospitals just outside the city limits to handle what they expected would be a flood of psychological casualties.

But the panic never came. London faced the bombing, not only with courage, but defiance. Yes, several thousand were killed. A million people lost their homes. The city crammed itself into bomb shelters every night. There was the constant thunder of planes, explosions, and sirens; but the bombing had the opposite effect intended. They were emboldened from within, not crushed from without.

"For God did not give us a spirit of fear," the Apostle Paul wrote to Timothy. "It's not a spirit of cringing and fawning terror. He has given us a spirit of power, of love, and a sound mind."

You can count on your world being shattered from time to time and fear will threaten to overwhelm you. Yet, you have within you the antidote. It is a God-given power, the sense of calm and confidence. Outer troubles will activate it from within, and though you may not know wit now, it will be there when you need it most.

September 8: Your Life Will Outlive You

My great-grandmother was Ola Whitfield, a simple woman born in the 19th century. She worked hard, was sparsely educated, remained anonymous to the greater world, birthed a farmhouse full of children, and died young.

Her obituary, written in the vibrant language of the time, captures her simple faith. It reads, "Ola left true evidence of her faith: She called her husband to her side and told him that she would have loved to stay with him and help raise the children. She told him to raise them right. Such a consolation to us all."

Granted, raising children "right," is no guarantee that said children will turn out well. That wasn't Ola's point. In her unpretentious way, she understood the profound truth that she would live on in those who followed her. So she was being intentional, planning for her life to outlive her.

In our "what have you done for me lately world," where time is measured by quarterly dividend reports or in two-year election cycles, we forget that the fruit of one's life may reach maturity only after many years, decades, or even centuries. It could be that those whom we will never meet, those who will walk in our footsteps generations from now, will be the ones to gain the most from our lives.

So when I read my great-grandmother's obituary, I am thankful; thankful for her and the ones who have gone before me. I am grateful that those who never dreamed of me or my children, made decisions and lived in a way that bettered our future.

And all this reminds me that, as the generations proceed, whether I like it or not, others will rely upon me and you for the same. Your life will outlive you. Make it a good one.

September 9: Keeping Your Hands Clean

Ask a group of people if they all washed their hands after using the restroom and most of that group will say "yes," and most of that group, disgustingly, will be lying. This includes medical professionals.

The administration at Cedars-Sinai Medical Center in Los Angeles knew this about their staff doctors and nurses, and sought to create a safer environment for everyone.

They used strongly worded memos about hand washing; offered rewards; threatened and compensated; but nothing seemed to work. Then one of the administrators had a brilliant idea: She placed her unwashed hand in a petri dish and sent it to the lab. It turned up a massive collection of bacteria.

The bacteria covered hand was converted into a colorful, digital image and disseminated throughout the hospital as computer backgrounds and screen savers. So when a staffer went to use a computer, there was this shocking, nefarious hand in his or her face, covered with bacteria screaming: "This is what your unwashed hand looks like!" The hygiene rate at Cedars-Sinai went to virtually 100% and the program became a tremendous success.

One of the takeaways from this case, besides the fact that medical professionals need to wash their hands more often, is that human behavior doesn't change easily. Threats of punishment or hopes of reward aren't enough.

Until a person sees up close and in shocking detail how destructive his current behavior is, that person is not likely to change. A person must be confronted with his or her ugly, unhealthy way of life; it must jolt him, knock him off balance, and shake a dirty finger in his face.

Then, there is the possibility that a person will make the first steps in the direction of vital, substantial change - but he must see it for himself.

September 10: To Be Godly

A man was going from Indianapolis, Indiana, to Louisville, Kentucky, when he was robbed and left for dead. A Baptist pastor, on his way home from the annual meeting of his denomination, saw the man. But he had a report to deliver to his congregation about the resolutions passed at the meeting he had just attended, so he did not stop.

A Bishop of the Methodist church drove by. She concluded that such meaningless acts of violence were likely perpetrated by dangerous gangs of teenagers who were without the proper Judeo-Christian guidance. She never looked back.

Then a third traveler came upon the victim: A illegal citizen, a man with booze on his breath, marijuana in his bloodstream, and who hadn't been to Mass since he was a child. He was moved with compassion, and triaged the wounded man, and drove him to the hospital. Which of these three was a neighbor to the man who fell into the hands of robbers?

Of course neither the question nor the story is mine. They belong to Jesus. In the parable of the Good Samaritan Jesus framed as radical a possibility conceivable by the community of his day - far more drastic than anything here. He took a known pariah and turned him into a hero - all at the expense of the upright church-goers.

Jesus told such a story to show what love looks like. Those who do not fit into our religious boxes or our precise definitions of right and wrong are sometimes the most godly.

For to be godly is to love. And to love, one need not have perfect doctrine or be morally pure. No, to love like God is to dirty our hands by helping our neighbors – "to do unto others" what we would want for ourselves.

September 11: The Last Word

Rabbi Irwin Kula collected an assembly of audio recordings in the days after the September 11th terrorist attacks; final conversations of those in the towers as they called to leave voicemails for loved ones. All the final conversations he had in his collection were about love.

Not a single person used his or her last breath to express hate or vengeance toward the perpetrators. Every last word was an "I love you" of some variety. Kula said, "Then I recognized that the real experience behind religion is love. It's no more complicated than that."

God isn't much into religion - not in light of Jesus. He's not interested in carving up the world along tribal lines, declaring winners and losers in who can most strongly declare how right they are.

Rather, Jesus came to reveal God's love to us, and to show us that love is the beginning, the means, the path, and the end; it's the only road to travel. I suppose this makes me an "exclusivist;" one who denies that all religious paths are equal and simply have their own unique twists and turns along the way.

No, I do not believe such a thing, for the morbid irony is that religion brought down those iconic towers on September 11th. Hard. Inflexible. Dogmatic. Immovable religion (And such religion can be perpetuated as easily by those called Christians as any other group).

God surely can't be associated with anything of the sort, no matter what name it is called or however right and correct it purports to be. God must be - absolutely must be - in what is loving, absolving, and just, not destructive. For love is what saves us. It is what gives us life. It is the only thing that overcomes hate and injustice. It is the last word.

September 12: Free Indeed

The enslavement of Africans was not unique to the United States. For three centuries, well before this atrocity culminated in our own Civil War, the British slave trade had been bringing Africans to the Western Hemisphere.

This trade is said to have drawn between ten and twenty million Africans from their homeland, with more than 500,000 going to European colonies throughout the greater Caribbean. These colonies belonged to the French, Dutch, Portuguese, and Spanish - making most of Western Europe culpable.

But the British carried many of these slaves to their own colony of Jamaica, where men, women, and children were worked to death on the sugar, coffee, and tobacco plantations. It was only through the lifelong determination of British leaders like William Wilberforce, Thomas Clarkson, Hannah More, and others, that the English slave trade was finally abolished.

British Parliament passed the "Slave Trade Abolition Bill" in 1807, and in Jamaica, effective January 1, 1808, the plantation slaves were set free.

A story is told that on the night before their freedom would be realized, a large group of Jamaican slaves gathered on the beach outside of Kingston. They were not there to protest or to wage revolt. They were there to celebrate.

They brought with them the strange combination of shackles and chains, musical instruments, drums, and a large coffin. Singing, dancing, and making music, one by one the set-free slaves filed by and dumped their chains into the coffin. Then, they dug a grave in the sand and quite literally, buried the chains.

An act of bravery and sacrifice across the sea, by men they had never met face to face, had won their freedom. And they would never go back to slavery again.

Neither will we, for those whom the Son has set free, are free indeed.

September 13: Right Here, Right Now

Kim Il-Sung, known as the "Great Leader" in North Korea, succeeded with his communist revolution in creating one of the more closed and oppressive societies in history; it remains so decades later under his grandson.

It did not have to be this way, for Il-Sung was raised in a Christian family. Why did Kim Il-Sung turn away from faith? He answers: "Many people believed that they would go to Heaven and Jesus would save them from their earthly misery. Thus, I thought Christian doctrines were too far off the mark to address our problems."

Il-Sung experienced a disconnection between the actual message of the Christian gospel and the sufferings of the world. This rendered the faith anemic and unable to address life's evils.

It does seem that Christianity has been neutered of its revolutionary power. It offers people a chance to forget their pain and suffering (and the suffering of others) for a little while, and focuses all of the faithful's attention on the sweet-by-and-by. This leaves only the "leftovers" for this world, a world that stands in need of true revolution today, not tomorrow.

This world is not well served by a faith that sleeps soundly in the confidence that believers will soon be evacuated, all because the world is so bad and the "end is near." And there is little time to celebrate our personal salvation when the urgent misery of our world calls out to us for help.

The love of Christ surely compels us to participate in the revolutionary transformation of the world; bringing the world-redeeming, evil-conquering, personal-transforming presence of heaven to earth today. There's no need to wait. We can join the revolution of love that will change the world – right here, right now – today.

September 14: What Love Fixes

Some time ago my wife was having a very bad day. Things at work were difficult. There were family issues. There was more month than money. The house was a wreck. Our children were defying her. I was ignoring her. She was reduced to tears.

I put my arms around her and said, "But honey, I love you." She pushed me away and said, "That doesn't fix anything!" And she was right. My love for her didn't shut up bawling children. It didn't magically put more money in our checking account. It didn't turn the dunce she worked with into Mother Teresa.

But what we ultimately agreed upon, after I got over the shock of being rebuffed, is that while love changes nothing about our circumstances, love changes us. It gives us the strength to face what is out there, even if what is out there appears unbearable. Love sustains us, encourages us; it gives us what we really need: The ability to keep going.

That's what God's love does. It keeps going and keeps us going. It endures forever, and for that, we are forever grateful. We are not alone. We are not abandoned. We are not forgotten. God is with us. We are loved.

If given this choice, which would you take: To have all your problems solved, all your struggles worked out, and all your troubles flushed away; or, would you choose to be deeply, unconditionally, and madly loved?

I think I know your answer. And that answer is the reason why we "keep on, keeping on," even in a world with more problems than solutions, more bills than money, and more questions than answers.

We won't get everything we want in this world, but we will be loved. That won't "fix" anything – but love is enough.

September 15: The Rabbi's Gift

A monastery fell into decline. Only a few old monks remained. The abbot decided to visit a rabbi who would occasionally seek retreat in a cabin deep in the monastery woods. Knowing the rabbi was a deeply spiritual man, the abbot would open his heart to him and ask for advice.

When he arrived, it was as if the rabbi had been awaiting the abbot's arrival. The two simply sat in the stillness. Finally, the rabbi spoke, "I know why you have come, but I have no answers. It is the same in my town; almost no one comes to the synagogue anymore."

The time came for the abbot to leave, so he pressed the rabbi: "Is there nothing you can say to help me save our dying monastery?" The rabbi whispered, "Well, there is one thing: One of you is the Messiah."

The abbot called his monks together the next morning. He told them bluntly, "The rabbi said that one of us is the Messiah." In the weeks that followed, the old monks thought about the rabbi's words and wondered whether it could actually be true.

Thinking like this, the monks began to treat each other with extraordinary respect on the off chance that one of them just might actually be the Messiah. A gentle concern began to grow among them.

Over time, as people visited the beautiful forest surrounding the monastery, they sensed the extraordinary joy that radiated from the place. People began to visit more frequently.

Then some of the younger men who visited began talking with the old monks. Then one joined them. Then another. And another. Within years the monastery had once again become a thriving community, thanks to the rabbi's gift, a gift that taught them to look for the very best in others.

September 16: The Pearl

John Steinbeck wrote a novella called *The Pearl*. It begins with a poor Mexican pearl diver named Kino who happily ekes out a living with his wife and son, owning nothing but a little canoe and a beachside hut.

When Kino's child is bitten by a scorpion, his world is turned upside down; he doesn't have enough money to pay a doctor to treat the child or to pay a priest to pray. At this moment, Kino discovers a pearl as big as his fist, the most incredible treasure the village has ever seen.

Now Kino will be rich. His son will be healed. Life will be transformed. But, things don't work out that way. Greed takes over the village. Thieves attempt to rob him. Kino's friends grow psychotically jealous. Kino begins to spend all his energies protecting his treasure.

In the end Kino loses everything: His home, his child, his little canoe by which he made a living, and his ability to escape to a better life. He and his wife stand on the shoreline and heave the evil pearl back into the ocean. Steinbeck's little story is a tale of human nature; it is about getting what one wants, only to discover that getting it, turns into one's undoing.

We all enter this world seeking. The search is intrinsic, natural, and good. Jesus spoke of it in a way that Steinbeck copied: We are searching for the "Pearl of Great Price." The glitch is that many of the things we seek are detrimental to us.

My guess is that much of our suffering is the direct result of misguided searching. We go "looking for love in all the wrong places," and when we go looking in all the wrong places, we end up with all the wrong outcomes.

September 17: First And Last

Jesus once told a story about a landowner who hired laborers to harvest grapes. Some employees worked all day, others labored for part of the day, and some arrived at the last hour. The landowner, inexplicably, pays them all the same wage. This doesn't seem very fair.

Imagine the scene: The tired workers form a line at the end of the day to receive their wages. When the Human Resources Director arrives with their paychecks, everyone is paid the same! There is the threat of a labor riot or at least a lawsuit for unfair labor practices. The landowner gives this response, "I haven't been unfair! Should you be jealous because I am kind?"

It is a direct and accurate reply, for the angry workers were not enraged over injustice. They were angry because the landowner was generous to those who had not "earned" their way. The landowner gave grace – making the last equal to the first – and this infuriated the other workers.

We often preach grace, but we don't always practice it. We talk about God's mercy, but we don't always want the people who need it most to get it. We say we are in the redemption business, but we are not eager to open the doors to all potential patrons.

Landon Saunders says it like this: "Figuring out who is in and who is out is just too much work. It's too heavy of a burden! Just try to treat every person you meet as if they will be sitting at the table with you in eternity."

That small change of perspective would do more to advance the kingdom of God on earth than a thousand aggrieved churches that pound their pulpits, point fingers, and exclude others from the love of God and the gates of heaven.

September 18: A Tale Of Two Statues

At New York City's Rockefeller Center, in addition to the legendary ice rink and television cameras, you will find a statue of the Greek Titan, Atlas. The ironworks piece of art is some 15 feet tall and weighs several thousand pounds.

You might remember that Atlas, in Greek mythology was a one of the Titans who waged war against the gods of Olympus. Zeus punished him for his defiance by placing the weight of the heavens and the earth upon his shoulders. As the legend goes, he is forced to groan beneath that burden for all eternity.

But leave Rockefeller Center and go across Fifth Avenue. There, you will find St. Patrick's Cathedral. There in a quiet enclave, behind the altar and away from the tourist traffic is a small stature of the boy Jesus.

It captures him as he made his visit to the temple and wowed the religious leaders of his day – stunned as they were that he knew the things he knew. This statue has Jesus holding the world in one tiny childish hand.

These two statues form a vivid and accurate contrast; even more so in the arena of faith. On the one hand we can live out the burdensome Christian life as if we were Atlas, condemned to groan under the weight of obligation, labor, and religious exertion. It's a weight that requires a Titan's strength to be sure.

Or, on the other hand, we can rest in the fact that Christ carries it all for us, simply and surely in the palm of his hand, if only we will let him.

Following Jesus is not about our personal strength. It is about our submission and dependence upon him, relying upon his power. Faith is not an obligation. It is the lifting of our burdens.

September 19: You Have To Trust Somebody

On a trip through the Midwest, I stopped for lunch in the megalopolis of Carmi, Illinois (population 5,240, but I mostly saw only scarecrows). While eating, my dog locked me out of my rental. My waitress said, "Don't worry. I'll call Rick. Trust me." I cringed.

Rick showed up, walking out of the cornfields like Kevin Costner, and for $20 and with the words, "Trust me" (There it was again!), he had me going quicker than you can say "Carmi." I kissed my waitress, tipped Rick $40, and jumped back on the road.

Then I had a blowout on the rental car in a place even more remote than Carmi. My joy drive through the American heartland devolved into a living hell, and frankly, I never want to see another Illinois cornfield ever again.

Still, it could have been much worse. Where would my dog and I have been without the helpful waitress who knew just who to call; without Rick, and his door-jimmying abilities; without the customer service rep at the rental agency who told me over the phone, "Trust me (Again!); it's going to be okay"?

It would have been an even more rotten experience without the unknown, unnamed person who wrote the rental van manual, explaining where to find the infernal spare tire; without the young man at a tire service center who was the epitome of kindness; and there was the waitress, who at the diner when it was all over, seemed to understand that ice cream makes all disasters just a bit more tolerable.

All along the way I met people – honest, good people – who asked only for my confidence, and I learned that you have to trust a few people every now and then if you are going to make it safely home.

September 20: I Knew You Would Come

Two young men, childhood friends who had grown up together, likewise enlisted together at the outbreak of World War 1. They ended up in the same Army unit and fought side by side.

During a vicious attack in the infamous "no-man's land" – an area full of trenches, foxholes, landmines, and barbed wire – one of them was cut down by gun fire. Mortally wounded, he couldn't get back to his trench line.

The area was under such pressure and gunfire it would prove fatal for anyone to attempt a rescue. Still, the life-long friend of the wounded soldier was going to try. But as he jumped from the trench to run across the battlefield, his sergeant grabbed him by the collar and sat him down.

"You will not go out there!" he ordered. "I need every man I have, and your friend is as good as dead. You can do nothing for him now." As soon as the sergeant turned around, however, the young man sprinted toward his dying friend.

The young soldier made it to his friend; he scooped him up and staggered back to the line, now mortally wounded by gunfire himself. His friend was already dead in his arms. The sergeant was furious, but he was also deeply moved.

Still, he blurted out to the young man, "What a waste! He is dead and you are dying! How could it have been worth it?" The dying man answered, "Oh, it was worth it, Sarge. When I got to him, he smiled and said, 'I knew you would come.'"

Friendship is nothing more than this: Being there for someone when they are most in need. If you have such a friend - just one - you are fortunate. If you have more than one, you are blessed beyond measure.

September 21: Kierkegaard's Parable

"A certain flock of geese lived together in a barnyard with high walls around it. Because the corn was good and the barnyard was secure, these geese never left the barnyard. One day a philosopher goose came among them. Every week they listened quietly and attentively to his discourses.

"'My fellow travelers on the way of life,' he would say, 'Can you seriously imagine that this barnyard, with its great high walls, is all there is to our existence? I tell you, there is a greater world outside, a world of which we are only dimly aware.

"'Our forefathers knew of this outside world. They would stretch their wings and fly across the deserts and oceans, the green valleys and the wooded hills. But alas, here we remain in this barnyard, our wings folded and tucked into our sides, as we are content to puddle in the mud, never lifting our eyes to the heavens which should be our home.'

"The geese thought this was very fine lecturing, poetic and profound. So often, this philosopher spoke of the advantages of flight and freedom, calling on the geese to be what they were. After all, they had wings, he pointed out.

"And what were these wings for, if not for flight? Often he reflected on the beauty and the wonder of life outside the barnyard, and the freedom of the skies. And every week the geese were uplifted, inspired, and moved by his message.

"They hung on his every word. They devoted hours, weeks, months to a thorough analysis and critical evaluation of his doctrines. They produced learned treatises on the ethical and spiritual implications of flight. All this they did.

"But one thing they never did: They did not fly. For the corn was good, and the barnyard was secure."

September 22: More Than We Can Bear

Chuck Jones created or produced some of the greatest cartoons ever made. His greatest creation might be the duo of "Wile E. Coyote and The Road Runner." In every episode the Road Runner would "Meep, Meep," escape, and Wile E. would go cascading off a cliff for the umpteenth time. But miraculously, he would never die.

Gravity wasn't his only challenge; he also suffered from those absurd contraptions he purchased from ACME, machinery he thought would help him catch his nemesis. None of them ever worked. But after each failure, and they were legion, Coyote would scrape himself off the desert floor and soldier on, "bloody but unbowed."

The Coyote's creator may have made him unflappable and indestructible, but our Creator did not provide us with such qualities. Life can be too much for us sometimes, and it's best to admit it. I know that cuts against the grain of our determined, conquering egos, but it is the truth.

There are simply too many falls off too many cliffs; too many stupid, self-inflicted wounds; too many times when we have had to spatula up what is left of us from the floor; too much exhausting pursuit without the pay off.

So, don't believe this proverb: "God won't put more on you than you can bear." The Bible never says such a thing, and life doesn't validate it either.

What do we do about it? Ask anyone who is in recovery. The steps that lead to healing begin with the confession that we "are powerless," and "only a Power greater than ourselves can restore us."

As this confession spills out on the ground like a catapulting Coyote going over a cliff, it is then - and only then - that God can do in us what we can't do on our own.

September 23: Heroes For Heroes

It was Dr. Alois Alzheimer who first diagnosed the "Disease of Forgetfulness." Today, the disease that bears his name affects more than 5 million Americans and the numbers continue to rise with our aging population.

Alzheimer's is no respecter of persons. It strikes the rich and the poor, the known and unknown. It even strikes our heroes. Like Pat Summitt, legendary coach of Tennessee's Lady Vols; Glenn Campbell, the award-winning country music artist; and famed boxer Sugar Ray Robinson.

There's my friend Betty who for 50 years has been her church's pianist. As Alzheimer's tightens its grip on her mind she still takes her seat on the bench to play Bach as confidently as she did decades earlier. Her church could afford a new pianist, but they want her to play for as long as she can, and they graciously accommodate her.

There is one of my personal and heroic mentors, Dr. Ron, who died from dementia. As his vigorous mind began to unravel, hundreds stepped forward to assist his wife and family – an entire community. And there is my own father-in-law who now wrestles with this disease.

The family will wrestle as well, at times smiling as he forgets a name; at other times weeping over stolen memories; and sometimes buckling beneath the weight of caring for one who was once capable of carrying the weight of the world on his shoulders.

But what other choice is there? When one has given his or her life to us, how can we not give a little of our life in return? Yes, some of our heroes will forget almost everything: Their accomplishments, the lives they once lived, and maybe our very names; but we cannot forget them, especially not now, because sometimes our heroes need a hero.

September 24: Holy Ignorance

Having lunch with friends we began talking about our earliest childhood memories. None of us could recall anything but flashbulb moments before our kindergarten years. At the time my friends' three-year-old son was sitting at the table with us.

His mother looked at him and said, "If something happened to me now, he would have no memory of me." Here was a child so devoted to and so dependent upon his mother that he can never be more than a few feet from her presence, and yet should she vanish, he would have no memory of her.

Does a child really know his mother? No. And yet, he does know her, better than anyone else. He is both in ignorance of the very one who gave him life and he cannot live without her. It is sancta ignorantia - holy ignorance. We all live in holy ignorance, even when we are "certain" about the things we believe. But we don't understand it all. We can't.

Paul recognized this when he prayed for the Ephesians, "May you have the power to understand how wide, how long, how high, and how deep Christ's love is. May you experience the love of Christ, though it is too great to understand fully."

When we speak of Christ we are speaking only of our limited experience with him. He remains out of reach. Yes, we know Jesus, but then we don't, and won't know him completely in this life. This doesn't weaken our faith. It pushes our faith forward. We press on in pursuit of more, because the faith we hold on to is incomplete.

So, the answer to the question, "Do you know Jesus?" is an absolute and positive, "Yes!" followed by an absolute and positive "No!" It's sancta ignorantia: Plead holy ignorance.

September 25: Recognition And Restoration

Denzel Washington starred in the movie "Flight," as Captain Whip Whitaker, a fictional, commercial airline pilot. When we first meet Captain Whitaker he is in a hotel room suffering from a terrible hangover, a hangover he remedies by snorting a line of cocaine, just before climbing aboard to guide his flight to Atlanta.

The flight crashes, not because Whitaker is drunk or jacked up on coke – though he is. The aircraft crashed because of mechanical failure. The Captain's efforts are regarded as heroic, as there are but a few casualties in the crash, but the curtain gets yanked aside on Whitaker's addictions.

While it could be said that the producers of the film took creative license with the flight and crash scenes of the movie, what the producers perfectly nailed is the nature of addiction. It devours. It gobbles up a person's well-being, uses up a person's identity, and enslaves.

In those moments of clarity, when one realizes that he can't keep living in these destructive cycles, he might decide to change. But such efforts to change almost always fail, because recognizing the problem is simply not enough. Rather, transformation is accomplished by giving up what is unhealthy, and replacing it with what is whole.

This is what Bill Wilson, co-founder of Alcoholics Anonymous, was talking about when he articulated the steps toward sobriety. There must be not only recognition, but acknowledgment of powerlessness and surrender to a Higher Power who can restore health and sanity.

This is the counterintuitive way of the cross; the paradoxical power of Christ: We only live once we have died. We only gain by giving up. We only win if we surrender. The quicker we get to that point, the quicker we can be restored and get to the joy of living.

September 26: On The Brink

On September 26, 1983, civilization came perilously close to ending. The Cold War was anything but cold, as the USSR had shot down Korea Air Flight 007 when it strayed near Soviet airspace, killing all 269 on board including Congressman Larry McDonald.

With passions running high, one of the greatest heroes of our time quietly went to work at a Moscow military base. His name was Lieutenant Colonel Stanislav Petrov. It was Petrov's duty to monitor the Soviet alert system in the event of a nuclear attack by the US, and launch an immediate counterattack.

On that September evening, Colonel Petrov's computer alarms sounded, warning of incoming American missiles. Petrov waited. Then a second warhead was detected; a third, a fourth, and a fifth. Still, Petrov had a "feeling in his gut," that the alert system was malfunctioning. Further, it was unthinkable, for him, that he would be the one extinguishing so much life.

So, Petrov did nothing but wait - a full agonizing hour - with alarms blaring the entire time. He was right. There were no missiles. The warning system had indeed malfunctioned. Singlehandedly, Petrov had prevented nuclear war, simply by not becoming a participant in it.

"Do all that you can to live in peace with everyone," Paul said. This is redemptive counsel for us all. No, not every individual skirmish has the potential to balloon into a global apocalypse, but worldwide wars are not that much different than private ones. It's the same reactionary game; the same wounded pride demanding to be assuaged.

Likewise, there is the same chance to step away from the brink. In every conflict someone has the opportunity to do nothing, and break the cycle of vengeance; someone can reject the established protocol of retaliation; someone can practice peace. Let that someone be you.

September 27: Unleashed

Two young men were scavenging a demolished medical clinic in Goianaia, Brazil, looking to salvage something whereby they might make a few dollars. They found a bulky machine which they sold to a junk dealer for $25.

The dealer disassembled the machine and found a stainless steel cylinder inside, about the size of a paint can. Inside the cylinder was a crumbly powder that glowed mysteriously blue. Thinking the magic material was "supernatural," he took it home and showed it to his friends and family.

It was not "magic," however. It was cesium-137, one of the world's most dangerous radioactive isotopes. The salvaged machine had once been used to give cancer patients their radiation treatments. Four people died of poisoning, hundreds were contaminated, and the Brazilian government had to screen more than 100,000 people for radioactive exposure. The Goianaia incident remains one of the world's worst nuclear disasters.

A machine intended to heal the body became an instrument of death. This is a powerful metaphor for what religion can become. Faith begins with material taken from a holy book, a source that brings spiritual healing and wholeness. But misapplied and mishandled, it can become an unleashed poison. Is there any better description for "religion gone bad" in our world today?

Extremists. Terrorists. Violence by Muslims, Christians, and Jews - none of the monotheistic faiths are immune - for the sake of ideology. Jihads. Crusades. Holy wars. It all becomes a deadly, toxic mess when religion is weaponized, regardless if the name Mohammed, Jesus, or Moses is invoked.

What is the solution? The answer is millennia old, "The Lord has made it plain how to live, and he has shown you all that is required: 'Do what is right, love mercy, and walk humbly with your God.'" That's enough religion for anybody.

September 28: The War Within

One evening an old Cherokee educated his grandson, who would soon become a brave, about warfare - the fierce war waged within each and every person. He said, "My son, the battle is between the two wolves that live inside us all.

"One is evil. It is angry, envious, jealous, sorrowful, greedy, and arrogant. It wallows in self-pity, regret, guilt, and resentment. It gains energy from feelings of inferiority, falsehood, and pride.

"The other wolf is good. It is joyful, peace-loving, hopeful and serene. It is energized by love, humility, kindness, truth and generosity. It is these two beasts that most often meet in battle."

The grandson thought about this for a moment and then asked, "Grandfather, which wolf will win?" The elderly Cherokee answered, "The one you feed."

The Apostle Paul said very much the same thing, summarizing the human condition. He wrote, "The power of sin within me keeps sabotaging my best intentions. I decide to do good, but I don't really do it; I decide not to do bad, but then I do it anyway. Something has gone wrong deep within me and gets the better of me every time.

"The moment I decide to do good, sin is there to trip me up. I truly delight in God's commands, but parts of me covertly rebel, and just when I least expect it, they take charge. There is a war within my mind."

Alexander Solzhenitsyn wrote the same: "The line separating good and evil passes not through states, nor between classes, nor between political parties - but right through every human heart - and through all human hearts."

We are all the combination of darkness and light, good and evil, right and wrong. We take heed to which of these we feed, for the strongest will always win.

September 29: A Better World

My friend Charles spent the last decade of his life as the Director of Student Services in my hometown school district, on the front lines of advocacy for some of the most vulnerable children in the community. When he died of leukemia some years ago, his friends gathered on a scraggly piece of land along the Tallapoosa River in north Georgia for his memorial service.

He loved that piece of land and the river that runs through it. He used it as his sanctuary. I use the word "sanctuary" intentionally, for Charles would rarely enter a church. He had lost a good deal of faith in politics, education, matrimony, and he seemed to have lost the most faith in religion.

Yet, Charles never lost his hope for living in a better world. He tirelessly worked for nothing less than the Kingdom of God (though he disagreed with my terminology).

I believe that one day all of creation will be remade; that the world will be washed clean and all things will be made right. But I do not believe such faith gives me permission to be a spectator waiting for utopia. Such faith compels me to act, as Charles did, living as God would have this world to be. Such faith invites me, not to wish for a brighter future, but to live it.

It never troubled me that Charles didn't go to church on Sundays. Rather, it encouraged me that he did God's work every day. I was never bothered by his claims to have no faith. Rather, I was challenged by how he actually practiced his faith.

Not all of God's work is done within the four walls of the church house. In fact, most of it is done outside. That is where it is needed the most.

September 30: Wounded Faith

Eli Wiesel, born on this day in 1928, survived the horror of the German Holocaust. After losing his entire family and six million of his countrymen, Wiesel also lost his faith in God. Who could blame him after all he had seen and experienced?

For years Wiesel refused to speak of his sufferings, but friends ultimately convinced him to put his pain on paper. He wrote, "Never shall I forget that first night in camp which turned my life into one long night, seven times cursed and seven times sealed. Those moments murdered my God and my soul and turned my dreams to dust. Never shall I forget these things. Never."

But over the years, God wouldn't go away. The heart that had been a stone cracked, and Wiesel's faith was reborn. Sixty years after the Holocaust, he said in a speech, "I have decided that one must wager on the future; and now believe it is possible to believe in God even in a world where there has been an eclipse of God's face."

After that speech a reporter asked Eli: "After seeing and suffering so much, do you still have faith in God as the ultimate redeemer?" He replied: "I would be within my rights to give up faith in God, and I could invoke six million reasons to justify such a decision. But I am incapable of straying from the path. My wounded faith endures."

Few people who read these words will ever suffer as Nobel Laureate Eli Wiesel, yet, many have had their faith wounded - those times that God seemed dead, or at least, it felt as if his face was "eclipsed." Don't put too much pressure on the wounded to "just believe." Let God do his work; only he can heal the most monstrous wounds.

OCTOBER

October 1: The Little Way

Jesus said: "The Kingdom of God belongs to those who are like children." If you want to get somewhere spiritually, you do not get there by clawing your way to the top. You humble yourself, because you have to get small to fit through the door that leads to the kingdom.

Thankfully, from time to time, God gifts the church with those rare individuals who remind us of Jesus' words. One of those people was a French teenager who lived a century ago named Therese Martin, better known today as St. Therese of Lisieux.

As a teenager Therese entered a convent with one ambition: To become a saint. But six years into her cloistered life in the convent, and suffering from poor health and debilitating bouts of depression, she realized that all her striving and religious go-getting was useless. She was exhausted by it all, and simply could not do it.

Giving up on sainthood altogether, and despairing of life, it was about this time that she read a single line from the book of Proverbs that changed everything: "Whoso is little, let him come to me." She named this discovery "The Little Way," realizing that the only way up, was down.

For the rest of her short life (she lived less than a decade in the convent), she quit trying so hard and learned to become a child once again. Often critiqued as overly simplistic and naïve, Therese and her "Little Way" are rejected by those who feel the need for greater complexity.

Yet, Therese was right on target, and not because, ironically, her way led to sainthood. She was right because her way reflected the way of Jesus. His way, "The Little Way," always leads us to abandon ourselves like a child, into the arms of God.

October 2: The Table

The Inter-Anglican Liturgical Commission on Eucharistic Food and Drink (what a terribly gawkish name for a study group) has found that for the reasons of allergies, cost, concern for alcoholics, lack of refrigeration or availability, all manner of commodities have been substituted worldwide for the traditional bread and red wine at the Communion table.

Banana juice, pineapple wine, Coca Cola, and Grape Fanta: These have all been used for Jesus' blood. And his body? Rice cakes, Ritz crackers, wheat toast, biscuits, and donuts. I'm all for a little irreverence in the church, but for lifelong wafer-chewers and juice-sippers, this sounds a bit bizarre. Maybe it shouldn't.

During the first week of October the church celebrates World Communion Day. In spite of our many differences, we recognize that the Lord's Table should bring us together, not tear us apart. It should invite, not restrict; appeal, not separate. It should welcome believers with certainty and safety, not alienate them.

This safety extends far beyond the avoidance of food-borne illnesses. All believers should find the Communion Table to be their own, as comfortable with the wine and wafer (or Fanta and Saltines), as they are sitting at their own dinner tables.

After all, that is where all believers call "home:" Gathered in the presence of Christ, filled and sustained by his goodness, and then sent out to serve the world.

We may come from different places and have different theological conclusions about a great many different things; but there is only one Church, one Faith, one Lord and one Body.

That body is neither made with refined flour nor does it froth with aged Port or Welches. That Body is a people, bound together not by elements of bread and wine, but by the sacrifice and love of Christ.

October 3: Hard Grace

A science teacher once announced to her class that it was physically impossible for a whale to swallow a human being. A little girl in the class protested, stating that Jonah had indeed been swallowed by a whale. The teacher reiterated that such a thing was impossible.

The little girl answered, "When I get to heaven I will ask Jonah." The teacher brusquely asked the girl, "Well, what if Jonah went to hell?" The little girl replied, "Then you will have to ask him."

Pardon the pun, but the whale in Jonah's story is too often a red herring. We get all tangled up in the scientific plausibility of such an act taking place, and miss the point of the whole story. Jonah's story is not a fishing tale. It is a story about God's relentless, patient, persistent, and sometimes hard grace.

If that big fish had not arrived to gobble down Jonah, he would have drowned in the depths of the sea. The whale was not Jonah's undoing. It was his salvation. The belly of that whale became the incubator – painful, disgusting, and cramped – in which mercy took root, rescued and transformed him. That is hard grace.

God's mercy often comes to us by painful means; as sickness, financial collapse, divorce, betrayal, bankruptcy, addiction, injustice, self-inflicted wounds, and foolish decisions. Hard grace is all those things that God allows into our lives that deconstruct us. Yet, our deconstruction is not our destruction. It is for the merciful purpose of our remaking.

God does not abandon us, but comes to us in strange ways, providing places to learn, grow, change, and get on with the life God has for us. Per Julian of Norwich: "There is the fall, then the recovery. Both are God's mercy." Both are hard grace.

October 4: An Instrument Of Peace

Saint Francis of Assisi may be the most beloved and written about figure in Christian history (outside of Jesus). His fame is well deserved. Patron saint of Italy, lover of animals and nature, defender of creation, founder of the Franciscan Order, champion of simplicity, advocate for the poor, and the first known church leader to create a live Nativity scene: There's much to love and write about.

For me, I can't think of St. Francis without returning to two pieces of literature that, traditionally, have been linked to him. The first is his poem, "Canticle of the Sun." We know it in English as the beautiful, enduring hymn, "All Creatures of Our God and King," which he wrote in the early 1200s.

The second piece is a prayer attributed to Francis, though it was likely penned by someone else. The prayer is often entitled, "Make Me an Instrument of Peace," or simply, "The Peace Prayer."

It may not be the verbatim words of Francis, but certainly he could abide by every word, for he believed that peace and all that is good does not magically arrive. We - the followers of Jesus - must become the agents of God's peace in the world:

"Lord, make me an instrument of thy peace. Where there is hatred, let me sow love; Where there is injury, pardon; Where there is doubt, faith; Where there is despair, hope; Where there is darkness, light; Where there is sadness, joy.

"O divine Master, grant that I may not so much seek to be consoled as to console; To be understood as to understand, To be loved as to love; For it is in giving that we receive; It is in pardoning that we are pardoned; It is in dying to self that we are born to eternal life."

October 5: Open Arms

In Jesus' day it was not uncommon to address God as Father; but Jesus made this way of speaking to God, normative. Jesus went so far as to call God, "Abba." This was an affectionate name used by the smallest of children. To think of God as "Papa" or "Dad" was a driving force behind Jesus' ministry.

After all, Jesus didn't come to change God's attitude about us. Jesus came to change our attitude about God, revealing him to be a benevolent Father welcoming us into his open arms. Embracing God as Father corrects the misrepresented images that have been put before us.

Now, I'll hurry to say that the use of "Father" should not be taken as exclusively paternalistic or masculine. The point is that God relates to us as a compassionate parent, mother and father, not that God is male.

In fact, to introduce God as "Father" to some folks isn't helpful; it is detrimental, as the word "Father" is far too baggage laden. This isn't an attack on God's parenthood. It is an acknowledgment that some people struggle with the image of divine parent, because they have no healthy model with which to compare it.

So let me be clear that this is a metaphor. It is a signpost pointing to something else, someone else; someone who is better to us than anyone else could be; someone who loves with an absolute love; someone who welcomes us into his arms without qualification or reservation.

You might call on the Almighty using words like God, Yahweh, Jehovah, Father, Mother, Parent, Papa, Protector, Provider, or Guardian – even Uncle Jerry or Aunt Lucille – whatever word is most associated with love, trust, welcome, and safety. Call God what you will; but call on him (or her). You will be welcomed, always.

October 6: God Is Good

I was sitting at my son's mid-week football practice watching with a group of other parents when a mother called to her youngster: "It's time to leave; we have to go to church."

Her son, five-years-old, had been busy playing with his friends. He was not happy with the interruption and popped off, "I don't want to go to church!"

His mother answered without blinking; "Then God will send you to hell with the devil and his angels." I immediately stopped being an observer and became an interfering, meddlesome busybody.

"Don't you ever say that to your child again!" I snapped, not realizing at the time how loud my voice had become. For her part, the mother I chided looked as if she could have stuffed me and my little fold-up lounge chair into the trunk of my car. I don't blame her, but I just couldn't let her comment pass.

My outburst arose from the fact that I had been subjected to just such religious threats as a child myself. This made me resentful and distrustful toward God. And when you don't trust God, it's hard to be enthusiastic about going to the building that bears his name.

Ironically, I have remained a church person my entire adult life, being in a pew or a pulpit most every Sunday. But I am no longer part of a rigid, hostile, fear-mongering faith because I no longer believe in a rigid, hostile, fear-mongering God.

This doesn't make me an enlightened expert sitting in my fold-up chair. I simply have learned that God is not one to be wary of or to be resented, because God is not a threat. The childhood prayer is correct: "God is good," and he is good all the time.

October 7: For Trevor

Tony Campolo was once on stage with Bishop Desmond Tutu and he asked the venerable man how it happened that he became an Anglican priest, instead of a Baptist or a Methodist. So Tutu told Campolo this story:

"We moved to Johannesburg when I was twelve. In the days of apartheid, when a black person met a white person on the sidewalk, the black person was expected to step into the gutter to allow the white person to pass. My mother and I were walking down the street when a tall white man, dressed in a black suit, came toward us. He stepped off the sidewalk and tipped his hat in a gesture of respect to my mother!

"I was more than surprised and asked my mother, 'Why did that white man do that?' My mother explained, 'He is a man of God; that is why he did it.'"

That man's name was Trevor Huddleston, an Anglican priest who worked in the slums of Johannesburg. When Tutu was later hospitalized with tuberculosis, it was Huddleston who came to visit the young boy; and it was Huddleston who would offer his own books and time to help Desmond catch up with his studies when he returned to school.

Years later, when Tutu began studying theology, he turned to Huddleston's Anglican Church, for he had experienced firsthand the love and service of this extraordinary man. Trevor Huddleston's name is almost forgotten in South Africa's freedom story, but not forgotten by Desmond Tutu. So influenced was he by the man, that when his first son was born, Tutu named him, "Trevor."

So when you think the little things you do and say don't matter, that your life will be easily forgotten, remember that there would be no Desmond Tutus without the Trevor Huddlestons.

October 8: Puzzles

When I lead retreats I sometimes divide the participants into small groups and give each group a children's puzzle to complete. While most puzzles are brand new in the box, I have tampered with one of them.

The puzzle in question will have a handful of wrong pieces mixed in, or I will have replaced the puzzle altogether, the pieces not matching the box at all. The group with the jacked-up puzzle will pour the pieces out, start working the edges, look at the box, and after a few minutes, be completely bamboozled.

When I reveal the dirty truth, they wail in protest, complaining that the assignment was unfair. "True" I say. "But the puzzles of life and faith rarely match the box we are given."

There are legions of people whose fitly-paired puzzles have gone scattering in the wind. Life no longer matches the picture they had imagined, and it is impossible to pretend otherwise. What is the answer to these misfitted and missing pieces puzzles of life and faith? Time and patience.

To keep working it out and to sift through the prefabricated pictures of what life once promised; to ask dangerous questions and to listen for unexpected responses; to curse, pray, cry, heal, and come through on the other side whole – even if a few pieces to the puzzle are never found.

So, if a friend is stuck trying to solve his or her puzzle, offer the right kind of help - not the latest book on puzzle-solving. Don't shout advice from the other room. Don't walk by as they stand and sweat over the mystery that is their life and lob out bombs of critique.

Rather, quietly sit down with them and patiently help them put it together, whatever "it" turns out to be.

October 9: Chosen And Loved

There are millions of adopted children living in United States' households. These children arrive in their homes in a myriad of ways, but most have this in common: They are loved. The adoptive parents want to provide a loving home for these children.

Two of those two million adopted children live under my own roof. When they were younger, and I suppose they need to hear it even more as they grow, I would tell them, "Everyone is born. Not everyone is chosen; but you were."

Granted, this doesn't settle all of their anxieties and identity issues – "Who am I? Where did I come from? Why am I in the world? How do I fit in? What is life?" (these questions seem injected with steroids for most adopted children) - but I hope their "chosenness" keeps them grounded.

Some of these questions will be answered now. Some answers will come in adulthood. But some questions may never be answered. Yet, they cannot let all the unanswerable questions of their existence rob them of this essential fact: They are chosen and loved.

One of the New Testament's more powerful images is, fittingly, adoption. "By his great love," Paul said, "we were chosen for adoption into God's family. You are not his slaves. You are his children."

God's choosing love might not squelch all our anxieties, but it's a good place to start. For if we know that God loves us, then we can make allowances for the things that we don't know; if we understand that we are chosen, then we can live with those things that can't be understood; when we are certain of our acceptance, then we can accept other uncertainties.

These facts can serve as a stabilizing force for all adoptees; and that, thanks be to God, includes everyone.

October 10: The Blessed Community

In the mid-1600s, George Fox gathered together a "Religious Society of Friends." A pious group made of seekers, disillusioned reformers, and free-thinkers, they often "quaked before the Lord" in reverence. Hence, this group was informally named, the Quakers. Today they mostly prefer to be called, "Friends."

Their beliefs range far and wide with no formal creed. Yet, they hold to a few essentials that can teach other people of faith a great deal. First, they believe unflinchingly in personal communion with God, not needing a mediator, priest, or pastor to speak to God on his or her behalf.

And second, Friends believe in the "Blessed Community," a living "reflection of the rule of God in the hearts of a people as they act out his peace and presence." Friends seek to create a social order that reflects God's grace, love, and compassion for and in the world. The goal is to be a people who have found a better way to live, and to invite others to participate in this life.

As the late Thomas Kelly, a Quaker mystic, said: "The Blessed Community is not something we create deliberately. Instead, we find it, increasingly within ourselves as we are increasingly within Him. The Blessed Community is the holy matrix of 'the communion of saints,' the Body of Christ which is His church. It is home."

If you have "found" a Blessed Community - whether it is a Baptist church down the street, a Catholic parish across town, an Alcoholics Anonymous meeting at the YMCA, or a group of Friends in a living room - then you, pardon the pun, have found a blessing. Any place where you are welcomed, treated with loving respect, and challenged to live out the kingdom of God, is a place worthy of being called "home."

October 11: Escalating Acquisition

You might remember from your college economics class that self-interest is the foundation of capitalism. If you are going to succeed in a free-market world, you have to look out for yourself. That's the truth, but most of us can't tell where self-care crosses over into self-indulgence. We don't know where the line is between carefully looking out for our interests, and greedily working all the angles.

Consequently, we move from survival to sustaining to hoarding, with no stopping rule or stopping place in the escalation of acquisition. Enough is never enough, so we keep charging ahead, even after we have more than we need.

It's hard to recognize personal greed, as it comes with most personal shortcomings: Greed is easier to recognize in others than in ourselves. Those awful corporate tycoons, those sharks on Wall Street, those dictators in the third world, those hedge fund maniacs, that slimy TV preacher: These are easy targets.

What about those of us who buy more house than we can afford? What about those who make $100,000 a year but live like they make three times that amount? What about the one who keeps rotating her debt just so she can maintain a higher and more lavish lifestyle? It's all the same disease - greed - driven by what we do not yet have, but want so badly.

Author and academic David Gushee calls our gluttonous, American way of life, "Affluenza:" Materialism, commercialism, and consumerism drive us, he says, to get the latest and greatest with no thought for the less fortunate, the least of these, and no thought for what this grasping does to God's good world.

Likewise, we give little thought for what "affluenza" is costing our souls; a cost that far exceeds the monthly payment on our debts.

October 12: Holy Huddles

Arnold Mandell once said, "Football is not a game. It is a religion" (Amen, and pass the pigskin). A crucial part of this religion is the huddle: The team circles up like a wagon train under siege. When the team huddles it is preparing itself to execute a play.

But wouldn't it be a shame if football were nothing but a huddle; a meeting to talk about playing, but it never involved actually snapping the ball? It wouldn't be much of a game. Isn't it a shame when Christianity devolves into the same?

On Sunday mornings many of us charge out of our locker rooms suited up in our clean uniforms. We sing our fight songs and wave our banners. We gather in our holy huddles to plan and plot, but most of us never actually play. That we attended the weekly pep rally seems to be enough.

But what happens inside our sanctuaries and houses of worship week after week, while important, is not where the "game" is actually played. Our weekly gatherings are more like locker room speeches. They are weight rooms that strengthen our spiritual muscles. They are rehab facilities in which we can get healthy. They are nutritional centers to feed our hungry bellies.

But when our muscles are strong, our wounds bandaged, our appetites sated, and our motivation roused, we have to leave the huddle and get out there on the field where the game is actually played.

Where people are hungry, thirsty, naked, sick, abandoned, and mistreated; where people are hurt, confused, in need of friendship, love, and redemption – that is the field of play for people of faith. If all our huddling doesn't empower us, if it doesn't translate into proper execution on the turf, then, indeed, we are only playing a game.

October 13: The Medicine Cabinet

Sometimes we treat our faith like it is a medicine cabinet or a pharmaceutical, going to it only when something is wrong, or if we are looking for a quick remedy.

"My head hurts," so I go to the cabinet looking for a pain reliever. "I have a stomach ache," so I reach in for a spiritual antacid. "I feel so uncertain," so I explore my therapeutic options. "I'm feeling a bit anxious," so I look for something that will serve as divine Prozac.

The faith that is peddled today is something of a sedative. It helps people to forget their pain and suffering, helps them sleep at night, and keeps them hanging on for next week's dose of tranquility; but it does very little to move people to a place of growing, spiritual health.

Thus, we can easily succeed in converting our faith into a first-aid kit, only turning to it when something hurts, and leaving it in the cabinet otherwise. Yet, the real power of faith is not its ability to magically stop our pain or to provide a fix to get us through a rough spot.

Rather, faith does more than medicate our boo-boos or make us happy when we have been made sad. Faith has the power to transform us, to shape and fit us for life, making us whole and well. As James said, "My friends, faith that does not lead to change is a faith that is dead."

It is possible to find great inspiration in our faith; but if such beliefs do not have transformative power in our lives, then we do not have faith at all. Instead, we are addicted to a spiritual tranquilizer that blinds us to the reality of our world and the renewal God seeks to produce.

October 14: The Game Of Tens

Here is a brainteaser called the "Game of Tens." Take a little time to answer the following questions (if you can):

Name the ten wealthiest people in the world.
Name the last ten Presidents of the United States.
Name the last ten winners of the Nobel Peace Prize.
Name the last ten winners of Time's "Person of the Year."
Name the current ten companies at the top of the Fortune 500.

How did you do? My guess is not as well as you would have liked. Now try these questions (I promise, they are easier):

Name the ten most memorable experiences of your life.
Name ten people whom you love.
Name ten people who have an influence on your life.
Name ten places you have visited that you will never forget.
Name ten holidays or celebrations you have recorded in a photo album, on video, or on film.

This "game" has been around for years in its varied forms, but the crux of the thing has always been the same: Huge, world-shattering events are laid alongside the familiar and common. When these lists are compared, the things that we think are so eternally important, turn out to be nothing but dust - we can't even remember them.

While the things so normal, those events so close to us we can no longer see them - experiences that are so routine and ordinary - these turn out to be the most important things in our life; and we fail to appreciate them.

The events that will most shape us won't be found on the front pages of the newspaper, go viral on the Internet, or be recorded in the *Guinness Book of World Records*. But common events and people will be forever recorded in our hearts. We must be careful to treasure them.

October 15: Heaven, At Last

One of my favorite hiking trails is a short two mile jaunt to the top of Blood Mountain near Blairsville, Georgia. The trail is marked, "moderate to strenuous," and it certainly is in places. It's best enjoyed, not as a race to the top, but as a steady enjoyment of God's creation.

In other words, you have to stop along the way, catch your breath, and look around. Otherwise, you'll only be huffing and puffing like a coal-fired boiler while staring at nothing but your shoelaces.

The last time I was at Blood's peak, rising to nearly 5,000 feet in the heart of the Southern Appalachians, it was a glorious spring day. The air was cool and clean. The valley below was lush and verdant. A few slivers of ice still clung to the granite dome where there was shade. The mountain laurel was in bloom, and the birds, squirrels, and bears seemed to be bouncing all over the mountainside.

It was as perfect a sanctuary in which I have ever worshipped. More so; this sanctuary was built by God, not man. I reached into my pocket for my "hymnal," a few poetic lines from Emily Dickinson:

Some keep the Sabbath going to Church
I keep it, staying at Home
With a Bobolink for a Chorister
And an Orchard, for a Dome

God preaches, a noted Clergyman
And the sermon is never long
So instead of getting to Heaven, at last
I'm going, all along

Heaven is all around us, and you don't have to hike a mountain, learn meditation, or go to church to find it. Do this: Stop along the way. Catch your breath. Look around. With a little time, you are certain to find heaven right where you are, right where you have been all along.

October 16: Spurs

Cenchrus echinatus. This is the scientific name for the scourge otherwise known as a Florida Sandspur. If you've never seen one (and more pertinent, never stepped on one), it looks like a tiny fossilized porcupine with menacing quills sticking in all directions. Stepping on one barefoot produces the same reaction as stepping on a ball of needles.

They are sticky little savages, dropping to the ground late in the year, where they wait to inflict pain on passersby or to hitch a ride in one's clothing. Then they can land in the carpet to ambush a sleepy walker in the middle of the night.

During this time of year, when I take my two dogs for a walk, we have to deal with sandspurs. They are forever attaching themselves to my dogs' feet. The dogs, curiously, react in completely different ways.

Toby refuses to stop when a spur lodges in his foot. The walk must go on. All this does is produce limping and whimpering, driving the spur deeper between the pads of his paw. When I force a stoppage to remove it, he growls, snarls, and nips at me - all while I attempt to stop his pain.

Mo, dog #2, without exception will stop, lift his afflicted paw in the air, and offer it to me for spur extraction. While he may whine a bit, it's never at me, but at the fossilized porcupine in his foot. Quickly it is removed, and off we go as happy as ever.

So there you have the two ways to deal with your pain: You can fight God, resisting, biting, and barking when he draws close to help and heal you. Or you can willingly offer it up without resistance. You already know which one works out the best in the end.

October 17: Disappearing Dump Trucks

In San Salvador, El Salvador there is a a housing project that is home to several thousand people. It is called La Chatarrería - the junkyard - for that is what it once was. The land had been filled with crushed cars, old buses, and dilapidated construction equipment. The new residents removed all the junk in order for new homes to be built.

My favorite part of this venture involved a dump truck that was too big and heavy to move. It sat in the middle of the job site untouched, until six eight-year-old boys attacked it. Every day these boys would arrive with their hacksaw blades, pieces of cloth wrapped around the edges for handles, and they would saw away. They would take whatever they cut off and sell it for a few pennies at a time on the street, helping to meagerly support their families.

This went on day after day, week after week, and month after month until one day, almost like magic, this dump truck weighing tens of thousands of pounds was gone. Six elementary school-aged children had consumed it, like vultures consuming a carcass.

One of the onsite missionaries told me that when he felt like quitting, that when he thought what he tried to do didn't matter, or when overwhelming odds made it all hopeless, he would revisit the memory of those little boys confronting that dump truck day after day.

We may not "build" a whole lot with the few years we have been given, and parts of what we build will get blown away. But with the blessed ignorance of children, we can keep sawing – keep parenting, keep teaching, keep fostering, keep nursing, keep showing up at whatever it is we do – until finally, almost like magic, the dump trucks disappear.

October 18: Doctor, Doctor

I despise going to the doctor. Backless gowns, vinyl examination tables, and being put into positions that rob you of all dignity, aside, I hate being so intensely examined.

When put under the stethoscope-bearing, X-ray-shooting, blood-sucking, prescription-writing interrogation of a skilled physician, your life has a way of telling on you. You can hide your secrets about as well as hiding your rear end while wearing one of those tie-behind frocks.

Have you been smoking? Your blood test will show it. Have you been boozing? Your liver will rat you out. Are you exercising too little? Your blood pressure will tell the tale. Have you been stretched out on the sofa eating cheesy puffs? Then your cholesterol will backstab you quicker than you can scarf down a Ho-Ho cake.

The examination, lab results, endless questioning, the rubber-gloved prodding: These all have a way of revealing our secrets. But honestly, I should appreciate - not resist - my physician's nosy persistence.

He annually runs me through the ringer with my wellbeing in mind. His goal is not to punish, embarrass, or shame me. By forcing me to face the truth about myself and how I live my life, he empowers me to make the changes that will lead to better health.

That is the same point made by the writer of Hebrews when he speaks of the Scriptures as "Sharper than any double-edged sword." The Bible isn't a giant stick used to bash in our brains or to shame us for our many violations. No, it is a powerful, spiritual tool of examination.

It opens up our hearts, spirits, and minds, and when necessary, it intervenes to improve our health. The Bible, like a skilled, healing physician, encourages us to get and be better.

October 19: From Morning Till Night

No doubt you have seen reproductions of some of Vincent Van Gogh's most famous paintings. "Starry Night." "At Eternity's Gate." "Sunflowers." But have you ever heard him preach a sermon?

"Hear?" No, but a few of his sermons have been transcribed. Yes, Van Gogh was a church pastor for a short time. His failure at the vocation led him directly to painting, and while I am thankful for his artistic genius, his sermons weren't bad either.

Here is an excerpt from his first sermon delivered in October of 1876. It sounds like one of his paintings, and it is the sound of Good News:

"I once saw a very beautiful picture. It was a landscape at evening. In the distance on the right hand side a row of hills appeared blue in the evening mist. Above those hills the splendor of the sunset, the grey clouds with their linings of silver and gold and purple.

"The landscape is a plain covered with grass and yellow leaves. Through the landscape a road leads to a high mountain far, far away. On top of that mountain is a city wherein the setting sun casts its glory.

"On the road walks a pilgrim, staff in hand. He has been walking for a good long while already, and he is very tired. And now he meets a woman, or an angel. The pilgrim asks her: 'Does the road go uphill all the way?' And the answer is: 'Yes, to the very end.'

And he asks again: 'And will the journey take all day long?' And the answer is: 'From morning till night, my friend.' And the pilgrim goes on sorrowful yet always rejoicing - sorrowful because it is so far and the road so long. But hopeful as he looks up to the eternal city."

October 20: The Fisherman And His Wife

A Brothers Grimm fable is about a fisherman and his wife who lived in a hut along the sea. One day the fisherman caught a magical fish who spoke to him: "Let me go and I'll give you anything you want." The fisherman quickly threw him back, wanting nothing to do with a talking fish. That evening the fisherman told his wife what had happened.

"Why didn't you ask for something! Go ask that fish to give us a comfortable house." the fisherman went down to the sea and called out:

"Oh, man of the sea!
Come listen to me;
For Alice my wife,
The plague of my life,
Begs a gift of thee."

The fish materializes and says: "Go home. She is in the house she wanted already." Indeed, there she was in a nice home and beautiful garden! Everything was great for a week or two. Then the wife wanted a stone castle. She sends him back to the water. And he conjures the magic fish again with his incantation.

Again the request is granted. But then she wants a moat, a draw bridge, soldiers, to be a queen, to be Pope! The fish grants her every request, only to have the fisherman return days later to ask for more. Finally she sends her husband to ask the fish to make her the lord over the sun and the moon. The fish answers, "Your wife will never be happy. Go home and live in your hut again." He returns home and that is what he finds; his little hut by the sea as things once were.

Waiting to be content only after you have everything you want, means to die waiting; and striving for what you can't have will only blind you to what you have been given.

October 21: Why Bother?

In 1775, the U.S. Continental Army invaded Canada in an effort to bring the French into the Revolutionary War. The army paused in western Maine to make camp along the Dead River, and there erected a flagpole adorned with the new American colors. That campsite became known as Flagstaff, decades before the city bearing the same name in Arizona.

Shortly thereafter, the campsite became a permanent village. But in 1928, the Maine legislature approved the construction of a dam on the river to produce electricity. This would also produce Flagstaff Lake, 22,000 acres of water that would flood the village of Flagstaff, Maine.

As the power company bought up properties one by one, the residents of Flagstaff stopped caring. They gave up on their homes, and over the course of two decades, relocated. During those spiraling decades all improvements and repairs in the entire town stopped.

All energy went into watching for the impending tide, dismantling everything, and using up what was left. All the trees were cut down. Roads deteriorated. Schools went unfunded. Every building was abandoned or torn down. Neighbors became selfish and self-centered, vying for the leftovers and the scraps.

The overall sentiment in Flagstaff became, "Why bother? Why should I care when the whole village is going to be wiped out anyway?" So, week by week and day by day, Flagstaff became more and more miserable; more and more abandoned.

If we give up on this world, how will the end result be any different? "Oh, it's all going to burn anyway; when the Lord comes back!" No, my friends, the world is going to be renewed, not destroyed. Until that day comes, we are the stewards of God's creation. Let us not give up on doing with it what is right with it.

October 22: Saving Presence

Dr. Phil Littleford was an accomplished cardiologist who revolutionized heart catheterizations. His innovations have saved many lives, over the years, but there was one life he did not save. Or did he?

He traveled to Alaska with his young son, Mark, for the fishing trip of a lifetime. The fishing was amazing and after several days in the backcountry, they prepared to fly out by sea plane. Unknown to the pilot, the plane's pontoons had taken on water. The aircraft crashed into the sea on takeoff.

The only hope, in the freezing waters, was to make the mile long swim to shore. Littleford was a strong swimmer and could have easily made shore (as the pilot did). But Mark, only 12, could not make it.

Phil chose to stay with his son. The two were last seen as a dot on the horizon, arm in arm, as they were swept out to sea. It doesn't take much imagination to put ourselves in Dr. Littleford's position, doing the same with our child or someone we love.

We usually think of "salvation" as a rescue; indeed, it is. But when the ending is not as happy as we had hoped, salvation still succeeds. Because salvation is presence as much as it is rescue.

A cancer patient may die of his disease. A faithful wife might be betrayed by her husband. A child might suffer abandonment by parents. "Salvation" may not bring healing, reconciliation, or joyful reunion, but it will always bring presence - the presence of a loving Father - who will stick with us and not leave us on our own.

Did Dr. Phil Littleford save his son in those Alaskan waters? Absolutely, because he refused to leave. It's better to have the company of supreme love than to live a storybook ending.

October 23: The Two Daughters

A certain woman had two daughters, one bad, the other good. The bad daughter was defiant and uncooperative. The good daughter, loving and cheerful.

One day while drawing water from a well a poor woman asked the good daughter for a drink of water. Being true and kind, she gave the old woman freely from the well. But the old woman was actually a fairy in disguise, and for kindness received, gave the girl a gift.

"Every time you speak," she said, "a flower or a jewel will come out of your mouth." When the girl got home, her mother scolded her for taking so long. When she opened her mouth to apologize, out came two roses, two pearls and two diamonds.

Her mother was astonished! But after hearing her story of what had happened, she quickly sent her other daughter down to the well to get the same gift. The bad daughter however, did not want to be seen engaged in such a lowly task as drawing water. It was beneath her. So she grumbled all the way to the well.

There, the same fairy came to her, not as an old beggar woman this time, but dressed as a queen. She kindly asked the girl for a drink from the well. But this daughter was sullen and rude, refusing to stoop to show kindness. As a result she received her reward as well. Every time she opened her mouth, out crawled snakes, frogs and toads.

The girls received the same gift, the gift of disclosure: What was in their heart was evidenced by their words. As Jesus said, "What comes out of the mouth gets its start in the heart." Thus, to improve one's speech, one must do more than "watch her words," but also mind her heart.

October 24: Wherever You Go

On March 10, 1943, Nazi soldiers began rounding up the Jews of Plovdiv, Bulgaria. They were to be sent to Treblinka, an extermination camp in occupied Poland. As the boxcars were prepped, 8,500 Jews were kept in barbed-wire enclosure at the train station.

When word of the deportation reached the Orthodox Bishop of Plovdiv, a man called Metropolitan Kirill, he led members of his church and other townspeople to the station. The pastor gently pushed through the armed soldiers, and let himself into the enclosure. The Jews surrounded him, weeping and crying.

Kirill raised his hands and shouted from the book of Ruth: "Wherever you go, I will go! Wherever you lodge, I will lodge! Your people will be my people, and your God, my God!" Then he began opening boxcars and locked gates, even lying down on the train tracks at one point, declaring he would die there should the train move.

By the following day, the enclosures were empty. The Jews were allowed to return to their homes and Kirill succeeded, with only his courage, in saving 8,500 souls from Treblinka's gas chambers.

Kirill's actions inspired many more to rally to the defense of the Jews. Defying their country's leadership, which had aligned with the Nazis, the Bulgarian Orthodox Church protected the Jewish community at every turn.

Because of such courage, there was not a single major deportation of Jews from Bulgaria during World War 2. On the contrary, at the beginning of the War, the Jewish population of Bulgaria was 48,000. By the end it was 50,000, making Bulgaria the only Nazi-occupied country to gain in Jewish population.

When a person is willing to take great risks to do what is godly and what is right, to oppose oppression and injustice, miraculous things can happen.

October 25: Minding Our Own Business

If you pay any attention to the world around you, you might conclude that the only voice we Christians have is that of a crotchety old man, angry that the neighborhood kids won't stay off our lawn.

Yes, some of what we say is healthy, principled dissent; but too much of it is an exhaustive collection of condemnation and angry finger-pointing, incensed as we are, at what everyone else is doing wrong. But by Jesus' own word, the church is not permitted to become this type of condemnation-meting society. We are not called to operate a business of inflicting punishment on others. In fact, we aren't called to mind others' business at all.

In my vocation I often come across those who are hostile toward the Christian faith. I try to engage such individuals and learn something from them. What I have learned from people such as these, more often than not, is their exasperation over how we Christians frequently come across as a kind of moral SWAT team.

We intrude into the lives of others filling the air with the ammunition of "ought, should, and must" when we would be better served by turning our energies and attention to our own hearts and examine our own lives, not the lives of others.

Dietrich Bonehoeffer said it best: "Jesus is the only standard by which disciples should live, but he is not a standard we can apply to others. He is a standard we can only apply to ourselves."

So, when we as Christians get blisteringly angry with those who sin differently than we do, we should remember to mind our own business. That business is to love, not condemn. That business is to begin with the self, for beginning there will keep us busy for a lifetime.

October 26: Maturity Over Monstrosity

Walt Disney is after your mother. Exhibit A: Bambi. Before his first birthday his mother is killed. Exhibit B: Dumbo. His mother is locked away as she tries to protect him from the jeering crowds. Exhibit C: Cinderella. She must suffer humiliation at the hands of her wicked stepmother and stepsisters.

Exhibit D: Snow White, a naïve, beautiful teenager, again, at the mercy of her wicked stepmother. She runs away to the woods, moves into a fraternity house with seven men, takes candy from a stranger, and finally runs away with the first man who kisses her. If she had a mother providing appropriate instruction, none of this would have happened. On and on I could go.

Some have tried to explain that Walt Disney is trying to show that a traditional family (whatever that might mean) is not necessary for happiness. Others believe that the elimination of the mother figure in so many Disney films is for dramatic effect (if Walt's characters all had loving, involved moms, there wouldn't be much of a movie plot left).

I think Disney is providing instruction for raising resilient, adaptable, successful children: People need to struggle to become strong, and protecting our kids from all adversity is a crime against their futures.

When a child (or adult) never suffers pain, rejection, or deprivation, this doesn't create maturity, it creates monsters. Beware of those for whom everything has come easy; who have never struggled; who have always had someone else clean up their messes. It's hard for such people to develop any depth of character.

To succeed, yes, we need instruction and guidance, but not so much that it ruins us. When wrestling against the "slings and arrows of outrageous fortune," this does more than make great movies. This makes for a great life.

October 27: Earning Courage

My teenage son, coming of age, has begun to see the world for what it is, both marvelous and dangerous. Or in the words of Frederick Buechner, "Here is the world. Beautiful and terrible things will happen." His eyes have been opened to the "terrible" things.

It's right on time, I suppose. I've said before that the emotional transition from childhood to adolescence is when a person realizes that the world does not revolve around him or her (a revelation some never get).

A person then moves from adolescence to adulthood when he or she realizes, "Not only does the world not revolve around me, I think it's out to get me!"

So we talked about economics, globalization, racism, terrorism and ISIS, the volatility of currency, the environment, the fleeting supplies of petroleum, the stock market, and pandemics. I told him that the challenges he and his peers will face seem insurmountable; just as they did for me when I was his age; just as they did for my parents, and their parents before them.

My point to him was that every generation faces a world that is hard, harsh, and unwelcoming. Every generation experiences the "beautiful and terrible things." The trick is to fulfill the last part of Buechner's quote: "Here is the world. Beautiful and terrible things will happen. Don't be afraid."

Here is how Malcolm Gladwell says it: "Courage is not something you already have that makes you brave when the tough times start. Courage is what you earn after you've been through tough times."

Few of us are born brave, but if we daily work our courage - and each beautiful and terrible day will surely give us that opportunity - we will build up the muscle to face the future, just as those before us have done.

October 28: Perfect Love

Years ago I accepted a friend's invitation to attend the "greatest Halloween celebration" ever. Upon arrival, much to my chagrin, it was a "Hell House."

A Hell House is an adaptation of a Haunted House. Attendees are led through designated areas and witness scenes of violence or tragedy. These scenes may involve a group of teenagers killed in a car accident, a frat house drug overdose, or horrid suicide.

The manifestations are many, but the outcome is always the same: Somebody is going straight to hell. The attendees watch as the dearly departed take their ill-prepared stand before the judgment of God, only to be dragged away by howling, soul-thirsty demons to burn in eternal fire.

This creates just the right moment for the Hell House organizers to present a brochure from the church, to give an altar call to repentance, or to conduct some plain old-fashioned fear mongering. My friend thought I would lead my own congregation in hosting a Hell House the next Halloween. Wrong. When the school shooting scenario began, I split.

Hell Houses portray a pagan God, an eternally angry executioner who demands blood. God, a terrifying hobgoblin rising in the night, or an insatiable Zeus hurling lightning bolts until someone can appease him. The message is clear: "Be afraid. Be very afraid."

The Disciple John had a different message: "God is love, and love expels all fear. Fear of punishment shows that we have not fully experienced God's perfect love."

Here is the contrast: Paganism imagines what we must do to keep God from destroying us. Faith joyfully celebrates what God has done through his mercy. The choice before us is the life of fear, or the life of love. The difference between these two makes all the difference in the world.

October 29: Koinonia

Clarence Jordan was born on this day in 1912, deep in the farming fields of Talbot County, Georgia. Growing up in the Deep South, Jordan was witness to bitter racism and acts of injustice against African-Americans that were as numerous as the Georgia cotton bolls.

But Clarence, by God's good grace, refused to become a participant. He could not understand how anyone could hate a man simply "because of the color of skin God Almighty gave to him."

What made the dissonance even more striking for Clarence was that many of the more zealous racists were prominent Christians. They were the very people with whom he attended church. But rather than blaming God and running away from religion because of the hard-heartedness of others, he boldly embraced a gracious faith.

After completing his education at the University of Georgia and Southern Seminary, he bought 400 acres near Americus, Georgia, and founded "Koinonia." This would be a farming community where blacks and whites would live together under the parenthood of God, choose love as the alternative to violence, and help the poor (With Millard Fuller, Koinonia would later birth "Habitat for Humanity").

This was no utopia, however, as it was the 1940s and 50s. Clarence was hated for his beliefs: His fields were salted; his fruit stands were bombed; his pecan trees were cut down; local communities instituted an embargo against his crops; gun shots were often fired into his home late at night. But through it all, Clarence persevered.

Jordan died in 1969, still reviled by many of his neighbors, so much so that the coroner wouldn't even drive to the farm to pronounce the man deceased. But the man was anything but dead. His deeds and words live on; his life a testimony of grace under fire.

October 30: Hope Over Hysteria

Today, in 1938, Orson Welles took to the radio airways as the usual host of the Mercury Theater. Using the science fiction book, *War of the Worlds* as his script, he described in dramatic and fictional detail how Martians had invaded Earth, landing in New Jersey.

There were 32 million radio listeners that evening, and the nation was thrown into a terrifying hysteria. Telephone lines were clogged; police stations were overrun; anxious mobs filled the streets; churches ran over with impromptu prayer meetings; and citizens armed themselves.

There is a Christian equivalent to this kind of unnerving panic. It is unbalanced apocalypticism that pours from radio, television, pulpits, and websites. The oft-presented Christian version of the Apocalypse is initiated not by a Martian invasion, but by Jesus' violent return to earth.

Entire congregations become so obsessively convinced that we are living in the final chapter of human history – on the last page, if not within the last sentence – that they give up on life today! But when you are convinced that the planet will soon be turned to ash, it's extremely difficult to do otherwise.

When one's view of the future is dark and sinister, it creates a kind of apathy and hopelessness toward the planet. We become little more than caricatures of today's politicians who choose to kick the worst problems down the street for another generation to wrestle with, long after they have left office.

We become freakish doomsday-preppers who misunderstand that the best preparation is joining God in his transforming work today, rather than watching the clock expire on the end of the world. No, "God is not slow in keeping his promises," but we have to be more than prepared for his imminent return. We must persevere, trading our misapplied hysteria for blessed hope.

October 31: Behind The Mask

That faint noise you hear is the sound of pint-sized spooks gathering on your lawn. They will soon be knocking at the door, plastic pumpkins outstretched. Give up the treats - the unhealthy, sweet, nougat-filled goodies in your cupboard - and don't deprive the little goblins of this rite of childhood passage.

Of course, adults don't get in on the fun, too. Americans spend $3 billion each Halloween, not on their children, but on themselves. Adults love to play dress-up, and not just in October.

We all hide behind masks, masks that veil the real person who lurks beneath. We so over-identify with our dress-up characters - the roles we play in life - that when the roles change, we experience miserable frustration.

One Halloween my son dressed as the spaceman Buzz Lightyear. It was fun - "To infinity and beyond!" - and that's how long I thought the boy would wear the costume. In his mind, this wasn't a temporary role he was playing. Buzz Lightyear was who he really was. It was as if he were losing himself, as if he couldn't live apart from that imaginary facade. Of course the real him was beneath that rayon spacesuit - everybody knew it - except him.

This is a common affliction. We build dramatic images of ourselves, who we think we are, who we should be, what we should accomplish, and once constructed, these have to be maintained and protected. We never let a tear or a crack show in our veneer, and the mask to which we cling slowly becomes a prison.

Here's a better way: Fulfill the roles that God has assigned you. Fulfill them with gusto. But never accept the masks you wear as a substitute for the person you really are; that's the trick to a sweet life.

NOVEMBER

November 1: For All The Saints

There are some 10,000 recognized saints in Catholicism. These are individuals who lived exemplary lives and who continue to inspire us. Each saint gets his or her own feast day on the calendar, but on November 1, all the saints are honored.

In Protestant traditions All Saints Day is used to remember all the Christian dead - every person who has traveled the road of faith before us. We thank God for their example, witness, and the influence they continue to have on our lives.

Together, Catholics and Protestants agree upon something called "The Communion of Saints." All of God's people, on heaven and on earth, are spiritually united. I love these two terms, though they are rarely used, that describes this:

1) There is the "Church Triumphant" - the saints who have prevailed. They lived, died, and have entered into the presence of Christ. 2) And the "Church Militant" - we striving sinners still engaged in the struggle of life. Together, those passed and we who remain, are one people vitally connected.

The most tangible way to stay connected to the "Church Triumphant" is by remembering; and not just remembering the Bible heroes of old or those who have "officially" been canonized - Patrick, Valentine, Francis, and the like. But also remembering those I call, "unsanctioned saints."

These are those people we knew personally, those who are no longer here but who remain an abiding presence; a motivating force; a comforting friend; a sustaining source of strength for our lives.

It could be a deceased parent or grandparent; a spouse, child, or friend. These saints remain with us, mysteriously, as we live our lives, there when we struggle, win, lose, prevail, and stumble. They may be gone, but how could they be forgotten, for we would not be who we are without them.

311

November 2: The Desert

Years ago a friend and I hiked through the Utah desert in Arches National Park. It is a remarkable, rugged place, and all the hiking trails made this clear. At each trailhead posted notices read: "Open slick rock. Exposure to heights. Narrow ledges. Trail not marked."

But the largest and most obvious warning sign read: "There is no shade. Carry and consume adequate water." Forget this whole "dry heat" thing. When it's triple digits on bleached sandstone and the wind is blowing like a hurricane, it's an inferno. Water was life, more important than anything else, and you had to have plenty of it.

For the Jewish people, their formation narrative was the Exodus out of Egypt. After centuries of slavery they were delivered and set out toward the Promised Land "flowing with milk and honey." But between slavery and salvation were 25,000 square miles and forty years of living in the Sinai Desert.

An entire generation endured the trials of the desert: Daily heat, nightly cold, no shade, prickly poisonous creatures on every hand, sandstorms, and thirst. So finding deep, cold, life-giving water became a theme embedded in the Jewish people's psyche. It was a symbol of joyful salvation.

Jesus made use of the theme when he said, "I will give you springs of living water so you will never thirst again;" and "Anyone who is thirsty may come to me. Rivers of living water will flow from his heart."

This world is a desert, a wasteland through which we journey on our way home. Yet, there is no secret in how to survive its harshness. Never wander too far from your water source. Never stray from the "fountain of salvation" that is Christ. He is all you need to be fulfilled in "a dry and thirsty land."

November 3: To-Do

A couple had a marriage that did not include much love. The husband was very demanding, so much so that he prepared a "to-do" list for his wife to follow. He insisted that she obey these demands to the letter.

His list indicated such details as what time she had to wake in the morning, when his breakfast should be served, and how the housework should be done. After several years, the husband died. As time passed, the woman fell in love with another man, one who dearly loved her. Soon they were married.

This husband did everything he could to make his new wife happy. One day she found in a drawer that old list of commandments her first husband had drawn up for her. As she looked it over, it dawned on her that even though her present husband never made such demands, she was actually exceeding her first husband's list. It was love, not obligation, that moved her.

Such is the challenge always set before us, to be motivated by love, not hardened demands, not rules. "Spirituality and faith without rules?" you might ask. "Is that possible?" Actually, it's the only way.

There is no joy in living a loveless Christianity (much like living in a loveless marriage). We might be committed, but committed to what? Obligation? Checklists? To the fawning and evaporating rewards of an inspector?

Our religious efforts and activities to please, praise, or placate God or others can become the very things that lead to resentment. For if Christian faith becomes a work-based, blood-sweat-and-tears burden, it's not a relationship that can last.

In the end there is only one item on our "to-do" list: Love. That's not just all you can do, it's the best you can do.

November 4: Calm Your Donkey Down

My friend Bryan Kennedy (songwriter, playwright, author, life coach and otherwise creative genius) has this little t-shirt he sells online. There are coffee mugs too. It is this cute, cartoon donkey sitting on its rear end. His front legs are folded across his chest, and his face is cross and frustrated.

The caption reads, "Calm Your Donkey Down!" It's Bryan's way of trying to remind us all to quit overreacting to everything we see and hear in the media, from our friends and families, on social media, and in news reports. "We can all use a calm donkey," Bryan says. And he's right.

We go off half-cocked and half-baked most of the time, ready to fight over the smallest of indignities, the slightest difference of opinion, the slimmest of religious or political disagreement. Every minor infringement is a call to arms, and we fail to see that more damage is done in this world by those taking offense rather than those who give offense (that last line is worth reading again).

Here is the late Henri Nouwen on the subject: "We spend an enormous amount of energy making up our minds about other people. Not a day goes by without somebody doing or saying something that evokes in us the need to react. Strangers and people different than we are stir fear, discomfort, suspicion, and hostility. They make us lose our sense of security just by being different."

Newsflash: Not everyone is like you or will like you. Not everyone agrees with you or will be agreeable to you. Not everyone will do what you want them to do, be what you want them to be, or appreciate what you do and how you are. But guess what? You can live with it. Calm your donkey down.

November 5: Opportunity

Bernard Lichtenberg was a Catholic priest serving in Berlin during WW2. Boldly, he spoke against the Nazi persecutions of the Jews, and for this he was arrested by the Gestapo.

During his interrogation Lichtenberg said: "I reject with my innermost the deportation of the Jews, because it is directed against the most important commandment of Christianity, 'Love your neighbor as much as you love yourself'. But since I cannot prevent this measure, I have made up my mind to accompany the deported Jews into exile. I ask the Gestapo to give me this opportunity."

Considered "irredeemable," his appeal was granted. He was condemned and consigned to the concentration camp at Dachau. Aged, frail, and in a weakened state, Bernard Lichtenberg died while in transit on this date in 1943.

Father Lichtenberg, almost single-handedly opposing the Nazis, was not acting in a sensible manner. He was not being practical. He was being loving. Such love can appear like madness, leading the follower of Jesus into all manner of impracticality in the "real world." But practicality doesn't seem to be Jesus' main concern.

We are instructed to love, following Jesus' own example, not because it is practical, reasonable, logical, or safe. And not for a minute should we think that unselfishly loving our neighbors will save the world from all hate and violence. Nor will it make our membership rolls at the church grow, achieve justice for all society, or make us popular.

We love our neighbors as ourselves not because it always "works," but because it bears witness; it is a clear reflection of the love of God for all. These "opportunities," as Lichtenberg called them, to join the weak, abused, and mistreated aren't realistic; because love doesn't always "succeed," but it always shines as a light in the darkness.

November 6: Under New Management

I was traveling a few days ago when I saw one of those strange church signs, maybe the most perplexing one I've ever seen. Certainly not the most clever, but perplexing. I think it was directed at the pastor. That's not unprecedented.

For example: 1) From Benton Heights Presbyterian Church - "Having trouble sleeping? We have sermons. Come hear one." 2) Cape Coral Community Church - "Now is a good time to visit. Our pastor is on vacation." 3) Mt. Pleasant Baptist Church - "Do you know what hell is? Come hear our preacher."

5) Clay City Christian Church - "Come hear our pastor. He's not very good, but he's short." 6) "Pastor Mason's sermon, 'I will not pass this way again' has given great comfort to the congregation." And 7) "Today the pastor will preach his farewell message. The choir will sing, 'Break Forth Into Joy.'"

This sign was similar. It read, simply, "Under New Management." I suppose that could refer to the elders or church board. Maybe there was a congregational uprising and they replaced the ruling body with others. Maybe the building was sold to someone else. But most likely, it represents a change in pastoral leadership. That's my guess.

It's just a shame that it became so public for the thousands of people who drove by each day, 99.99% of whom have never set foot inside that church. It was obviously a dog whistle to a small segment of the community. "Come on back," they were saying. "That preacher you had so much trouble with - he's gone! We are under new management!"

Honestly, no minister, priest, or pastor is in the "management" business. Shepherding? Yes. Teaching? Absolutely. Management? Not really. People aren't managed. They can be coached, loved, directed, or led. But managed? That's above any spiritual leader's pay grade.

November 7: He'll Take Care Of The Rest

My grandmother was a simple, poor, woman from the Georgia Mountains. When she died she had less than $500 to her name. But there was a lot more to this woman than her small "estate." She was a giant of faith and resolve, possessing an exceptional peace and strength.

At her funeral her oldest son, my uncle, described her well: "She had two sons, three grandsons, a son-in-law, and a grandson-in-law who became preachers." And then motioning to her coffin he said, "But the best preacher in this family is right here in this box."

Her greatness crystalized for me long before a college history project (our class was charged with formally interviewing a living grandparent); but that project forced me to chronicle the major events of her life. I knew these events, but had never really put them together in a timeline.

Her mother died when she was an infant. Her older brothers went away to fight the Great War. She married my sharecropping grandfather at the height of the Depression, a man plagued by alcoholism and given to violence. She gave birth to eight children, and none were born with a physician's assistance.

Electricity and indoor plumbing didn't arrive to her clapboard home until one of her sons was in Vietnam. She survived Reconstruction, World Wars, abject poverty, the death of a child, decades of domestic violence, and witnessed the advent of everything from air travel and fast food to penicillin and cell phones.

At the end of the interview I asked her: "How did you survive?" From the front porch she stole a glance at the massive oak tree in her front yard. Then, with a smile she said, "I just did what I could, son. God Almighty took care of the rest."

November 8: Are You Reading?

It was John Spach who first told a story about a young man heading off for his freshman year at Duke University. His parents loaded him up with everything he would need: Clothes, computer, detergent, linens, food, food, and more food.

As he was about to drive away, his car creaking beneath the load, his mother handed him a Bible and made him promise that he would read it. "This book will bring you great comfort, keep you from trouble, and help you adjust to your new life," she said. He agreed to read it and toward the hills of North Carolina he drove.

After a few weeks the boy began to complain that he didn't have enough money. "Living alone is expense," he said.

"I told you it would be," his father answered and sent a little money. His mother would always ask, "Are you reading the Bible and staying out of trouble?" His answer was always the same, "Oh, yes ma'am, I'm reading it every day." These calls repeated themselves over the course of that first semester.

When he came home at winter break, his mother confronted him with the fact that he had not been reading his Bible. "Yes, I have!" he said.

"Oh no you didn't," she answered, and she knew it to be a fact. Because she had laced the pages of that Bible with $5, $10, and $20 bills - more than enough money to get her son through the semester. Had he been reading the Bible, he would have known this.

Reading the Bible won't necessarily put dollars in your pocket (no matter what that slick televangelist says), but if you take some time to read it, you might find a few welcome surprises. You might find what you need to get you through.

November 9: Two Kinds Of People

A little boy kept getting in trouble at school for running around the room. With scolding and threats, the teacher finally succeeded in making him sit in his chair.

After a while he raised his hand and when the teacher called on him he said, "I might be sitting down, but inside my head I'm still running around the room."

A little defiance from time to time is healthy. "It is a medicine necessary for sound health," said Thomas Jefferson. But there's a mighty chasm between justified dissent and defiant rebellion. The problem within our hearts is not that we want things to be better. We want things to be our way.

C.S. Lewis, the writer who gave us *The Chronicles of Narnia*, also gave us a little story entitled, *The Great Divorce*. It's about ghosts who live in this cold, dark, polluted town. It's hell, actually, but they don't know it.

They catch a bus to heaven and are invited to stay, though most of them can't do it. They are stuck in their little, dirty town and in their frail, ethereal bodies. Most of the ghosts go back to the darkness even though they are promised joy, transformation, and the answers to all their questions.

For the narrator of the story, this is more than he can understand. He asks one of the heavenly beings to help those trapped in themselves, to rescue them from their blindness and foolishness, that they might experience life.

His guide answers: "There are only two kinds of people in the end: Those who say to God, 'Thy will be done,' and those to whom God says, 'Thy will be done.' We are where we are because of this choice." And that choice - to rebel or to surrender - remains ours every day.

November 10: Settle Down

Here is a reason why many of us can't be happy: We want life to be perfect, and we will sacrifice satisfaction to try to make it that way. We will wander away from what is good, fulfilling, and sustaining because we think we can do a little better. We choose the false idea of perfection over concrete and real satisfaction.

An example: A man plans to go to his high school reunion and feels pretty good about it; because he feels good about his life. He's aged, but he's looking alright. He has a wife he loves; his kids are busy with their lives. He has a successful career, good cars, a nice home.

When he gets to the reunion it appears as if his old friends have surpassed him. They look more fit, younger even. Many have traded in their starter spouses for younger, hotter upgrades. They have smart kids at Ivy League schools; make more money than he does; drive newer cars and live in nicer homes. The man leaves the reunion feeling miserable.

What changed in this man's life in the course of a three hour reunion? Absolutely nothing. The change was only in his perspective. The monstrous idea of a more perfect life robbed him of the joy of the excellent life he has. In the words of Voltaire: "The perfect became the enemy of the good."

So is it any wonder that some people can't be happy? They can't be satisfied with their house, family, marriage, or career so they are always chasing after something new, better, or more perfect.

I'm not saying we shouldn't dream, seek improvement, or reject mediocrity. We should't "settle," but we must settle down if we want to be happy. After all, perfect does not exist, but satisfaction does.

November 11: Unconditional

On this Veterans Day it is right to honor all who have served in the military, and especially those who gave their lives. But we do them all a disservice if we do not remember them in such a way as to stop filling the ground with the fallen dead of war.

Yes, let us fervently honor those who unselfishly gave their lives, but let us vigorously refuse to glorify the violence that took those lives. And let us work with all our holy might to end our dependence upon warfare, for war is not the answer.

War promises us that when the last battle is fought, the last bomb is dropped, the last enemy is slain, and the last soldier is put to rest in sacred soil, then we will have a world at peace. Yet, war is waged without end, and our cemeteries continue to fill.

The world we want, a world where swords are beaten into plowshares, where mercy and justice flow down like the waters, where every tear will be wiped away from our eyes, and where there will be "no more death or sorrow or crying or pain" is the world constructed by the unconditional love of God, not the unconditional surrender of our enemies.

I believe that Jesus, in showing us how to live and die; how to sacrifice without hate or hostility; and how to love others and ourselves, has shown us the path to be at peace with God and the world.

So let us gather at our cemeteries and memorials of stone, around the living and the dead. And as people of faith, let us also gather around another stone; the stone rolled away by the power and love of Christ, the only love that will bring peace to the world.

November 12: Good Neighbors

The community in which I once lived experienced incredible growth as families from Atlanta fled to the countryside. This created a clash of cultures. On one side were the long-established, generational farmers. On the other were new suburbanites fresh from the city.

The quickest place to see the divergent value systems was a county zoning meeting where land use was heatedly debated. At one such meeting a newly established Home Owners Association (HOA) took a local farmer to task. They wanted the county to shut him down because his chicken houses produced a rather noxious odor that the new home owners found offensive.

It was a gaggle of middle-aged, latte-sipping suburbanites up against one old farmer who, true to form, had come to the meeting in his overalls, boots, and wearing a John Deere hat. The lady representing the HOA was going on and on until finally the farmer said, "If you had your way, you'd shut down every farm in this county. Where would you get your eggs then?"

She answered - and I kid you not - "Well sir, I would buy mine at the store!" Needless to say, that ended the argument. Ultimately, that particular neighborhood learned to inhale the smell of chicken litter as well as the folks who were homegrown.

Look, we are all in this together. Who? We. Everybody. All. Those next door, those across town, and those on the other side of the world whom we will never meet. We are all connected.

And where are we? Together. For good or bad, right or wrong, and for as long as we live. The colonization of other planets has not yet begun, and until it does, we are stuck with each other. We might as well find a way to be good neighbors.

November 13: Renovation

Do you know you? I find that most of us have lived with ourselves our entire lives and still have little self-awareness; no sense of who we really are. We only know what others know about us. The exterior, the shell we have manufactured. But that isn't the real self. That's not the real person.

Spiritual growth, at its most basic element, is the deconstruction of what is false. It is ripping and tearing away, like a renovation project.

When you start ripping out walls, rewiring circuits, and refinishing floors, you don't know what you are going to find. You thought you were just going to put on a little spackling and paint, but you might find that termites have almost consumed the place.

Home "improvement" feels like a daily setback. But it's not really. If you are going to have a self worth living with - and for others to find safe and inviting - it's necessary work. Underneath all that ripping and tearing away is the real you - the person God made - the one you were created to be.

That's why the words of Jesus are so necessary. They are like a summons from the building inspector: "I've looked over things here, and well, do you want the good news or the bad news? The bones of the building are sound; no problems there. But this roof, it's gotta go. Your appliances are all good but there's a leak in the water line. You're going to have to dig it up and replace it."

It's hard to take this kind of assessment about who you are; and even harder to do what has to be done, but that's what transformation is. That's what spiritual formation is. Honest assessment. Tearing down and rebuilding. Becoming who we were created to be.

November 14: The Life You Have

One of my sons decided he was going to leave home. "I'm done with you people! I'm moving out!" he angrily said. I answered, in the heat of arguing with an adolescent, "Really? I wouldn't be so lucky!"

Then I remembered what an old man had once told me he did in this same case. I calmed down and said, "Well, get on out - and take your stuff with you." The boy started packing. I let him get into a few minutes, and then went to his room where he was feverishly stuffing a duffle bag.

"What have you got in there?" I asked. "Oh, no. I bought those clothes. They aren't yours. They stay. No, the Xbox stays too. It belongs to the family, not just one of you. Put those boxes of macaroni back in the cupboard. I bought those with my money. In fact, I bought that duffle bag you're packing. Mine, mine, mine - it all belongs to me."

You get the idea. For all his stubborn, egotistical, childish ranting and raving, what did the boy actually possess that he could take with him and start a life somewhere else? Nothing. Where was he going to go at age 14 to start this magical life of independence and freedom? Nowhere. How was he going to provide for himself; feed himself; shelter himself? He couldn't.

Without the benevolence of a father - and without a daily dependence upon that father's care - he would end up naked, hungry, destitute, and poverty-stricken. No amount of shouting or posturing about how he was going to make it on his own would change that.

All his resistance, pride, and opposition didn't lead to a better life. It kept him from enjoying the life he had. It will do the same for us.

November 15: On The Rock

The writer of Matthew's gospel seems to have collected what we call the "Sermon on the Mount" as a summary of Jesus' teachings. This is why Ben Witherington calls the Sermon the Mount, "Jesus' Greatest Hits." It is the most practical synopsis of what it means to be his disciple, the bedrock of the Jesus life.

At the conclusion of Jesus' great sermon, he invites us to take his words and build our lives upon them. Of course Jesus would end his most memorable talk this way; he was a carpenter. But so are we all. We are all builders.

Some of us see all that we have built collapse into a great disastrous heap, unable to bear the strain of driving rain, rising floods, and hurricane-force winds. Others survive the inevitable storms of life. Sure, their windows get knocked out. A blue tarp may have to cover a shingleless roof. Some carpet may have to be replaced, but the house remains firmly fixed to its foundation.

What is the difference between those who collapse and those who survive? Not the building or its materials. It's the foundation. Those who build on the rock – that rock being the words and way of Christ – survive the hard times. Both houses experience different outcomes but the same storm. The one that survives does so only because it is resting on solid ground.

Following Jesus and building upon his teachings and words will not prevent the storms of life from making landfall at your front door. Having Jesus in your life doesn't place a magical forcefield over your life, your family, or your circumstances, keeping all the bad stuff on the outside. Storms are certain. But in these words of Jesus we find what it takes to withstand the storms of life.

November 16: Looking At The Heart

Over the years I have received my fair share of corrective emails from those who read my syndicated column. I write about faith and you know what they say about religion and politics. Those are the two subjects that will most easily ruin a dinner party.

But it wasn't my theology that offended one reader. It was my looks. He wrote, "The photo of you above your article totally turned me off. I did not even continue reading. If a so-called representative of Jesus Christ doesn't care any more about his personal appearance than to roll out of bed and not shave or wash his hair and style it, then surely his viewpoints on life are way off base.

"You should be ashamed of yourself (followed by these 14 exclamation marks) !!!!!!!!!!!!!! My prayer for you is that you will come under conviction of the Holy Spirit and begin treating God with reverence, starting with your own personal appearance. I pray that you will see the light."

Bizarre? You better believe it. Unprecedented? No, I'm afraid not. That is why God gave specific instructions to us all: "Don't judge by appearances. People judge by outward appearance, but the Lord looks at the heart."

It's a never ending human exercise; to come to conclusions about people based solely on their appearance. And it's not just those who look or act in a way we find questionable. In a narcissistic culture where image is everything, we judge those who look, dress, smell, drive, and live in elegance and naturally assume they have storybook lives. But if we knew the truth, such people might be miserable (or insane).

In the words of the proverb: "Never judge a book by its cover." This goes for everyone, not just scruffy columnists with perpetually unruly hair.

November 17: Mirages

You are driving along on a bright sunny day and what looks like water appears in the road a couple hundred yards away. As you move closer, it disappears, only to reappear in the next dip in the road. So you go further and further and further, always reaching for it

But is it water? Of course not. It is a reflection of the midday sky. It is a mirage. If you chase it looking to satisfy your thirst, it will only lead you to trouble. You will end up lost and dry, confused and disoriented, unable to figure out where life went wrong. It went wrong the minute you started chasing illusions and hallucinations instead of what is real and certain.

Many of the things we chase in life are nothing but mirages. That perfect boyfriend; that woman to satisfy all our fantasies; that storybook marriage; an ideal career; the magazine-cover home. These will never do the trick; they can't satisfy.

Richard Alpert, also known as Ram Dass, says that desire is like eating ice cream. One has to keep eating it, faster and faster, because it is constantly melting; it is always getting away, and never fulfills true hunger. I would only add to this apt description that even if one is able to "eat the whole thing" before it melts, then he or she will only feel sick, nauseous, and guilty when it is over.

But maybe desire isn't the real problem. It's not that "we want," or that "we chase," but that we want and chase the wrong things. After all, desire is simply the search for happiness. What is the object of those desires; what is it that we are after that we think will make us happy? Those might be the better questions.

November 18: Fire With Fire

In 1942 Clarence Jordan founded a countercultural, redemptive community just outside the town of Americus, Georgia named "Koinonia."

Koinonia is the Greek word for "community." And Jordan set out to create just that: A farming community where men, women, blacks, whites, rich, and poor would live together under the parenthood of God, using love as a substitute for violence, and sharing their possessions with the poor.

The whole "using love as a substitute for violence" didn't go over too well in the days of WW2, the Korean, and Vietnam Wars. One day a man showed up at Clarence's house angry that he and the people on his farm wouldn't fight.

Clarence answered, "You've got that wrong. We'll fight." And then he looked across the field where a mule was sticking his head out of the barn. Clarence said, "Suppose you walked by the barn and that old mule reached out and bit you in the seat of your britches? Would you bite him back?"

The man answered, "Of course not! I'd get a 'two by four,' and hit him in the head!" Clarence, with his Southern-fried wisdom answered, "See, you would fight, but you wouldn't use that old mule's tactics, 'cause you ain't no mule. You wouldn't bite or kick him because he would win. You would choose weapons that a mule can't compete with."

Then Clarence delivered the clincher: "Yes sir, we will fight, but we will fight with humility, grace, justice, and forgiveness. But we're not going to fight with the enemy's weapons, because if we do, the enemy will whip us."

We have to fight in this world, let there be no doubt about that. But let us choose our weapons carefully, for fighting fire with fire will only burn the whole world to the ground.

November 19: What's Most Important

A dear friend of mine passed away on this date in 2014. His name was Chris. Below are a few words I gave at his eulogy:

"Chris often quoted a line from 'The Shawshank Redemption': 'It comes down to a simple choice, really; get busy living or get busy dying.' True. Now that urgency is placed on us - to live - and to live for what counts.

"What counts? A reading from the New Testament is an appropriate answer, one of Chris' favorites, from Philippians 3:7-9, from the Apostle Paul: 'Nothing is as wonderful as knowing Christ Jesus my Lord. I have given up everything else and count it all as garbage. All I want is to know the love of Christ and to know that I belong to him.' There is no higher ambition; no better way to live.

"A story Chris would tell involved Karl Barth, likely the greatest theologian of the twentieth century. Born in Switzerland, Barth went on to be a pastor and theology professor in Germany, though he was forced to leave Germany when Adolph Hitler came to power.

"Ultimately he traveled the world giving lectures to the smartest and brightest theologians on the planet. Anyone who has studied formal theology - as Chris did - has read his works. His Church Dogmatics took more than 30 years to complete and is more than six million words long.

"Late in his career, in the 1960s, Karl Barth gave a final lecture at the University of Chicago. He was asked: "Dr. Barth, of all you have experienced, written, and lectured, what is the most important insight to God you have ever discovered?"

Barth paused for only a moment, closed his eyes, smiled, and answered, 'Jesus loves me this I know; for the Bible tells me so.' Amen."

November 20: John Martin

An old story circulates in my family about my great-great grandfather, a fiery circuit-riding preacher named John Martin McBrayer. "The Preacher," as he was known, traversed the Southern Appalachians on horseback, going church to church, camp meeting to camp meeting, and revival to revival.

Ultimately he settled down (I think his wife got tired of him leaving her with the 12 children each week) and started a Baptist church in North Georgia. He would fill that pulpit for much of the remainder of his life, and when he died, he was laid to rest in the red dirt of that church's cemetery.

It was the early 1900s and drought was smothering the Georgia countryside. A Saturday prayer meeting was called, a meeting to pray for rain. Old John Martin came riding up on his pony and then dragged his heavy Western saddle and saddle blanket into the church with him.

"Well, Preacher," one man asked, "Why'd you bring your saddle in? You stayin' all night till service in the morning?" Everyone laughed. I'm told that John Martin gave a mischievous chuckle himself. Then he answered, "No, I thought we'd be a prayin' for rain? I do believe the rest of you will be ridin' home wet."

Sure enough, before they all left the church that afternoon, the rains had come and the drought had been broken. And just as sure, most folks left on wet saddles and in drenched wagons while The Preacher trotted toward home as dry as dust.

I often tell this story, not as a means of convincing people that they will always get what they pray for, but as an illustration of what faithful prayer looks like. While many gathered to go through the motions, John Martin prayed as if God was really listening.

November 21: Given Much

I met Marta Torres and her daughters while standing on a street in the city of San Salvador next to the shack she had built with her own hands. It was a collection of rusted metal and termite-infested timbers shared with cockroaches as big as your hand and regularly washed with knee-deep rain water, sewage, and mud.

Marta was discovered by an American missionary who felt that something had to be done to help. Thus, I found myself plunged into Marta's story. We tore down her old shack and built a sturdy wooden home in its place.

Finally, we gathered in a circle, dedicated the home to God, thanked him for bringing us all together in a glorious orchestra of grace, and handed Marta the keys. But what Marta gained was minuscule compared to what my friends and I received.

As we worked, the joy dripped off our cheeks tasting of the words of Jesus: "It is more blessed to give than to receive." I also learned that faith like Marta's is almost impossible to emulate.

I have infinitely more than Marta; more than most of the world. Faith, for me, is hardly ever a living reality. It is something invoked when life is simply not going my way, not something required when desperate.

I don't have faith like Marta's because I've never had to employ such faith. My life, though not without its challenges, by comparison has been quite comfortable, and comfort does not grow faith. Faith, like any muscle, grows by means of use, application, and exercise.

"God has given me little that I might learn to trust Him more," Marta said to me. We who have been given much might learn a great deal from those with such faith. They just might save our souls.

November 22: One By One

Johnson Oatman, Jr. was a failed singer so he began writing songs, songs to be sung in church. Over two decades he authored some 3,000 hymns.

You probably know Oatman's music, even if you are unfamiliar with his name. His most lasting work is a song entitled, "Count Your Blessings."

Growing up, I think we sang this song every other week. I can still recite the first stanza from memory: "When upon life's billows you are tempest tossed; when you are discouraged, thinking all is lost; count your many blessings, name them one by one; and it will surprise you what the Lord hath done."

Have you counted your blessings lately? I know all the "big things" on the list. Family, nation, shelter, food, children or grandchildren, employment; for these we are thankful. But to list all of our blessings, even the little things, would take a considerable amount of time.

Maybe you could start with A and work through the alphabet to Z, concentrating on the little, often assumed, godsends. I'll get you started: Air conditioning. Band aids. Coffee. Dogs. Electricity. Football. Garrison Keillor.

On and on it goes, and this list could be reproduced a thousand times over with little thought, just observation, because blessings constantly rain down upon us. God's ever-present grace surrounds us. Heaven smiles down, if only because we are fortunate enough to live at a time and in a place like this.

Take the time to look around your life and count your blessings - one by little one. Give thanks to God for what you have, what you have experienced, for the grace you have received, and for the people you have known. Try to remember that Thanksgiving is more than a circled date on a calendar. It is a way of life.

November 23: Truly Satisfied

An old Quaker came to the end of his days as a farmer; so, he placed a sign on his land that read, "This farm will be given to anyone who is truly satisfied."

A wealthy merchant came riding along and saw the sign framed by the rolling hills, the dark soil, the barns and silos. He said aloud, "If this man is so eager to part with his land, I might as well claim it."

He guided his pony to the farmhouse, hopped from the saddle, and walked to the front porch. The farmer came to the door and the men shook hands. Immediately the merchant explained why he was there - to claim the land being offered.

"Art thou truly satisfied?" the Quaker asked the merchant. The merchant responded, "I am, indeed. I have everything I need." The old farmer answered, "My friend, if thou art satisfied with everything ye have, why doth thou need my land?" And with that he closed the door.

We have been duped. We think that acquisition will satisfy us. We have been fooled into thinking that a shinier car, a bigger house, a younger wife, a better neighborhood, or the newest piece of technology will make us happy. But it's an evaporating illusion. When you are chasing after what will never ultimately please you, getting more of it won't get it done.

I think that's what Jesus was getting at when he said, "Seek first the Kingdom of God, and all these other things will be added to you." He was saying, "You're going to desire, you're going to want; just point those cravings in the right direction."

Then you discover that living a satisfying life requires very little. You will discover that the hungry life can be replaced by the happy life.

November 24: Gratitude

A man went to his rabbi and complained, "There are ten of us living in one room. Life is unbearable!" The rabbi answered, "Go home and take your goat into the room with you. Come back in a week."

A week later the man returned more distraught than before. "Rabbi, we cannot stand it. The goat is so filthy!" The rabbi told him, "Go home, let the goat out; come back in a week."

A radiant man returned to week later. His perspective had been astonishingly altered. "Life is beautiful," he cried. "We enjoy every minute of living together without the goat – and there's only the ten of us!"

Jesus once encountered a group of ten, living together, with little for which to be thankful. These ten had more than a stinking goat in the room. They had leprosy. Life was unbearable. Jesus did more than change their perspective. Mercifully, he healed them. This group turned together from death's door. But they did not turn together toward their healer. Only one of the ten came back to Jesus.

Even Jesus was surprised by this. "Were not all ten cleansed?" Jesus asked rhetorically. "Where are the other nine?" Maybe one waited to see if the cure was for real. Maybe another intended to go back later. Maybe one ran to the family from which he had long been separated.

I don't know for sure why the others did not return, but I do know that we can become so absorbed in our blessings or good fortune that we fail to consider the Source of those blessings. During this season of gratitude, may the Source of every good and perfect gift give us the greatest gift of all: A grateful heart. In return, may we fall at his feet with joyful thanksgiving.

November 25: How Much Land Does A Man Need?

Leo Tolstoy wrote about an unhappy farmer in, "How Much Land Does a Man Need?" This farmer never seemed to have enough, so he traveled to a distant tribe that possessed more land than anyone could walk over; and it was all there for the taking.

"Pay a thousand rubles and begin walking in a circle," the tribe instructed the farmer. "Everything within that circle, so long as the circle is completed by sundown, is yours."

At sunrise the following morning the farmer began running as quickly as he could, making a large circle, to get as much land as possible. Late in the day, realizing how far from the starting point he was, he began the desperate return trip.

He ran with all his waning strength back to the beginning of his circle. Just as the sun was setting, he collapsed where he began. The tribespeople cheered and celebrated. Never had anyone acquired so much land in one day!

In joy they bent down to rouse the farmer from his exhaustion, but he did not stir. He was dead. Tolstoy concludes the story by saying: "The farmer's servant picked up a spade and dug a grave and buried him. Six feet from his head to his heels was all he needed."

How much land (or you can insert different words here) do you really need? It is a lie to believe that killing ourselves in the chase to get just a little more will bring some satisfaction. Such thinking is a death-spawning run in a circle.

Yes, we can enjoy the good things that come into our life, and we may be able to afford the monthly payment on a lot of different luxuries, but the cost of acquisition is often measured in currency more expensive than dollars.

November 26: Bless The Name

Elmore's Department Store was one of the three more enjoyable places for a young child to visit in my small, Southern, home town. There was the Super D which had the best popcorn and hotdogs anywhere around; Western Auto with its mechanical horse that one could ride for a dime; and Elmore's.

Elmore's was the local department store. And, while it was likely not much bigger than a closet in comparison to today's big box stores, for a youngster with a couple of dollars, it was a shopping nirvana.

My dad took me there one afternoon and while searching for those magical Matchboxes I got lost in the clothing department, dwarfed as I was, by the towering racks of dress shirts and blue jeans.

I called for my father. "Daddy! Daddy!" I said. Nothing. On the verge of panic I changed tactics: "Roy! Roy!" He showed up within seconds. There were a lot of dads in Elmore's that day, but I needed the one with a unique name. I needed the father to whom I belonged.

Jews have a marvelous way of spontaneously giving thanks. They exclaim, "Blessed be the Name!" They are doing much the same as I did when I was lost in that department store. The "Name" represents all the extraordinary goodness they have come to know about the one to whom they belong.

They know God as someone who is better to us than anyone else ever could be; someone who loves us with unconditional love; someone who welcomes us to the table without qualification or reservation; someone who provides us with what we really need; someone we can call on when we have lost our way.

For that, and so very much more, we should bow our heads in sincere thanksgiving, and "Bless the Name."

November 27: No Obligation

My friend went to work for one of the largest missions organizations in the world. For nearly twenty years of faithful service he was among indigenous people groups living out the love and witness of Christ.

It all came to a grinding halt while he was serving in one of the more oppressive Islamic nations of the world. His organization shut down the hospital where he worked. Why? Not enough locals were becoming Christians.

My friend pleaded with the mission's executives to reconsider. This was a hostile, dangerous country that required Christians to go "underground." Further, the hospital treated thousands of patients a year. and a part of the world that previously hated "western Christianity" was finding it increasingly difficult to hate those who were loving, medicating and saving their children, sick and elderly.

A mission executive responded to these pleas with this: "We have no obligation to the bodies of those whose souls are going to hell."

Is this really the gospel? To disregard the crushing misery of people if those needs are not spiritual in nature? Can we say we are following Jesus if we focus exclusively on the heaven to come while ignoring the hell of this world?

Jesus taught, lived, died and lives again, not so a few select people could earn a seat on a heavenly evacuation pod while everyone else is tossed into the galactic trash can. No, he came to create a community of people who would make it their vocation to live out heaven on earth so that redemption, in all its magnificent and diverse manifestations, will be experienced today, not just tomorrow.

We have the opportunity - the obligation - to become catalysts and conduits of the kingdom of God here in today's world, because today – not tomorrow – is "the day of salvation."

November 28: By The Rules

In the winter of 1988, Mother Teresa was walking through the snow in the South Bronx looking for a building she might convert into a homeless shelter. She found two fire-gutted buildings on 148th Street, and the city of New York offered one of the buildings to her Missionaries of Charity for one dollar.

Immediately they began repairing the buildings, but after two years, Teresa was told that New York's building code required their building to have an elevator. She explained that because of their vows, they were prohibited from using modern technology. So even if an elevator were installed, it would never be used.

Plus, an elevator would add an additional $100,000 to the cost of the project. The Mission was told the law could not be waived - no matter what. So Mother Teresa did something she rarely did: She gave up. She could not, in good conscience, devote that much extra money and time to something that would not really help the poor.

She wrote to the city of New York: "The sisters feel we could use the money much more usefully for soup and sandwiches instead of elevators." She went on to thank the city for their efforts and intentions, and that the entire episode had "served to educate us about the law and its many complexities."

Philip Howard observed the story and said, "No person set out to oppose or spite Mother Teresa. It was just the law." Yet he rightfully says that the story of the Missionaries of Charity in New York reflects how "order can get in the way of what is right and just."

Legalism easily replaces common sense. Be sure that in all things, you attempt to do what is right and merciful, not what is orderly or allowable by rule.

November 29: The Good Life

My family has a furry little pup named "Mo." We took him in temporarily, but he so effectively wormed his way into our hearts, he became an irreplaceable part of the family.

Mo isn't very bright. Lift one of his ears, look in, and you will see straight through to the other side; zero brains. But what he lacks in IQ, he more than makes up for in happiness.

He wakes up every morning like he just won the lottery, full of joy at the prospect of another day. He attacks every single meal as if it were filet mignon. He becomes deliriously euphoric when taken for a walk. He greets every newcomer with wet kisses and a wagging tail.

And his favorite thing in the whole world is to crawl into your lap while you drink your morning coffee or beg for a belly rub while watching the evening news. In fact, that's about the extent of his demands. All he requires is a little affection, and he has no other expectations.

Maybe that's the secret to both canine and human happiness - to find satisfaction in what we have. Like the "birds of the air" and the "lilies of the field" (or dogs sleeping at the foot of your bed). They don't toil or spin, sow or reap, fear or worry, because they simply take what life gives them.

Ask yourself this candid question: How different would your life be if you were truly content with what you have, instead of being disappointed over what you don't have?

No, you don't have to be very smart to be happy: Greet each morning with gusto. Savor the little enjoyments. Take a walk. Love the people around you without reservation. Slow down. That's a dog's life, and that's a good life.

November 30: The Catch

There is a story told a hundred different ways but with the same punch line; it is about a man who falls off a cliff. He slips over the edge, careening and banging downward. Then, as if by miracle, his pants snag on the skinniest of tree branches. He quickly grabs hold of it, and for the moment remains alive, though he is hanging thousands of feet above the ground.

He can't climb up, and he can't lower himself to the canyon floor below. Stuck as he is, with no one else to call upon, and powerless to save himself, he looks heavenward and prays: "Dear God! Please help me!" A thunderous but calming voice answers from heaven: "Do you trust me, my beloved son?"

The man cries out in return, "Yes, God, I trust you! Please save me!" God answers, "Okay, just let go of the branch and I will catch you." The man thinks about this offer and his situation for a moment, and looking at the jagged rocks below him, calls out: "Well, is there anyone else up there who can help me?"

It's often that we want God to intervene. To help us, save us, because we have no other option. And don't be too hard on yourself for calling on God only after you have exhausted all other avenues. I'd say he's used to that, and it's human nature to do our own thing until we can't do anything else.

Grace means God will help anyway - on one condition. The "catch" to grace, the only requirement to receiving God's help is faith (not a skinny tree branch that grabs the seat of your pants). You will have to simply let go of whatever it is you are clutching, and fall into the arms of God.

DECEMBER

December 1: Let The Singing Begin

The following is from Pastor Peter Loughman:

"We were new to town and heard that a church had a fantastic Christmas Eve service. So, we went with some friends. The usher gave us the bulletin and warned us that there should be no talking before, during, or after the service. Those in the congregation were also forbidden from singing, as the choir found it difficult to perform with unprofessionals.

"The service started with the hymn 'O Come All Ye from Faithful.' Our row couldn't help but sing. An usher appeared, quite menacing, and hushed our unprofessional row right up. The second hymn was 'Hark The Herald Angels Sing.' The choir was quite good, but unlike the rest of the congregation our row couldn't resist singing. Immediately the usher was upon us: 'One more time, and you are out,' he scolded us.

"Christmas hymn, after Christmas hymn, and we couldn't sing a word. We were like prisoners in our pew. It was miserable. Finally, the service was ending and the carol 'Silent Night' was just beginning. It is irresistible and we started singing once again.

"A heavy hand fell upon my shoulder, 'You have to leave. You're singing again,' our ever vigilant usher said. I didn't move. We were on the last verse" and in unified defiance, our whole row sang the hymn with increasing gusto.

"We finished the hymn, extinguished our candles, and headed for the door, where we were met by the usher. He shook our hands and exclaimed, 'Merry Christmas, please join us for service this week.'"

As you might guess, Pastor Loughman found a different place to worship the following week. Advent is upon us, the season of the year that we celebrate the arrival of Jesus. Let the singing begin - and don't let anyone stop you.

December 2: A Third Option

Philosophers can be divided into two groups: The optimists and the pessimists. The optimists believe that people, at their core, are good. They believe that given enough time and opportunity, humanity will progress toward utopia. The pessimists, however, believe that we are animals; irretrievably evil, incapable of changing.

These two conflicting philosophies have pulled and tugged against us for all of human history. But there is a third option. As followers of Jesus and believers in his Advent, we accept neither blind optimism nor jaded hopelessness.

We believe the blind optimists are wrong, because "progress" has been a failure - technologically, no - but spiritually, an absolute fiasco. But pessimism has no future either. Yes, evil is real – in our world and in our hearts - it is a dirty, four-letter word. But love is a four-letter word too. And it is the love of God that is the only real option for our world, a love born manifested in the Christ Child, born for our redemption.

God's love that sent Christ into the world is not naïve. His love recognizes that the world is a hard, difficult, unjust place. It recognizes that we are incapable of getting off of the merry-go-round that leads to our own destruction.

But that love also recognizes that humanity is the crowning achievement of God's creation, and we are of such value and worth to God, that he cannot leave us without salvation and a path to transformation.

Love transcends both our misguided optimism and our desperate cynicism because love actually changes us. Ultimately, that is why we believe, hope in, and follow Jesus. In him we experience the love of God that leads to redemption – not progressive utopia, not cynical annihilation – but redemption, God's "good tidings of great joy for all people."

December 3: Out Of The Box

I received a cartoon that made me laugh; and think. Jesus and God have gathered around the Christmas tree to exchange gifts. I'm sure the Holy Spirit is there, but as a Spirit, he is unseen.

Jesus appears disappointed with what the Father has given him. So God says, "What's wrong Jesus? You said you wanted a church for your birthday!" Jesus, who is looking with confusion at his gift, answers, "Yeah, I did. But I'm having trouble getting it out of the box."

Having trouble getting the church out of the box? Indeed, it is a difficult task. Not that there is anything wrong with boxes, that is, the containers that hold us from time to time. But where we gather - what we mistakenly call a "church" is just a box. The real church is a people, and if the people stay boxed in, never getting out, then it must be frustrating for our Lord and detrimental for our world.

Samuel Escobar said the "forgotten Commission" of John's gospel provides both a mandate for engaging the world around us, and a model. In John 20:21 Jesus says to his disciples: "As the Father has sent me, I am sending you!"

Jesus was sent by God as his loving, redemptive agent. Now Jesus sends us out to be the same. In a most authentic way, the church is the continuation of the incarnation. It is the expression and embodiment of Advent. We are the next chapter in the Christmas story. We who call Jesus our Lord, take on the very real presence of Christ in the world.

If - and it's a fairly big "if" - if we are willing to get out of the box and into the world, we can go where Jesus went, for that's where we belong.

December 4: A Little Help

"Marley was dead. There is no doubt whatever about that. As dead as a doornail." This is how Charles Dickens' classic, *The Christmas Carol*, begins, a holiday favorite for decades.

Certainly, you know the story; Ebenezer Scrooge, a miserly, tight-fisted old man "bahs" and "humbugs" his way through the Christmas season with no concern for his fellow man. So he is haunted by three spirits: The ghosts of Christmas Past, Christmas Present, and Christmas Future. This was Dickens' creative and prophetic effort to correct the attitude of a hardened, curmudgeon of a man.

Scrooge's words epitomized his crustiness. Confronted by the suffering of those whom he felt were not deserving, he wished simply that the poor would perish as quickly as possible "and decrease the surplus population," so that there would be less panhandling for charity.

When we refer to a "Scrooge," it should be remembered that this is not a person who doesn't enjoy the Christmas season (We all grow weary of the crass commercialism, materialism, and end-of-year pleas). No, a "Scrooge" is one with callouses around his or her heart, one who could help others in need, but won't.

When we are comfortable, possessing all we need, it's easy to throw around words like "handout" or "lazy." At such times it's also easy to miss how much like Ebenezer we are. Sure, some people will never help themselves, but there are many, many more who just need that little help we can give.

It might be wise to remember that we've all had help to get to where we are. If you don't believe that, just look at your navel. That umbilical stump proves that your life began with someone else's help. No, there are no "self-made" people, only people made to help others.

December 5: What Counts

Joseph, by far, is the least recognized member of the Christmas family. Mary, deservedly, gets a great deal of attention. And Jesus? Of course the story is all his. But Joseph is often overlooked, his role in the whole affair seemingly so small. But somebody has to play the small part, and those who do, can make a big difference.

A teacher in front of a classroom. An artist behind the canvas. A coach on the sidelines. A grandparent on the front porch. A missionary in an inner city. A foster home with a new child. An aunt, uncle, or older sibling raising a child. A carpenter fathering a curly-haired Jewish boy. You never know what the future will bring.

A great man said: "What counts in life is not the mere fact that we have lived. It is the difference we have made in the lives of others." That great man was Nelson Mandela who died on this date in 2013.

Mandela's legacy is well known: His personal transformation, his decades of imprisonment, his ending of apartheid, his Nobel Peace Prize, all his publications and rise to worldwide statesmanship. But his life could have been much different.

Mandela's father suddenly died when the boy was young. An African child without a father is destined for poverty and obscurity. But a tribal leader adopted Mandela as his own. This resulted in his education, acceptance into college, eventually his campaign for black African rights, and everything that followed.

Everyone has heard of Nelson Mandela. Hardly anyone has heard of Jongintaba Dalindyebo. But without this quiet, unrecognized man, Nelson Mandela's legacy would have never been possible. I think God gives out such assignments more often than we recognize. He gave one to Joseph. He just might have given one to you.

December 6: Joy, Joy, Joy

"I've got the joy, joy, joy, joy, down in my heart." So goes the children's tune I first learned in Sunday School. "It's down in my heart to stay," the familiar refrain ends. But joy, leaking out of these fractured human containers, has a way of escaping.

The car breaks down. The boss needs you to work the entire weekend. The school calls about your misbehaving child. Bills clog the mailbox. It's like having an emotional vacuum cleaner hooked up to your chest. Before long, the "joy, joy, joy," is gone, gone, gone.

But if you listen, you might hear joy's beautiful song. Listen for it in the ringing bell outside your favorite department store as you're invited to give to the poor. Hear it in the giggle of your children as they wait in line to sit on Santa's knee. Look at it sitting around your holiday table, the faces of your friends, family, and loved ones.

Joy is in every Christmas caroler, every gift given, every holiday meal shared, and in every reading of the nativity story. Joy waits, like all well-mannered guests, to be invited in.

The angel in the Advent story appears to the quaking shepherds and says, "Behold, I bring you good tidings of great joy. For unto you is born a Savior, which is Christ the Lord." This sent those shepherds tearing through the dark Bethlehem streets, unable to still their joyful hearts.

Eventually, they had to return to their sheep and go back to work. But they did not lose their joy in the process. They went back to the fields "glorifying and praising God for the things they had heard and seen." The "joy, joy, joy, joy was down in their hearts to stay." May it be in yours as well.

December 7: The Best Of Things

"Let me tell you something, my friend. Hope is a dangerous thing. Hope can drive a man insane." So said Red Redding to Andy Dufresne in that masterpiece, "The Shawshank Redemption." If you have never seen the movie, find time to view it, as it will be worth your time.

Shawshank is about life in prison. It is a story about guilt and innocence. Friendship and love. Vengeance and absolution. Struggle and injustice. It is a story about hope, and how hope can keep a man alive, even though Red had given up on hope long ago.

What is hope exactly? A cruel joke? An ethereal smokescreen that convinces gullible people to long for something that is impossible to attain? No, it is patience. It is perseverance, endurance. We might call it resilience.

We exhibit hope when we persist; when we refuse to quit; when we keep believing, even though any reward for our belief is not quickly forthcoming.

Vaclav Havel, the Czech playwright who was eventually elected the first president of the Czech people after the fall of the Soviet Union, defined hope as well as Andy Dufresne or anyone else could for that matter. He said, "Hope is not optimism. It is a state of mind. It is the certainty that life has meaning, regardless of how it turns out. I am not an optimist, because I'm not sure everything will end well. I just carry hope in my heart."

Yes, "hope is a dangerous thing," but not because it "can drive a man insane." It is a dangerous thing to the status quo; it gives people the tenacity to "keep on keeping on." It gives people the power to change the world. And that is why, in this world, Andy Defresne called hope "the best of things."

December 8: The Manger

"Mary brought forth her firstborn son, wrapped him in swaddling clothes, and laid him in a manger." There was nothing extraordinary about this. The extraordinary thing is this is God "laid in a manger." God, born with the stench of animals. God, born into a backwoods village with third world germs and bacteria. God in a feed trough.

We have made religion an exercise in gaining elevation. We have turned it into a spiritual mountain climb, a Jack-and-the-Bean-Stalk ascent, pulling ourselves up to the top. Then we will be enlightened; we will be better; we'll make ourselves stronger, more worthy, and more God-like.

I'll not argue with the intended goals. But the means to becoming more like God isn't in climbing higher. What the birth of Jesus says to us, is not that a man can become a god, but that God has become a man.

Go to Bethlehem and see the wrinkled, olive skin and the wet curly hair of a newborn boy. Hear the midwife shred a feed sack into strips and wipe Mary's brow. Look at all of Joseph's buck-toothed, bug-eyed cousins, peeping into the stable. Listen for the sandals of the shepherds, clippity-clopping along the streets, running to kneel at the manger as quickly as their angel-struck feet can carry them.

There God is. He is in the mud and in the manure. He is among the poor and the ordinary. He is down on the earth, and down to earth. There is no climbing up any ladder to get to this God. There is only kneeling down to find him. You only meet him in the grime and the grunge of this world. There is no hiking to the top; there is only letting him in.

December 9: Who Will?

On December 9, 1965, Charles Schulz's "Peanuts" was brought to life on national television for the first time. A half-hour special aired entitled, "A Charlie Brown Christmas."

Charlie Brown, the beloved anti-hero of the "Peanuts" gang, is feeling down and out at Christmas time. It's just too commercialized, he concludes, so he becomes the director of the annual Christmas play to make a difference.

He's not much of a director, so Lucy sends him to get a Christmas tree. And not just any tree, mind you: "Get a big, shiny aluminum tree," she says.

What does Charlie Brown bring back? The smallest, puniest, ugliest, scrawniest piece of pine wood anyone has ever seen. And the "Peanuts" gang is merciless in response, and Charlie is so distressed he exclaims, "Isn't there anyone who knows what Christmas is all about?!?!"

It is then that trusty Linus steps forward – him, his blanket and his wilted, saliva-soaked thumb – to save the day. He quotes the Christmas story from Luke 2, the King James Version, in fact. In the end, Linus picks up his blanket, walks over to his friend and says, "That's what Christmas is all about, Charlie Brown." And with that, the mood, the tree, the poison-mouthed Peanuts, and the despondent Charlie Brown are transformed.

The executives of CBS took a huge gamble when they aired that Christmas program in 1965. Emphatically, they did not want to have Linus reciting the story of the birth of Jesus from the Bible. It was too preachy; too old fashioned.

But for all their resistance, Charles Schulz was even more adamant that the scene be kept in the program, for in the words of Schulz to the executives: "If we don't tell the true meaning of Christmas, who will?" Indeed, who will?

December 10: The Innkeeper

I've always sympathized with the innkeeper in the Christmas story. He couldn't have known he was turning the Messiah away. So I was glad that Jeffery Dillinger rewrote the tale, based on his own experience. Dillinger wrote about a sweet 7th grade boy named Wally.

"Wally was bigger than any other kid in his Sunday School class. He was also limited. His mother had been an alcoholic, and as a result, Wally had fetal alcohol syndrome. He was loved and loving, but as a child with developmental disabilities, was regarded as "slow."

"Christmas time came and since Wally was the biggest and had the hardest time with memorization, he was selected to be the innkeeper. The class coached Wally to be as ugly and as mean as he possibly could be.

"The night came for the Christmas play, and Mary and Joseph came to Bethlehem. They went to the inn and knocked on the door. Wally opened the door and said, 'What do you want?' just as gruff as he could. Joseph answered, 'Sir, we need a room for the night.'

Wally the innkeeper said, 'You'll have to stay someplace else. There's no room here!' Joseph pleaded, 'Please, sir, my wife is expecting a baby. Don't you have someplace where we can be protected from the cold and where she can deliver her child?'

"Silence. Wally had forgotten his lines. From behind the curtains you could hear someone saying, 'Be gone. Be gone.' Finally, Wally slammed the door.

Mary and Joseph turned, sadly to leave. But just as they did, Wally opened the door and said, "Wait a minute. Wait a minute. You can have my room."

And if the innkeeper had known who was at his door that first Christmas night, he would have done the very same thing.

December 11: Tangled

Here I am, twisted up in the same desperate situation again this year. I planned carefully to avoid it, but to no avail. When I put the Christmas lights away last January they were in perfectly arranged order. I knew the strings of blinking colors would burst from their boxes unfettered. Instead, every strand looks like a giant bird's nest.

Maybe Joseph felt this way on the first Christmas, like a big tangled mess had just landed in his lap. One day everything made sense. The next day nothing did. One day Joseph was driving nails, doing what carpenters do, and the next he was in the middle of a divine conspiracy.

What did Joseph do with this tangled web? He went to work untangling every twisted strand of it. He took on the responsibility that had found him. Joseph chose to play the role of father to his adopted son. He kept driving nails and doing what carpenters do, unraveling each stubborn strand as he went.

I'm sure there were a few knots that never came undone for Joseph, as there are often not enough answers to go around, just twisting questions and more impossible knots.

What do we do in times like these? We sit down with whatever life, God, or destiny has dealt us and we untangle what we can. We keep doing whatever it is we do, staying with it. Because if we are going to live life, it will mean persisting through the confusion. There's no other choice.

So when your well-ordered, well-kept life explodes into a tangled mess – and it will – what are you going to do? You can point fingers, blame others, curse the Fates, ask a million unanswerable questions, or you can get on with untangling things as you go.

December 12: For Lottie

She was born December 12, 1840, into an affluent Virginia family. She was named Charlotte Moon. Everyone called her Lottie. At 18 she committed herself to Christ, became fluent in six languages, and shortly thereafter was appointed as a Southern Baptist missionary to China.

The Baptists had never sent an unmarried woman to the mission field, and it's still a divine mystery how Lottie pulled it off. But she did. She reported to the North China Mission Station in the port of Tengchow, and began her ministry by teaching in established missionary schools, but she gave up teaching and moved into the interior to plant Christian churches.

Alone in the interior and deprived of Western companionship, Moon increasingly retreated into the "inner chamber" of her heart, developing a near mystical relationship with Christ. Immersed in the culture, Moon became one the Chinese, and during a famine in 1911, she gave all her food and money to famine relief.

By the time her assistants discovered that she had been starving herself to feed the Chinese, she weighed only fifty pounds. Moon died at the age of seventy-two, on December 24, 1912, in the harbor of Kobe, Japan, while en route to America. The official cause of her death was malnutrition.

In 1918, the "Lottie Moon Christmas Offering" was established, for Baptist churches, and since then, that collection to aid the international world has collected more than $1.5 billion dollars.

Lottie was a shining example of incarnation: She went into a dangerous world, rife with famine, violence, war, and injustice, simply to love people. And while she was more often maligned, misunderstood, and lonely, her good works do follow her. May we all be compelled by this kind of love, the same love of God that birthed Jesus into the world.

December 13: The Waking God

Annie Dillard said of those of us who casually enter our church sanctuaries each week, "Does anyone have the foggiest idea what sort of power we so blithely invoke? We should all be wearing crash helmets. Ushers should issue life preservers and signal flares; they should lash us to our pews. For the waking God may draw us out to where we can never return."

Advent is no exception to this experience. It is the rule. God has awoken. More so, God has arrived. And even though it is in the form of a helpless baby, the world is turned upside down. Shepherds quake. Angels sing. Mary trembles. Awe-inspired Magi bow in reverence. Joseph, a stunned carpenter, scratches his head.

Everyone is asked to believe that the baby, "wrapped in swaddling clothes and lying in a manger," is indeed the Promised One of God, a uniquely born gift to the world. Are we not all asked to believe the same? Are we not asked to believe that God has spoken?

I am very much aware that when one speaks of "God speaking," it might be time to call the paddy wagon. Great lunacies have been committed by individuals convinced that they were on a divine mission. But to hear God speak, deep within our hearts, is not necessarily a sign of mental illness.

It can be; just like finding Jesus's image in a bag of cheese puffs or an icon of the Virgin Mary on the back of a piece of raisin toast. It can be a manipulative way to dupe the spiritually naïve.

Yet, on those rare and unusual occasions, Annie Dillard is right: "The waking God may draw us out to where we can never return." He has spoken and nothing will ever be the same again.

December 14: Undoer Of Knots

A man named Irenaeus, an early church father, was one of the first Christians who did serious thinking about the Advent season and its greater meaning. He thought a lot about Mary and came to the conclusion that Mary's example of holy surrender to God's will was a pattern for us all. He used a scintillating title for her, one I had not heard until a few years ago. He called Mary, "The Undoer of Knots."

Mary took the tangled mess she had been given - young, unwed, "found with child," and subject to ridicule and condemnation, and persistently worked it out, overcoming all her challenges in redemptive, surprising ways.

Pope Francis, who has loved Irenaeus' title since he first saw Johann Georg Melchior Schmidtner's baroque painting "Mary, Undoer of Knots," as a young student in Europe, says the same.

Speaking of that little girl from Nazareth and the model she gives us, he says: "There are problems and struggles we face for which we do not see any solution. They form a tangle which gets more and more painful and difficult to undo. But even the most tangled knots are loosened by God's grace. All the knots of our heart, every knot of our conscience, can be undone."

And then Pope Francis tells us how: "Mary first conceived Jesus in faith when she said 'Yes' to the message God gave her. And what took place in the Virgin Mary also takes place within us. Believing in Jesus means giving him our flesh with the humility and courage of Mary, so that he can continue to dwell in our midst.

"May Mary help us to say 'Yes,' to be open to God's surprises, for everything he gives us is a gift - even our weaknesses - so that he can become our strength."

December 15: Can't Stop Christmas

In the 21st century we take the celebration of Christmas for granted. We exchange gifts, sing carols, light candles, spend obscene amounts of money, enjoy family and friends, and eat to the point of embarrassment. But this kind of inhibition has not always been so easy.

For the first centuries of Christian history there was no Christmas. Christians celebrating the birth of the King of Kings and Lord of Lords, with Caesar still very much in power in Rome, was a recipe for extermination. No one was stringing lights around a tree while singing, "Happy Birthday, Jesus!"

But finally, it became safe enough to celebrate so the early church picked a date when shepherds would have been keeping watch over their sheep at night - in the spring - the most likely time of Jesus' birth. It was the 4th century before December 25th became the Christian celebration of the birth of Christ.

But in 1643, British Parliament outlawed Christmas because of its connection to ancient paganism. Massachusetts did the same, levying a fine against anyone caught celebrating. It was not until 1836 that the first state legalized Christmas as a holiday in the United States. Any guesses what state that was? It was the land of boll weevils, Bear Bryant, and boiled peanuts: Alabama.

By 1900 all other states had followed, due largely to the dedication of Lutherans, Catholics, and Anglicans who recognized the need to celebrate the Advent season. All the early Baptists, Presbyterians, Quakers and Congregationalists opposed the celebration of Christmas. They said it was too worldly (If they could only see it now!).

The laws to stop Christmas celebrations never held up. How could they? The need to celebrate the birth of Jesus was just too strong because no one can stop Christmas - not then - and not now.

December 16: The Missing Jesus

Many Christmas seasons ago I was very busy as a hospital chaplain. The entire staff was busy, and we were all on the verge of overlooking the "reason for the season." One of the hospital volunteers brought us back to our senses. She came rushing into the office with the panicked words, "Jesus is missing!"

I thought someone had taken a crucifix out of one of the hospital rooms. Sometimes Jesus finds himself among a patient's personal belongings when they leave. The hospital kept a whole box of Jesuses to replace the stolen ones, figuring if a person needs Jesus enough to steal him, then please, take him.

But this missing Jesus was the baby one from the Nativity scene. Everyone was there: Mary, Joseph, shepherds, angels - all the usual suspects - except for Jesus. The manger was empty. Our volunteer concluded that Jesus had been stolen from his crib while sleeping.

It was quickly clarified that Jesus was not missing. He simply hadn't arrived yet. Baby Jesus was wrapped, not in swaddling clothes, but in shrink wrap and stuck in a drawer. He was safe and sound waiting for Christmas Day to make his grand entrance. We, along with all the Nativity scene characters, wait for him until then.

In your own heart Jesus may be locked away, collecting dust in some dark little corner. You may have grown so busy that you have not even thought of him during this season.

Break the packaging. Knock off the dust. Get him out of the drawer. Let him take his place at the center of this season, and at the center of your life. We may be busy, but not so busy that we forget to "praise God for all we have heard and seen" in this child born in Bethlehem.

December 17: Is There Any Hope?

On December 17, 1927, a Navy submarine was trolling beneath the waters of Cape Cod Bay. A Coast Guard cutter was traveling across the surface. The vessels never saw each other.

The submarine broke the surface just in time to receive a deathblow from the cutter. Rescue attempts began at once, but it took hours for the first diver to descend to the wreckage. When he found the hull he heard tapping. There were survivors pounding out a question in Morse Code on the hull: "Is there any hope?"

Humans need a few essentials for survival. Food. Water. Air. Without these we can't live, not for long. And then, hope. No one can live, truly live, a millisecond without it.

Is there any hope? I can hear this question echo from this craft we call Earth. We find the New Testament to be correct when it says that all of creation groans for renewal and relief. The world hopes for something better.

Hope is fastened to this child we find lying in a Christmas manger. Advent is a season to remember, yes, the coming of the Christ child into the world. But it is also a time to anticipate. Christians gather in houses of worship and around Advent wreaths to reflect upon the day when Christ will come again. A day when all things will be made new; a day when hope will become certainty, when what we can only pray for now, becomes definite.

In the meantime, we are called to live lives of anticipation as we look forward to that day and "speed its coming." The arrival of hope depends largely upon us, the decisions we make and the lives we live. Will we live in such a way to bring redemption to the world? I hope so.

December 18: Worth The Risk

In December 2013, American Ronnie Smith was shot and killed in Libya as he took his morning jog. He had been a high school teacher at the International School in Benghazi.

What was Smith doing in one of the most dangerous places in the world? By his own testimony, "to spread a spiritual message and go where no one could find a church if they wanted to, where no one has access to the gospel."

Ironically, he died at the same age as his Lord, 33. And he died in likewise fashion, having traveled an incredible distance, taken on the culture of a different people, immersed himself in the grit and grime of their troubles, and scorning safety, gave it his all.

His wife, Anita, wrote an open letter to the Libyan people just after Ronnie's death: "We came to Libya because we saw your suffering, but we also saw your hope, and we wanted to partner with you to build a better future. We stayed because we believed the Libyan people were worth the risk.

"To his attackers: I love you and forgive you. How could I not? For Jesus taught us to 'Love our enemies' - not to kill them or seek revenge. Jesus sacrificed His life out of love for the very people who killed him. Jesus did not come only to take us to paradise when we die, but also to bring peace and healing on this earth.

"Ronnie would want his death to be an opportunity for us to show one another love and forgiveness, because that's what God has shown us."

"Worth the risk:" These words can only be spoken through the power and love of a God who took on flesh, entered our world, suffered, and died. Because we were "worth the risk" too.

December 19: Let It Be

For a long time I thought a "Hail Mary" was a desperate, last-ditch throw at the end of a football game. Having been raised in one of the more contrary factions of Protestantism, you can't blame me; we weren't allowed to talk to Mary.

The prayer that bears her name goes: "Hail Mary, full of grace. Our Lord is with thee. Blessed art thou among women, and blessed is the fruit of thy womb, Jesus." It's Gabriel's announcement in Luke's Christmas story. Mary's response is not as well known but just as remarkable. She answers Gabriel, "Let it be."

Paul McCartney wrote his song by that same title at a difficult time: The Beatles were breaking up, individually they were all suffering, and McCartney was lost and confused. He began to feel this wrenching misery, longing for his mother – named Mary – who had died when he was fourteen.

Paul's mother came to him in a dream, he says. And she said, "Paul, let it be." McCartney awoke, went to the piano, and wrote the now classic song: "When I find myself in times of trouble, Mother Mary comes to me; Speaking words of wisdom, let it be."

When Mary – the mother of Jesus, not McCartney – said, "Let it be," she was willingly receiving the way of God for her life. She was admitting that her designs for living would be set aside so that God's design for her life would come to fruition in and through her.

Hers, like McCartney's, was a song of surrender. It was a song of submission to a higher and better way. Now, this sounds like losing, like we are giving up, but we lose nothing. We gain everything. "Let it be." To confess such a thing is to indeed be full of grace.

December 20: Mercy, Mercy

Charles Brown's plane had been shot to pieces by German anti-aircraft guns. Half his crew was dead or wounded, and he could hardly keep the plane aloft. Brown looked to his left and locked eyes with Franz Stigler, an ace German fighter pilot flying just feet off Brown's wing. Brown knew this was the end.

But Stigler, one hand on the trigger and another on his rosary, couldn't shoot. Instead, he escorted Brown to the edge of Allied airspace, saluted, and peeled away. Brown landed safely, survived the war, and returned home. But the older he got, the more Brown thought about that December day above Germany. He decided to find that German pilot.

Shortly thereafter, he received a letter from Franz Stigler! It read, "Dear Charles, all these years I wondered what happened to you." Stigler was now making the same improbable search, and the two pilots became best friends.

Brown was forever grateful for Stigler's gift of mercy - his whole life had been possible because of it. But the event changed Stigler too. Stigler said, "The war cost me everything. Charles Brown was the only good thing that came out of it."

A book found in Charles Brown's library after both men's deaths had this written on the flap: "On the 20th of December, 1943, I had the chance to save a B-17 from her destruction. The pilot, Charles Brown, is for me, as precious as my brother. Thank you Charlie. Your Brother, Franz."

Few stories illustrate so well the transformational power of mercy. It is a shared gift, a gift for both the offender and the offended; for the violator and the violated. When we replace vengeance with compassion and retaliation with grace, then, like no other moment, we are giving life to the world.

December 21: All Means All

"We three kings of Orient are," begins a favorite carol of the Advent season. Favorite or not, the song is completely inaccurate. First, we don't know exactly how many kings there were. Second, they were not "kings" from the Orient. They were magi – primitive astronomers - from modern day Iran.

Third, these men did not find the Christ child while "following yonder star." They saw the star "in the East," but then proceeded west. The star did not reappear until they were already in Bethlehem.

And finally, the Magi do not belong in the Nativity scene at all. They were latecomers, maybe as late as Jesus' second birthday. The quaking shepherds, singing angels, and lowing cattle were all long gone.

My critique is to simply point out that we know extremely little about these mysterious men. And these traditions prevent us from embracing what we can learn from them – for the journey of the Magi is a fascinating exercise in unexpected faith.

Not many people would launch out on a dangerous journey through the Middle East based solely on a celestial hunch. Not many people would put their lives on hold to pursue their mystical intuitions. And the most shocking of all, not many Iranians would worship at the feet of a Jew.

Yet, in God's way, these all belonged together. Divisions of race, religion, nationality, distance, or ethnicity did not factor into the equation. This is a foreshadowing of what the Apostle Paul would say later.

"In Christ," he said, "there is no difference between Jew and Greek, slave and free person, male and female. You are all the same in Christ Jesus." And "all" does mean "all." All are welcome into the presence of the One who will "reconcile everything – all things in heaven and on earth to himself."

December 22: Shalom

"On earth peace, goodwill toward men," sang the angels on the first Christmas morning. The Hebrew word for peace is shalom. It is more than a word. It is a vision for how life could be, should be, and the life God is pulling his whole creation toward.

Thus, peace is not merely the absence of war or conflict. It is not simply quietness or calm. It is overall wellbeing. It is health and wholeness. It is personal, communal, and cosmic harmony. It is a satisfied and blessed life.

So, when someone blesses you with "Shalom!" they are wishing you the best that God offers. "Be at harmony with yourself, your world and your God. Have a fruitful, robust life," they are saying. All of that in a single word, and shalom is God's intent and will for the world.

If this is true, then what in God's world has gone so terribly wrong? This world is anything but peaceful. Tyrants rule. Violence is routine. Political opponents fight, argue, vilify and wrangle. Peace, much less the broader idea of shalom, doesn't seem to be how the "world really works" at all.

Yet, the problem is not God's, for he has provided the path to peace and goodwill. The problem is our lack of practicing peace. Such practice isn't easy, I know. Deep within my own heart, I am a violent, revenge-taking person. But stuck with Jesus, what choice do I have but to confess, "Let there be peace on earth; and let it begin with me."

If we believe that one day the lamb will lie down with the lion; that swords will be beaten into plowshares; that mercy and justice will flow down like the waters; then we must live that belief and put peace into action today.

December 23: No Limits

King David began his career as a singing cowboy of sorts, a rock-throwing, shepherding whippersnapper; shockingly, he became a giant slayer. There is Moses, a foreign-born, stuttering, impatient murderer of a man; wonder of wonders, he was God's chosen deliverer.

Rahab is the biblical version of Calamity Jane, running a brothel in Jericho; she saved an entire nation. Noah was a drunk; but he also built the incubator for humanity. Simon Peter was a loud-mouthed, hot-headed rambler who couldn't shut up and wouldn't show up when he was needed; he became a Rock.

Paul was a hump-backed, bug-eyed little weasel who made a living killing Christians - then he became one - and changed the trajectory of Western Civilization. And consider the Virgin Mary. While girls today are engrossed with whatever comes from Hollywood or Cupertino, she was busy birthing the Son of God.

Who could have anticipated such a thing, given her limitations. In her day, a woman would enter a prearranged marriage even before sitting for the SAT or getting a driver's permit. So she was nothing but a novice. And she was a woman. Women in first century Palestine were not very liberated. In fact, they were often considered property.

And Mary was from Nazareth. In Mary's lifetime, there were no fewer than three major rebellions in her hometown, and each of these insurrections were cataclysmically crushed by the military. So Mary was the wrong age, wrong gender, and from the wrong neighborhood, but God chose her to be "the most blessed among woman."

We think that our liabilities and weaknesses will prevent us from being used by God. Nothing could be further from the truth. Our limitations are the very things that birth the power and love of God into the world.

December 24: Silent Night, Holy Night

"Silent Night" is the most recognized Christmas song in the world. The story behind this beloved carol is well-known, but it deserves repetition.

It was December 23, 1818, and Pastor Josef Mohr was walking home after watching a Christmas play. His walk took him up a hill overlooking his village, a peaceful, snow-covered town with candles burning in each window.

Inspired, Mohr hurried home and wrote a poem thinking it would be good to sing for Christmas Eve if he could find some music to put with it. Franz Gruber, the local music teacher, attached a simple melody to the song the next morning. It had to be simple because the pipe organ at the church wasn't working.

So on Christmas Eve 1818, with only a guitar, Mohr's church heard and sang "Silent Night" for the first time. A few weeks later the repairman showed up to fix the church organ. When finished, Gruber sat down and began playing "Silent Night." The repairman, impressed, asked for a copy of the score.

Within 15 years the song had spread all over northern Europe. Within 50 years it had made it to New York City. Within a century, it was being sung by the troops during World War 1. From both sides soldiers along the Western Front left their trenches on Christmas Eve 1914, and met in "no-man's land" to celebrate an impromptu truce. "Silent Night" was the only carol they all knew and could sing in their native tongues.

Today, "Silent Night" will be sung in more than 300 different languages all around the world. So with Josepf Mohr, Franz Gruber, voices raised in every country, and with the declaration of the angels on that first Christmas, may we "sleep in peace" – for "Christ the Savior is born."

December 25: One Solitary Life

Dr. James Allen Francis wrote the following words almost a century ago, words that capture like few others the "good tidings of great joy, which shall be to all people, the birth of a Savior, which is Christ the Lord. Merry Christmas!

"He was born in an obscure village, the child of a peasant woman. He grew up in another obscure village where he worked in a carpenter shop until he was thirty. Then for three years he was an itinerant preacher.

"He never owned a home. He never wrote a book. He never held an office. He never had a family. He never went to college. He never visited a big city. He never traveled more than two hundred miles from the place where he was born. He never did one of the things that usually accompany greatness. He had no credentials but Himself.

"While still a young man, the tide of popular opinion turned against him. His friends ran away. One of them denied him. He was turned over to his enemies. He went through the mockery of a trial. He was nailed upon a cross between two thieves.

"While he was dying his executioners gambled for the only piece of property he had on earth - his coat. When he was dead, he was laid in a borrowed grave through the pity of a friend. These long centuries have come and gone, and today Jesus is the central figure of the human race.

"I am far within the mark when I say that all the armies that have ever marched; all the navies that have ever sailed; all the parliaments that have ever sat; all the kings that ever reigned, put together, have not affected the life of mankind on earth as powerfully as that one solitary life."

December 26: The Day After

Theodore Geisel was accepted into Dartmouth College just as Prohibition was passed into law in the early 1920s. But young Theodore was a third-generation brewer.

Therefore, it was no surprise when Theodore was busted by Dartmouth for throwing a drunken bash in his dormitory with a dozen or so of his friends. Theodore didn't get thrown out of school, but he was forced to resign all extracurricular activities, and this included his writing for one of Dartmouth's college newspapers.

Well, Geisel was an enterprising, creative young man, so he kept writing for the newspaper, just under an assumed name. He started signing his articles with his middle name: Seuss – and Dr. Seuss was born.

Dr. Seuss went on to write some of the greatest children's literature of the 20th century. My favorite is, *How the Grinch Stole Christmas*. Dr. Seuss is actually the Grinch, or at least the inspiration for the character.

Seuss says, "I was brushing my teeth on the morning of the 26th of December when I noticed a very Grinch-ish countenance in the mirror. It was me! So I wrote about my sour friend, the Grinch, to see if I could rediscover something about Christmas that obviously I had lost."

Christmas is over, and with it comes an almost unstoppable letdown. With so much anticipation for so much of the year, how could there not be a little air let out of all our hearts? It's to be expected.

This is no reason to let the Grinch steal your joy, however. It could be, perhaps, "that your shoes are too tight. Or it could be that your head isn't screwed on just right," to quote Seuss. Just make sure your heart isn't "two sizes too small." Christmas will stick with you much longer that way.

December 27: At Odds

In December of 2001, the Jews of Afghanistan celebrated their first Hanukah free of the Taliban in almost a decade. It was a small celebration, for there were only two Jews left in the entire country -alone.

At separate ends of a rundown synagogue, Ishak Levin and Zebulon Simantov lit their candles and said their prayers with a heavy, dark curtain dividing the room so that they would not have to see each other. Neither of the men could accurately remember what started their feud.

Levin said, "For a thousand and thousand years, our forefathers have celebrated these nights, and now Jews all over the world are celebrating too." And then speaking of his antagonist on the other side of the heavy curtain, he said, "But with him - it is not possible."

A decade later Levin was dead, leaving Simantov alone, the only known Jew left in the country, living in a single, tiny room, at odds with his neighbors, estranged from his family, cursing former friends, and demanding money or whiskey from reporters who came to interview him. He was a bitter, old man, the ugly product of his own hatred and lack of reconciliation.

Zebulon Simantov may be alone in his dilapidated Kabul synagogue, but he is not alone in his alienation, even as the celebrations of Hanukah and Christmas linger. Untold thousands are at war with those around them, be it the army across the border, or their neighbors across the street. These holidays of shalom and peace aren't enough to break the hold of ill will.

How long will you allow old animosities to keep you at odds with others; often others with whom you have so much in common? There is only one place that resentment will ultimately lead you: A place of complete isolation.

December 28: Grow Old, Grow Strong

New research from the US Geological Survey has uprooted decades of established dendrological study. What? You're not familiar with dendrology? It is the scientific word for the botanical studies related to trees. And it turns out that science has been barking up the wrong tree for some time.

The conventional understanding has been that young trees are healthier and grow faster than old trees, not unlike human beings. Then, when a tree reaches maturity, it stops growing. But not so, says the new research. Trees reach a limit as far as height goes, yes, but they never stop growing out. In fact, trees grow faster the older they get.

Again, this sounds most human-like. Eventually we stop growing up, but we start growing out – thickening in the middle. But trees aren't putting on fat, as it were; they are packing on pure botanical muscle. When properly rooted, getting the sustenance needed, trees get stronger the older they get.

Researcher Nate Stephenson said, "We're not talking about the tree equivalent of an aging crowd with beer guts. Old trees are more like active, healthy bodybuilders. It's as if, on your favorite sports team, you find out the star players are a bunch of 90-year-olds. They are the ones scoring the most points." Growth such as this, according to the new research, could go on indefinitely.

This "discovery" isn't new. We know this about people. Some of the strongest, most vibrant specimens are those with more than a few tree rings under their bark. They are sturdier than the many saplings whipping in the wind because they are older.

It's because they have stayed rooted in faith for a long time. That's how faith works. Stick with it; it will grow on you and you will grow with it.

December 29: Fuel For Tomorrow

The Old South Congregational Church in Boston sold one of its hymnals for a staggering $14.2 million. Obviously, this was no ordinary hymnal, but one of the first books ever printed in North America. The sale almost tore the church apart.

On one side were those members of the congregation who wanted to preserve the church's history. On the other side were those who felt that the resources of the church should be repurposed, not preserved.

I watched this story unfold and was sympathetic to both sides until I heard the church historian say that the church had two of these exceptional books, actually using them was impractical – they were much too fragile for that.

He further revealed that the hymnals weren't even in the church's possession. They were stored in a book museum at the Boston Public Library. Most church members have never even laid eyes on them. They had not been used, literally, for centuries.

One thoughtful parishioner said, "I have two sons, and looking forward I want my sons to learn that it's not about objects. We can take those objects from the past and turn them into fuel for tomorrow."

What a fantastic perspective, and what an applicable lesson for us all. As one year ends and another begins, a profound choice is put before us: Will we hold on to the past – preserving, protecting, and perpetuating it – even when doing so becomes much more work than it is worth? Or will we use the past, its gore and its glory, as fuel for the future?

Let's not make life a museum built to what used to be, but a mission to bring about what can be, for life is not so much about preserving the past as it is living with power and purpose today.

December 30: Puzzles Of The Past

It was on Christmas morning 1980 that I discovered Erno Rubik's magic puzzle under the tree: The Rubik's Cube. With a few twists I was hooked, but I never figured the thing out.

Theoretically, it is easily solved. No matter its configuration, it can be tidied up in twenty turns or less. But I suspect that of the 350 million cubes sold over the years, most of them are in the same condition as the one I received - unsolved.

There are some puzzles that cannot be solved, and most of these conundrums have a common denominator, described with one word: Yesterday. For every person wrestling with what is happening today; for every person anxious about what might happen tomorrow, there are a dozen people stuck in what happened yesterday.

We take our past experiences and we work them over and over and over again, getting bogged down, wasting life, and we can't seem to let the past go. But we can't keep attempting to solve what can no longer be solved, and live a free and peaceful life today.

This is almost impossible to believe, but according to Erno Rubik himself, there are 43 quintillion ways to scramble a Cube. So if you turned the Cube one turn every second, it would take you nearly 1500 trillion years to go through every permutation!

When viewed from this perspective, it makes perfect sense to give up on solving some of problems, for we don't have the time to obsess with unending analysis of how our lives could have been different. We don't have the years to navel gaze at our pain and our problems.

We are granted only so many days among the living, so we had better spend those days, living, not scrutinizing every twist and turn of our past.

December 31: Seasons Change

Your life will pass like the seasons of the year. The season will be, roughly, a period of time between 20 to 25 years each.

First, there is spring. Life is new and young. Everything is just beginning and your life calls you forward. You plant the seeds that in time will grow, bloom, and eventually be harvested.

Then comes summer. The days are long and warm. You have time to work, love, and play. Everything is growing, sometimes productively, and sometimes in a weedy, tangled mess. You fight floods and drought, good times and bad, but the weather is warm and welcoming.

The third season of your life is autumn, the great time of harvest. In your 40s, 50s, and stretching into your 60s, you begin to reap what you have sown. Your children become adults, and move toward the summer of their own lives. Your career and ideas about life reach maturity. The colors begin to change, on top of your head and on your chin.

Finally, there is winter, the last twenty or so years of life. There are still crops to harvest, and there are still a few seeds to plant, though not on the sprawling farm of life. You cultivate in little flower pots and hanging baskets, your days much shorter.

You cannot stop the movement of your life. Like everyone, you are moving toward winter. Consequently, the question is not, "How can I stop time?" The question is, "What am I doing with the time I have?"

Mark Twain said, "Twenty years from now you will be more disappointed by the things that you didn't do, than by the things you did." He's right. Seasons change, but while today is still called today, we have the time to do and to live. Get busy.

ACKNOWLEDGEMENTS

I would be remiss without offering a words of thanks to the following people:

To Tim Ryals for his excellent layout, design, and print work. Thanks "Willie" (for both your work and friendship)!

To Bridget Bergwall for long-sufferingly proofing this manuscript.

To David Beavers for your friendship, constant encouragement, and invaluable coaching and mentoring.

To the late Chris Hale, to whom this book is dedicated, who first inspired the idea for a "daily devotional" book. I wish I had completed it before you left us, my friend.

To the people of my congregation, "A Simple Faith" in Santa Rosa Beach, Florida and the readers of my syndicated column, "Keeping the Faith," nationwide. You are the guinea pigs upon whom I bounce everything first. Thank you.

To my boys Blayze, Bryce, and Braden who inspire so much of what I say and write.

And most of all, I thank Cindy Cooper McBrayer. She is my partner, best friend, love, and life. Without her, you would not be holding this book in your hand.

ABOUT THE AUTHOR

Scientists say that the beautiful, sugar-white beaches of the Florida Panhandle are the result of erosion from the Appalachian Mountains. A sand dune that we enjoy today, as we are told, was once a mountain top in Georgia, but over time that mountain washed all the way down to the sea. There's no better description for writer, Ronnie McBrayer.

Before making his home near the beautiful beaches of Walton County, Florida more than a decade ago, Ronnie was a life-long Georgian, born and raised in the foothills of the Appalachian Mountains. Today, having washed down to the sea, he is the author of multiple books and publications, a talented musician, a local pastor, and a nationally read columnist. His weekly feature, "Keeping the Faith," has been syndicated nationwide since 2006.

Ronnie maintains a contagious faith, a cheerful schoolboy wit, and an applauded storytelling style that invites his readers and listeners to discover new ways to experience personal freedom and grace. With his wife Cindy - a talented artist in her own right - and his three sons, Ronnie might be a long way from home, but he is never far from his roots.

Visit his website at www.ronniemcbrayer.net.